Praise for *NLP: The Ess*
to Neuro-Linguistic Pi

"In our fifty years of publishing important works on self-improvement, NLP Comprehensive's programs have been among our most well-regarded and bestselling. This new book *NLP: The Essential Guide* continues that fine tradition. It is a pleasure to recommend it."

—Vic Conant, president, Nightingale-Conant

"*NLP: The Essential Guide* is a richly personal journey. You'll enjoy the anecdotes as you're guided through exploring how applying the principles and teachings of NLP anywhere and everywhere can make life easier and happier. A unique introduction to NLP where you will experience NLP not so much as a set of concepts, but alive and living."

—Connirae Andreas, author of *Core Transformation*

"This is a book written to teach the reader 'how-to' put the principles of NLP into practice. It was written by two of the most interesting and passionate NLP practitioners in the world. This comes across in a fashion that makes it easy reading and 'real' learning, i.e. the explanations and exercises impart new and useful skills. It will teach a serious reader the nuts and bolts of the 'operating software' with which the mind works while dramatically improving their lives and communications with other people. It's one of the best introductions into learning NLP in print."

—Frank Bourke, president and founder,
NLP Research & Recognition Project

"A well-organized, practical guide to making NLP work in your life, the personal stories make it easy to relate to and bring the book alive."

—Joseph O'Connor, author of *Introducing NLP*,
The NLP Workbook, and *Coaching with NLP*

"There must already be at least two hundred introductions to NLP, including our own book, *Heart of the Mind,* published twenty-three years ago. Why yet another? What is special about this book is that the authors apply the patterns and methods in many different areas of their own lives—thoroughly, and with care and creativity. It may seem a bit wandering at times, but the journey always ends with a heartwarming and human resolution."

—Steve Andreas, author and publisher of the NLP Classics

"Tom and Tom can explain anything and make it clear, motivating and doable. I highly recommend this book. Great stories and techniques to live your life by." —Shelle Rose Charvet, author of *Words That Change Minds*

While there are many excellent technical introductions to NLP. *NLP: The Essential Guide to Neuro-Linguistic Programming* is instead a personal journey of using and applying NLP in real everyday life, to the ups and downs, to other people and with one's self. As you read it, you'll find yourself thinking in new ways and applying the techniques to your own personal challenges and opportunities.

In addition to the book, we have created a special website where we have online examples and demonstrations of everything in the book and more. You'll find links to it throughout the book, and we will be adding to it as you request. This is also an online community and support system. It's a place where you can ask questions and get answers.

NLP Comprehensive:
Founded in 1979, NLP Comprehensive has been at the leading edge of NLP ever since. From developing training to publishing, the company has maintained a reputation for the highest quality throughout its endeavors. To date it has published over fifty NLP titles including Nightingale-Conant's highly popular *NLP: The New Technology of Achievement*. Most recently it has compiled and published to rave reviews its thirty years of training experience in the form of the **"Portable NLP Practitioner Training,"** a thirty-seven-DVD-based home study program. For these and other titles from NLP Comprehensive, go to www.nlpco.com.

Praise for NLP Comprehensive

"I have taken training with over 30 different NLP organizations, including founders of NLP. Your Practitioner training is by far the best I have experienced, head and shoulders above the quality of trainers and content offered elsewhere." —Alix von Uhde, certified NLP trainer and Life Coach, Colon, Germany

"NLP Comprehensive's trainers and training gave me invaluable tools to model my own excellence and the excellence of others. As a result, I have built a 6-figure coaching practice which is improving the lives of thousands. I consider it required curriculum for life." —Jason D. McClain, founder and CEO, IDEA ::: Evolutionary Companies

"[After my Practitioner Training] you can imagine how eager I was to learn even more NLP to enhance my skills even further. I made the mistake of signing up for training with several different organizations because they happened to fit my schedule at the time. It was not until 'suffering' with boredom through poor facilitation, repetitive, low-level 'get that kind of information anywhere' classes that I realized what a quality training I had received from your organization in the first place. **What others were offering as 'Master Practitioner' material, had already been thoroughly covered in your Practitioner Training!** *I have found the superb quality and variety of trainers you provided at your training to be unsurpassed."* —Mary Miscisin, M.S., Sacramento, California

NLP

The Essential Guide

TO NEURO-LINGUISTIC PROGRAMMING

From NLP Comprehensive

Tom Hoobyar and Tom Dotz with Susan Sanders

wm

WILLIAM MORROW
An Imprint of HarperCollins*Publishers*

FIRST EDITION

Designed by Diahann Sturge

Library of Congress Cataloging-in-Publication Data has been applied for.

ISBN 978-0-06-208361-6

13 14 15 16 17   OV/RRD   10 9 8 7 6 5 4 3 2

CONTENTS

TRIAL BY FIRE: MY PERSONAL INTRODUCTION TO NLP
Tracy Hoobyar

NLP has been a part of my life since the mid-1990s. My father began studying NLP to learn more about himself and those around him. Because my dad was the son of a preacher, anything he learned, we *all* learned!

As time went on and I listened to Dad tell me what he had learned, it all sounded interesting, but, after all, it was Dad's thing. I was busy with a toddler and didn't have time to worry too much about it.

In early 2002, things changed drastically for me. My then eleven-year-old daughter was hospitalized at Lucile Packard Children's Hospital, at Stanford University, for anorexia. Her heart had been affected and was weak, her bones were brittle, and we were given a *very* bleak prognosis. After three weeks and more than sixty thousand dollars' worth of care, they wanted to admit her to a residential psychiatric hospital out of state. We would get to visit her occasionally. We were told there were no other options—she wouldn't survive if we didn't follow their suggestions.

Against medical advice, we decided to check her out of the hospital. As you might imagine, the primary doctor was not impressed. He invited my entire family to find other care in the future, and wished us well. Outpatient services were unsatisfactory. Counseling was not productive. It really began to look like this was going to be as bad as they told us.

Unwilling to accept that, I talked to Dad about changing her prognosis. After a lot of hours, Dad and I devised a plan to help my daughter—to defy all the rules and statistics—and help her get better. Our plan? Use everything he knew from NLP, everything I knew about psychology, and work with her to help her recover. While we used a combination of techniques, the most effective, and the quickest, tools came from the NLP world.

We worked with my daughter to understand, and *accept*, the part of her that was struggling for control by restricting her food intake. With her, we explored what she was thinking and feeling. We "played" with different techniques until we found what worked.

We went to her doctor three times a week at first, then twice, and then only once a week. He monitored my daughter for the typical challenges anorexic kids encounter upon release from the hospital. He checked her vitals and urine tests, and evaluated her for improvement.

She was never hospitalized again, gained weight steadily, and worked through her "demons" with the support of NLP and those who loved her. The doctors thought we were crazy when my daughter would talk about how she pictured anorexia, how she was able to make changes in her relationship with this disease and with food by playing with the size and color of the picture—and other things that sounded equally odd to those trained traditionally.

It was not an easy road back, but it was well worth traveling.

Today, my daughter has spent more than ten years in recovery. I'm convinced that without NLP, we would have lost her. With my newfound belief in the power of NLP, Dad and I worked harder than ever at real-world, practical applications. We found ways to help kids dealing with abusive histories, elderly people dealing with chronic pain, and businesspeople dealing with day-to-day issues.

Our dream was always to put together a program to help real people deal with real problems. Dad had such an amazing way of presenting information. He would use stories to help people understand what he wanted them to learn. His genuine compassion for others, and desire to help them live better lives, guided his actions and writings.

What you hold in this book is the realization of the dream we shared. He spent countless hours in trainings, reading books, working with the experts, testing theories, and applying techniques to everyday challenges. He researched NLP and its applications in more detail than most people could ever imagine.

The amazing thing is that you're going to benefit from *all* of that. He literally helped hundreds of people overcome their challenges; here, he shares the tools he used to do that. Whether the struggle you're concerned with is a fear of public speaking, dealing with the hurdles of major life changes, living with chronic pain, or some other issue, Dad has used NLP to positively impact something like it—and he is going to show you how to do the same.

This book will show you how to use NLP to become the person *you* want to be. You will learn the skills and tools to reduce stress, manage your thoughts and feelings, improve your communications with anyone in your life, and live the life you want to live.

You will hear stories that will enlighten you about your own stories. You may even discover something you didn't know about yourself. I know I did. Here's what I can tell you. NLP offers many powerful tools to change your life—tools that can also change the lives of those around you, if they're open to that.

This book takes years of information and presents it all in a friendly, simple-to-read format that is easy to understand, learn from, and implement. Every once in a while, you find a book that really speaks to you, that is just the right "teacher" at the just the right time. I think author and speaker Garrison Keillor said it best: "A book is a gift you can open again and again." I'm very happy and proud to share this special gift from my father with you.

Authors' Note and Appreciation

Tom Hoobyar was an avid learner and adventurous explorer who embraced life's mysteries and questions. He was the originator of six patents and the majority of his forty-five years in business exposed him to diverse issues in small businesses, Fortune 500 firms, as well as twelve start-ups that grew to be number one in their industries.

While he was CEO of a Silicon Valley manufacturing company, Neuro-Linguistic Programming (NLP) became a vital tool that enhanced his leadership skills and his company's success. He later used NLP as the foundation for his writing and coaching practice, which enabled him to touch and change the lives of hundreds of people.

While compiling his secrets of success for this book, Tom died from pancreatic cancer. Tom dreamed that his message would live on long after him, and asked us to transform his notes and transcripts from his teachings into this book. To honor the confidentiality he promised clients, we've changed the names and situations of the people in his stories.

Tom's wide-ranging background and rich life experience enabled him to bring a special perspective and approach to NLP, which makes his insights and message more useful outside the training room or coaching session. We've done our best to preserve how easily accessible he made NLP to others.

Because Tom Hoobyar had a unique gift for communicating and making complex subjects fun and easy to understand, this essential guide is written in the present tense—enabling you to have an engaging conversation with him that can change *your* life.

Many people contributed to making this book possible. With this in mind, we'd like to especially thank:

- Robert McDonald, whose precise and heartfelt teaching style inspired Tom Dotz to train with NLP Comprehensive and then found NLP California, where Tom Hoobyar and Susan Sanders were likewise inspired with the possibilities NLP made real.

- Steve and Connirae Andreas for their creativity in developing new processes, their generous spirit of teaching, and their leadership in the NLP community. Without them, Tom Hoobyar and the two of us would not have met or shared our journeys of learning NLP.

- The NLP Comprehensive Training Team for continually bringing NLP concepts, skills, and processes to life for thousands of students—in particular, Charles Faulkner and Steve Andreas, who were the chief editors on NLP Comprehensive's first book, *NLP: The New Technology of Achievement*.

- Adam Korn and Trish Daly at HarperCollins for embracing this project and shepherding it through to completion.

What You'll Get Out of This Book

There are hundreds of potential turning points in each person's life—and this book will be an important one in *yours*. How's that possible?

Here's how. You'll discover HOW your one-of-a-kind, never-to-be-duplicated special mind *actually* works. You'll find out how you were able to use your brain before you could even say a word. Even better, you'll be able to "get under the hood" of your own thoughts and adjust them to fit your current needs. Since most of our beliefs and values were created when we were children, this is a good thing. Some of those patterns might benefit from a little updating, don't you think?

In this book, you'll get specific processes for updating these old patterns and creating new ones. You'll explore simple, solid solutions to issues including anxieties, procrastination, and motivation. You'll learn and practice powerful strategies for immediate, lasting results in areas like self-confidence.

These may seem like pretty big promises, and yet the possibilities are *not* overstated. The basis for this is NLP, or Neuro-Linguistic Programming. It's a funny name for an essential function of life: understanding and managing your own mind. NLP is famous for its fast fixes for phobias and long-held fears and anxieties—and much more.

Like many great ideas, the concepts of NLP have been embraced by many leaders in their fields—now, several decades since its inception, echoes of NLP appear in all kinds of books, training courses, coaching, and motivational speeches. As you go through this book and learn more about NLP, you'll find yourself recognizing the many places and people who have adopted it as part of their work.

This essential guide provides you with *multiple* ways to create and maintain motivation to keep you moving forward toward your goals. You'll also learn two tremendously important processes for selecting and validating your goals. That alone is worth the price of admission. When you truly know what you want, and that what you want is worth having, you'll find all your internal resources aligning. You'll find the friction, distractions, and hesitations melting away. You'll learn what NLP calls internal congruence, and that gives you a strong running start.

You'll discover new ways of relating to and understanding other people that will make getting cooperation and giving direction easier and more satisfying than ever before. And I'm speaking as a guy who used to have real issues with shyness and public speaking.

You see, I know firsthand what a difference using NLP has made in my own life. Using its concepts and techniques can have powerful and long-lasting effects. I have trained hundreds of people in NLP concepts and techniques—and have seen people make remarkable changes in their lives.

You'll also get a new understanding of *other* people because you'll have a better idea about what's going on inside them. For the most part, many people don't know how they work *inside*. They really are unable to tell you what makes them think a particular thought, or do what they do. You'll learn about other people's inner workings by simply observing behaviors and noticing the right key signals.

Having this awareness also helps you to be a little more approachable, a little more "simpatico," and a little smoother when you're communicating. Of course, the reward here is the power of influence. The knowledge you'll gain about how people work gives you real persuasive power.

Your relationships will improve across the board because you will become more understanding, and more understood. That combination makes you an easier person to be around. Frankly, it makes you more attractive.

You'll find your performance at work improving. Mine certainly did. I became a better team player. And, even though I was the boss, I became much more approachable to my employees. You'll become healthier, too, because you'll be better able to manage your motivations to exercise, to eat well, and to reduce or do away with some of your poor health habits.

The bottom line is that by reading this book and doing the recommended activities, you'll develop the skills to become better at just about everything you do. You'll gain powerful tools to be able to overcome whatever you believe is your number-one problem.

If I were you, I might be thinking, "Why should I trust this guy—and invest my time exploring these ideas?" Here's why. For most of my career, I've made my living as an inventor, engineer, and entrepreneur, and after NLP training, as a consultant to people dealing with personal and professional performance issues.

I *know* what's proved most useful to me over the last fifteen years and *that's* what I'm going to share with you. This book is not simply an encyclopedia of NLP. Instead, this is an interactive user guide that puts the power of NLP at your fingertips *right now*. I am, first and foremost, an NLP user. It's how I navigate life.

Let me start with how NLP really got my attention. It's the story of how, after thirty-six years, I found a way to stop smoking. I had been trying to quit for eighteen of those thirty-six years. Nothing worked for me. I tried hypnosis, putting money in a jar every time I would break down and have a smoke, telling all my friends and family that I quit, drinking myself to sleep for one stretch of six nonsmoking months. Nothing worked. Every time I "quit," I would find an excuse to start smoking again. Once I even used my dad's death as an excuse to stop on the way to his house to buy a pack of cigarettes. "Emergency," I told myself. "I'll quit again when I get through this."

Yeah, right. And I felt like an idiot. Here I was in charge of a start-up firm, and I was the only smoker in the company. Out of consideration for our employees, I had declared our offices a nonsmoking zone. So I would be alone, standing outside in all kinds of weather pounding down a quick cigarette before meeting with my staff, stinking like an ashtray and *knowing* that I was broadcasting my weakness. Then, one day, I saw an NLP process in a book. I thought I might as well try it.

That was more than twenty years ago and I haven't lit a cigarette since. A few years later, when the company was on solid footing and I had a little breathing space, I started taking NLP training. Wow.

I had spent my entire adult life figuring out processes and technologies, but this new discipline blew those strategies away. As my questions about human nature (and my own inner workings) were answered for me, I realized that I had stumbled on to the coolest technology yet—the technology of human behavior.

What Is NLP?

NLP is a revolutionary study of the PROCESS of human thought. In other words, it's the study of what's actually going on when we think. I don't mean the physical or electrochemical reactions, but what we would notice if we looked at the *step-by-step* activity of thinking.

The interesting thing about the mind is that if you take a brain and cut it open, you can't find the mind. You can't find a poem or the taste of chocolate or the feeling of a first kiss or the music from the prom dance. All you find is a bunch of nerve tissue. The nerve tissue in your brain acts as a substrate. It's almost like your computer. It acts like your hard drive or your motherboard, and basically it's designed to store various bits of data and to assemble, reassemble, and rearrange them and call them up whenever you want.

NLP is an understanding—not of the brain—but of how the *mind*, using the brain, expresses itself in your life and creates what you call your experience.

Right now, for instance, you're reading these words. But these words by themselves are not your experience. Your experience is these words blended with what else you're seeing around you at the moment, where you're sitting, and how your body is feeling. Part of your experience right now is composed of the things you're saying to yourself, like, "Geez, I wish he'd say more about that point," or "That's interesting," or "I don't know if that's true or not," or "Am I really going to get my money's worth out of all this time I'm spending?"

The comments you make as you go on, coupled with your visual and your physical sensations as you read, blended with my words—all of that combined becomes your experience. Now, how does your brain do all *that*? Before I answer that, let me give you a little background information about NLP.

NLP started at the University of California, Santa Cruz in the early 1970s and has grown rapidly since then. NLP differs from psychology because its philosophy and techniques are derived from a specialized form of studying people called "Modeling." NLP researchers interviewed and observed people doing many activities—and then shared the huge body of knowledge they accumulated about how people think when they're falling in love, grieving a personal loss, shooting a gun, flying a plane, learning a language, or falling asleep. Thousands of people have been studied over the years, and much has been learned about how we think, and how we can adjust our own internal thought processes.

NLP popularized the "Visual, Auditory, and Kinesthetic" learning styles in addition to many new technologies utilized in education, psychotherapy, and communication. It's used in business for interviewing, hiring, training, management, and sales. Entertainment and business professionals, as well as athletes and coaches in amateur, professional, and Olympic sports, use NLP coaching to improve performance.

In the beginning, I studied NLP because I wanted help inventing products and being a better CEO of the high-tech company that I had founded, and I got it!

Every day I was managing people, making phone calls, negotiating with vendors and customers in the business world. NLP really influenced my view of my employees. Even though I could see that some of them could probably resolve some issues and be happier (not to mention, be better employees), I wasn't licensed to be their therapist. I was their boss.

Even though I was getting very excited by the things I was learning about human nature, I couldn't really talk much about my discoveries. I certainly couldn't ask other people, "What pictures are you making in your head right now?" or "Are you hearing a voice?" It wasn't safe to try that and it certainly wouldn't have been very effective.

So I decided to use this growing knowledge for my own personal development, and allow it to change *my* language and *my* gestures to get results for me first. Then I discovered how this also allowed me to get results with other people. You see, the funny thing was that when I changed, the people around me changed, too.

It actually turned out remarkably well—and that's what I want to share with you. My goal with this book is for you to learn about the operating principles of NLP, about how you think and how others think. You'll be able to manage your life more easily, and to dramatically improve your communications with other people.

What I didn't know back then was that there would be so many additional benefits from using NLP skills. NLP has helped me be a better husband, father, and grandfather. It's helped me be happier, easier to get along with, a better family member, and more productive in my professional work.

Since retiring from manufacturing, I've worked with clients as a consultant and coach. NLP has helped me to share my skills and experience with thousands of people in many walks of life and in many situations.

I'm an NLP Master Practitioner and Training Coach. I have a lot of other certifications for NLP and related training because I found the field so fascinating. In my home library, there are hundreds of books on the subject. I'm also the founder of the international NLP alumni group, the NLP Café. In this book, I've distilled the best of everything I've learned from NLP—which is a lot! You don't have to be as focused on NLP as I am to reap many benefits from this information. You're sure to find a payoff within your first hour.

ᴡo Important NLP Principles of Human Nature

NLP researchers originally studied therapists who were famous for getting almost miraculous results with their clients. One of the psychotherapists initially studied was Fritz Perls, who developed "be-here-now" Gestalt therapy. He was a genius at reading body language and at getting immediate changes. His unique approach was the direct opposite of psychoanalysis, which requires years of therapy and self-study to develop an understanding of how one came to be who they are.

The second therapist was Virginia Satir, the brilliant developer of family therapy. Instead of working with just the one person in the family who was disruptive or troubled, she dealt with the *entire* family. She felt that each person and their behavior were part of the family dynamic. She found that if she addressed only the one person, they'd go back to the family structure and get a little crazy again, so she worked with the entire family.

The third person they studied was Milton Erickson, a medical doctor who was the primary developer of clinical hypnotherapy. A genius, with a completely different approach to therapy from Perls and Satir, Erickson also produced results that appeared to be magic. The fourth subject of initial study was a man named Moshe Feldenkrais, a body worker who did brilliant healing work with his hands.

NLP's underlying operating principles, called "Presuppositions," reflect the underlying unifying beliefs of these key individuals who were studied to discover what was most effective—and *these* became the operating principles of NLP.

The interesting thing about these distinctively different leaders was that their deep beliefs about human nature were pretty much the same. Two of the beliefs I want to emphasize for you are important because they flow through everything we do—and they contradict *a lot* of what most of us have been taught.

THERE IS NO SUCH THING AS AN INNER ENEMY.

One belief is "There is no such thing as an inner enemy." There's no monster within. You're not broken. You can really let go of old beliefs like this.

When people do things that are not good for them—and it doesn't matter whether it's biting their fingernails or committing serial murders—they are doing what they are doing because some part of them thinks it's essential. A part of them believes that it's necessary for survival, for their well-being. While some behaviors may not be sane, healthy, or anything most people would condone, it's important to understand that in that individual's worldview, in *their* mind, that behavior is absolutely necessary.

BEHIND EVERY BEHAVIOR IS A POSITIVE INTENTION.

So suppose you have an issue—let's say there's a certain person you just can't confront. Every time you see them, your knees turn to jelly and you start stuttering. Maybe it's an attractive coworker, somebody's boss, your mother-in-law, your spouse, or maybe it's one of your children. The thing is, you're not broken, and there's nothing wrong. The reason you have such a reaction is that part of your mind thinks that *not* confronting them is what's essential for you to do to survive.

Maybe the behavior is intended to keep you safe. Maybe it's to preserve your self-respect, or self-love. Maybe it's to get "justice." No matter how weird or inappropriate it may seem, for that person there is an inner logic that makes perfect sense. It sounds a little crazy, doesn't it? Why would this "logic" be true? Well, in the example above, if we did a little looking, we might find that your mind reached that conclusion when you were three or four years old.

Long ago, you might have had a difficult experience with someone who reminds you (in some way) of the person in your present life. It doesn't have to be obvious—it could be how they look, their tone of voice, their role in your life, or just the way your unconscious sees them in relationship to you. When we use NLP, we look *inside* the mind, to find out exactly what pattern is operating to produce that response, and then we can alter it. By reading this book and putting the principles into practice, you'll be able to do this, too!

The two things I'd like you to hold in mind are that *there is no such thing as an inner enemy* and that *behind every behavior is a positive intention.* Your mind—as well as everybody else's mind—is operating the best way it currently knows how. It may be wrong and it may need an adjustment, simply because most brains decide how to operate when people are four or five years old.

But enough about NLP and me. Let's talk about what's ahead for you.

What Is an NLP "Power User"?

There are many reasons people study NLP. Some people are just curious about how human nature operates. Others want to discover how they themselves think. Power Users want to use NLP in the real world, where this skill set makes a tremendous difference for them.

There is a world of difference between "knowing how" and "being able." My goal is to make you able. I've known many NLP Trainers and Practitioners who were pioneers and Power Users in this field. I've also studied the methods taught to hostage negotiators, Navy SEALs, and Army Rangers. I've studied other skills that I've found useful in life, such as the self-management skills of entrepreneurs, actors, and therapists. I've adapted the best of these here for your use.

NLP is more important today than ever before. Here's why. In our world of ever-evolving technology, we are *constantly* connecting—with people we work with, people we love, people who have information and/or access to others. We're so busy responding, we hardly have time to think. So in the following pages, I'm going to guide you through dozens of "Discovery Activities," where you will be able to explore your personal thinking patterns—and learn how to manage and change them if you wish. You'll also learn about whole new ways of dealing with other people and understanding how *they* are thinking and feeling.

Ready? Curious? I hope so—this oughta be fun.

NLP

The Essential Guide

TO NEURO-LINGUISTIC PROGRAMMING

Section One: It's All About You

CHAPTER ONE: UNDERSTANDING HOW YOU THINK

What's going on in there?

Life consists of what a man is thinking of all day.
—Ralph Waldo Emerson

You know *what* you think, right? We all do. You're thinking about what you like or don't like, and what you want or don't want. You also probably think of what you wish you wanted *less* of, like gorging on chocolate ice cream, TV, Web-surfing, shopping, drinking, or working.

In fact, when anyone talks about thinking, they talk about *what* they're thinking about. They don't talk about *how* we go about thinking those thoughts. What you'll learn from this book is how you go about forming your thoughts, the effect that has on you and others, and how to change it to better suit you.

The understanding you'll gain here is largely based on Neuro-Linguistic Programming, which is commonly referred to as NLP. NLP is based on the theory that all human thinking occurs in pictures, sounds, feelings, smells, and/or taste: the five senses. No one has yet ever effectively challenged this theory by giving me an example of a thought that *isn't* expressed in some combination of words, pictures, smells, tastes, or feelings.

Can you do that? Right now, try having a thought that's *not* an image, sound, feeling, smell, or taste. Just kinda makes your brain stop for a minute, doesn't it?

After you have a thought, you have a response. Maybe it's a funny feeling, followed by a comment like "This guy is nuts," or some other internal dialogue, picture, or feeling.

All and each of us operate this way, and yet each of us is distinctively different in the exact thought patterns we have created as a result of our sensory-based thinking. We all live inside our self-created minds. Our unique reality is a result of our individual biology *and* the influence of our individual, mostly random personal history. Understanding that we all live in and operate from a personal model of reality is the key to making our lives better serve us.

By understanding this, you can truly understand yourself and other people, how you and they do the sometimes strange and sometimes pleasing things people do. You can figure out how to give yourself more of what you do want and less of what you don't.

Most important, you're going to find out how to assess what you really want and how to know that it's really right for you. In this book, you'll be introduced to processes you can easily put to use right away to give you relief from what you don't want and more satisfaction with what you do.

An inner picture or sound can truly be a resource. Rather than just talk about how this is true, let's play with this concept by doing a process together. Having a little experience with this concept now will give you an understanding of how valuable this book can be for you. The approach you're going to learn is especially useful anytime you want to have a greater sense of comfort and ease when you are doing something you need to do.

A Taste of NLP: A Firsthand Experience

In this first activity, *Accessing Personal Resources,* I'm going to ask you to remember a time when you had a strong sense of ease and flow in your work. Think of a vibrant memory, one that you will enjoy reliving. Choose a time when everything just seemed to move easily and you were really able to do what you wanted to accomplish. By vividly remembering that time, you'll be drawing upon your personal resources and past experience. Then I'll show you how to create a special memory trigger, so you can have that feeling again whenever you want or need to.

What could you accomplish if you could easily step into that sense of focus on your work, free from distractions, so everything flowed smoothly and almost effortlessly? What other positive feelings would you want to reexperience if you could simply transfer them from the time they actually happened in your life to where you really want to have them again? The "Circle of Excellence" process will do just that. This process is adapted from the popular book *NLP: The New Technology of Achievement.*

 **Discovery Activity:**
Accessing Personal Resources

Ready? Let other thoughts about the day move into the background as you focus on this activity. First of all, this is a real contrast to the way you probably do most of your thinking. In these Discovery Activities, the only way to go fast is to go slow, to start. You want to really s-l-o-w d-o-w-n your thoughts as you follow the instructions, especially the first few times. This will make it much easier and more successful for you as you do these processes. So take a breath, relax, give yourself some time, and enjoy.

Now go back in your memory to a time in your work when you were really experiencing a sense of excellence, a sense of easy flow, a sense of accomplishment. Relive that experience—seeing what you saw, hearing what you heard, feeling what you felt.

As you feel that sense of flow building within you, imagine there's a circle on the floor, like a spotlight, right in front of your feet. Notice how it's big enough that if you were to step into it right now, your feet and your whole self would easily fit inside it. What color is the circle of light? If you want to, you can change the color and make it more blue, golden, or even sparkly.

Listen carefully for a moment; is there a sound that goes with your circle? Maybe it has a soft, steady hum that echoes the powerful energy of the moment. Maybe you hear a song or applause. What do you notice?

As you recall this experience and imagine the colored circle and this sound, what feelings are you aware of? Maybe you feel kind of tingly or your posture is more erect. Perhaps you have a feeling of confidence or pride. What feelings do you notice now?

Once you've really relived that feeling of excellence, that feeling of ease and flow *at its fullest,* step into that circle, bringing everything you see, hear, and feel *into* the circle.

In a moment, you're going to step out of that circle and leave all those feelings *inside* it, knowing you can come back to them whenever you want to. This is an unusual request, and you can do it. Do this now, just step out of the circle, leaving all those mental pictures, sounds, and feelings inside it.

Now, as you are standing outside the circle, think of a specific time in your future when you want to have that same feeling of excellence, that same focus, ease, and flow. Take a moment to see, hear, and feel what might be happening in that upcoming situation—what happens just before you want to reexperience your feelings of excellence. Perhaps you see your desk. Maybe you hear a voice introducing you as the speaker at an event. Maybe you feel excitement about what's going to happen. Whatever comes up for you, just notice that now.

As these cues are coming up in your mind, step back into your circle and relive those feelings of excellence, focus, easy flow. Notice, as you imagine that *future* situation unfolding, how these feelings of flow and easy confidence are fully available to you—that you can easily access those same powerful feelings of excellence, focus, and flow.

Now step out of the circle again, leaving those powerful feelings *in* the circle. Once you're outside the circle, take a moment and think about that upcoming event. You'll find you automatically recall those feelings of confidence and flow, that sense of ease. This means you've already reoriented yourself for that upcoming event. You're feeling better about it and it hasn't even completely happened yet. When it does arrive, you'll find yourself naturally responding with more focus and confidence—you'll have that sense of easy flow.

Whenever I experiment with a new approach, I know the first time is likely to be less than perfect—simply because I've never done it before. You know the old saying, "Anything worth doing, is worth doing poorly to start"? That's especially true when making personal changes. If, after doing the activity, you were only partly successful, just do it again, paying close attention to each step, because the sequence and timing are important.

When you apply NLP concepts and techniques, you're taking the initiative. You are deciding for yourself how you want to react to the events in your life. In this activity, you took the feelings of ease, flow, and confidence from a past experience and attached them to a future situation that you might have felt uneasy about. This is a process you can do for as many different future events as you want, with as many different kinds of feelings as you want.

If you've ever experienced a resource, even if it was only for a second, that means you have access to it forever! Using the "Circle of Excellence," you can choose to use your resources any way you want— whenever you want. In any situation, you can choose how you want to feel and how you want to respond. You can choose to live your life on purpose, by choice. You really do have all the resources you could want or need. Isn't that great?

You First: Understanding How *You* Work

Now that you've had a little taste of NLP, I sincerely hope you're hungry for more. So let's get started.

All humans have pretty much the same wiring in their central nervous systems. Because we're born with the same wiring, we learn many of the same things in the same way. We may all be concerned with similar things, *and yet* we don't all think the same way. In fact, each one of us thinks in a slightly different way from any other human who has ever lived, or ever will live. Each of us is as unique as a snowflake or a fingerprint.

In this chapter, you'll learn how humans think, and you'll learn how to discover *your* personal thought processes. Most important, you'll start learning how to change your thought processes to get you more of what you do want in life. As you go through the first section of the book, you'll learn how to apply this knowledge to yourself. The second section focuses on how to use these understandings and processes with others.

You might be wondering, "Why should I care how I think?" Here's why. Most of us go through our lives getting used to small discomforts, as well as emotional and mental limits. We say, "I've never been good at numbers," or "I just don't have a green thumb." These thoughts are no problem, unless you have a reason to want to become good at numbers or at gardening.

But what if it's more serious?

Suppose you're just not able to handle necessary confrontations with a coworker or a family member. Everyone needs to be able to set and protect his or her boundaries. That's how we create our personal feelings of safety and get other people to respect our choices.

What if you "just can't get anything done on time." Or you're not able to keep your poise when speaking in front of an audience. Or you'd like to change your health by stopping some old habits and building better ones. Or some other behavior that you'd like to change, but haven't succeeded at doing so.

The thing is, we can all be more of who we *want* to be. But most of us just give up after a few decades of life, and accept that "we are who we are and that we can't change." Not true!

It's just that until recently, people didn't have the right tools for personal change.

When you discover your personal thinking patterns, you can "get under the hood" of *your* vehicle and change old unwanted habits. You can choose new ways to behave in situations that make you uncomfortable. You will discover new skills and become easier to be around. Essentially, you will become able to redesign yourself. Many of my coaching clients have done just that. So have I, and so can you, if you want to.

You can change whatever you want to change. And, if you later decide the change isn't desirable, you can put things back the way they were, or choose a new way. So come along with me, and allow me to guide you on an exploration of your personal thought processes.

Most of us experience our feelings like we experience weather. "Oh, I'm having a bad day . . . Oh, so-and-so made me mad . . . Ah, I don't know, I'm just off today . . . I just can't get it." It's kind of like being caught out in the rain without an umbrella, isn't it? You're at the mercy of whatever come along, or you try to suck it up and be a good soldier. Maybe you tell yourself, "Don't be a crybaby. Push through anyway." That's the hard way; that's like trying to open a door using the wrong end of the key.

An easier way to do it would be to understand how those feelings were created in the first place. If you'd like to know, I'll tell you.

"Ouch" or "Yahoo": How We Create Our Feelings

Here's how feelings are created. The first thing that happens is that you get some kind of external stimuli. For example, when you woke up this morning, the first thing you had was your inner commentary. That was just you, right? But then, you began meeting the world—a whistling coffeepot, a crying kid, a dog that needs to be let out, the newspaper in the front door, the TV on. Whatever your world consists of, you had that stimulation coming into your brain.

As soon as sensory input comes into your brain, it's interpreted. You assign a meaning to it. This is really important because this happens so fast you aren't even aware of it. The interesting thing is that *as soon as* a meaning is assigned, you have an emotion. You create a feeling about it.

You might think, "It's going to be a crappy day . . . There's gonna be traffic . . . It's smoggy . . . I hate politics . . . The economy's down . . . We ran out of coffee . . . Doesn't anybody else take care of the damn dog?" Sound familiar? Or, if you're as lucky as I am to be happily married, it might even be "Good morning, sweetie. What's on your docket for the day?" Bottom line? There's one thing or another going on in your mind.

Whatever the stimulus is that's coming in, you assign a meaning to it, you have an emotion, and it's *those* emotions that generate your reaction. That's the way it happens for most people. As you begin to understand that your emotions come from the meaning you make of some thought or some external input, you can go back to that thought, "unpack it," and change it. This is where the ability to slow down your thoughts will actually allow you to think more effectively, and to choose better responses.

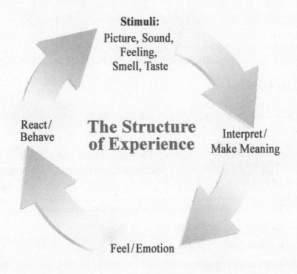

Stimuli:
Picture, Sound,
Feeling,
Smell, Taste

React/
Behave

**The Structure
of Experience**

Interpret/
Make Meaning

Feel/Emotion

So, stimulus to meaning . . . meaning to emotion . . . emotion to action. This whole cycle happens in an instant. It happens millions of times every day, and almost always without our awareness.

Remember, the tricky part is that we're usually only aware of the first stimulus and then the emotion; the meaning is typically out of our awareness.

Try on the following statements: "I feel great when I'm around you." "He made me mad." "That customer ruined my whole day." Despite how these emotions are stated, the real author of our feelings is NOT that other person. The *real* author of our feelings is the meaning we make out of whatever caught our attention.

Autopilot: The Mind's Three Favorite Options

There's another really important thing that happens in the mind: it does certain things automatically—and without our awareness. It generalizes, deletes, and distorts information. Let's explore a few examples.

GENERALIZATION

Generalization is noticing how an experience is similar to other experiences. It's a natural process. We perceive people, things, and events by noticing *aspects* of the experience that are like *previous* experiences. There are many kinds of doors, right? Revolving doors, automatic doors, sliding doors, screen doors, the list goes on, doesn't it? But, they're *all* doors. An upscale restaurant may have nicer ambience, a specialized menu, more attentive service, and higher prices than a family-style restaurant, but they both have food, tables, and servers—so they're both restaurants. And, of course, certain people remind us of other people. Experiences remind us of other experiences. This is how our brain generalizes. We experience a new thing or skill consciously a few times and after that we delegate it. We do this all the time.

Even though generalization is useful and efficient, it can also get us into trouble. For example, someone who *reminds* us of a friend may well be a very different kind of person. A pepper in your food may look like a mild pepper you've had before, but in fact be a very spicy pepper. Something that looks familiar, a generalization, can lead to incorrect conclusions or ineffective actions.

Generalizations can also contribute to limiting beliefs. For example, all people with green eyes are sexy or tall people wearing big boots are threatening. Such generalizations submerge and become beliefs. And those beliefs then start to run your life. Actually, beliefs are so strong that when you have a belief, it starts to alter what you perceive. Now all these external stimuli coming in have to get through these belief filters. Your mind doesn't really get the raw information. It doesn't get to choose anymore.

Rather than getting the *actual* sound waves coming in, your brain just gets what it *hears*. And hearing, like seeing, takes place in the brain, not the eyes or the ears. The eyes and the ears are just channeling in vibrations, essentially electromagnetic waves. It's just raw data coming in, but your *mind* is filtering that raw data and saying, "Is it dangerous? Is it safe? Is this interesting? Is this significant?"

Your mind is filtering your experience to allow you to survive; so this is a good thing. It's just that you might want a little more flexibility in this area. That's one thing you'll get as you explore the different Discovery Activities in this book—because the more choices you have, the better off you are. Of course, to create, examine, and make different choices, you have to *use* your brain, which means not living on autopilot. That becomes a problem when beliefs that were formed when you were a kid (knowing only what you knew then) are *still* making your choices. Those old beliefs have largely chosen your work, your politics, your mate, and your lunch.

As you explore your beliefs and start modifying them using the approaches in this book, you will be able to have more choices available to you in the future, and that is a very good thing. But, I digress.

DELETION

What's deletion? Deletion is dropping away aspects of an experience. Deletion is natural. When we perceive or remember someone or something, we often leave out the background, other people and so on. That's deletion. When we focus intensely on something and everything else disappears, that's deletion. When we can't remember something, that's another form of deletion. When used effectively, deletion helps remove the noise, distractions, and minutia of life, so we can concentrate on what's important.

Here's a "deletion" experience you might be having right now. You're probably focused on reading these words, thinking about what they mean, arguing with the ideas, or taking notes. What you're ignoring perhaps is the feeling of your body sitting wherever you're sitting, on a hard chair, a comfortable couch, or a cramped bus seat. You may not be paying attention to your body, your environment, or what time it is. You may not be paying attention to the way your feet feel at the moment. When I mention it, maybe you notice them, but not until then.

Another example is when you're looking for someone in a crowd, you're focusing on specific things and you're deleting the background. You might scan a group of people searching only for a certain thing—the color of a sweater, the shape of a hat, or long blond hair—everything else in the picture is just background; you've deleted the other elements.

DISTORTION

Distortion is changing an experience from what it *actually* is to some modified form of what it is. (Let's put aside whether you can really *know* what something is and just explore distortion further.) Distortion, too, is natural. We perceive and remember people, things, and events based on *aspects* of the experience: the typical dog, the ideal friend, the worst vacation, and so on. This is a distortion. It's a bit of the experience, but we have dropped out a whole lot of details and filled in the rest with imagination.

When we perceive a particular characteristic about someone, good or bad, and apply it to *all* aspects of that person, that's distortion, too. With distortion, when we perceive someone as a slow talker, we might distort things so we imagine that they're also a slow thinker. Similarly, we may conclude that someone who's a sharp dresser is a sharp thinker. When you remember a moment of an event as representing the whole thing, that's distortion. When you tell the story of that experience and leave things out and embellish others, that's distortion. We do this quite frequently.

These three ideas don't really operate independently—they interact. For example, generalization requires deletion, and is a form of distortion. It doesn't matter that you remember these terms, what's important is that you recognize that there are billions of bits of information flooding into your brain every second—to manage all this, your awesome brain *automatically* generalizes, deletes, and distorts information.

A Well-Oiled Machine: Body, Brain, and Mind

Each of us is a blend of three different parts: the body, the brain, and the mind. These all work together and influence each other. A problem in one area affects the others. For our purposes right now, here's how to think about these parts:

THE BODY

The body is your physical body, your nerves, muscles, and circulation. Your body includes your endocrine system and other organs that are constantly adjusting your bloodstream to make you as effective as possible. Ever miss a meal or a good night's sleep and then discover that you just aren't "up to par" the next day? You may have all the information you need to solve a problem and yet the solution just doesn't come. What's happening is that your body is producing fatigue toxins, your blood sugar is low, or you're having an insulin reaction, and that chemistry is affecting your mind.

THE BRAIN

The brain is the three pounds of stuff inside your skull. This amazing organ is where most of your consciousness takes place. The brain uses 25 percent of the total amount of oxygen you breathe. It is composed of about 100 billion neurons. Each neuron has one to ten thousand connections to other neurons. A single human brain equals the entire computing power of our planet in 2007. The human brain can perform 100 trillion calculations every second. What's it do with all of that processing power? A staggering amount of work!

The brain handles all of the information about how your body is working and feeling, *and* all of the information about the outside world that is fed into the brain. That's a total of two million bits of incoming information per second! But most of this data is handled automatically. We are only aware of a tiny fraction of this information at a conscious level.

If we have a brain malfunction, either physical or chemical, it affects our feelings. Things seem real to each of us in a way that no one else can possibly understand. And once our mind is engaged with a negative thought, the body is triggered to produce chemicals that can increase the negative effect and we spin out of control. Physical brain problems can be the result of disease or injury. Chemically, this can happen with too many martinis, prescription drugs, and even some foods.

THE MIND

When someone has a sudden scare or flash of anger, it triggers a re-action in the body. Their bloodstream is flooded with hormones and chemicals. Their heart races and their eyes narrow. Their breathing increases and they get ready to fight or run away. Chemicals like these go into the brain and change the way it works. Then those parts of the brain devoted to higher functions, like creative thought, shut down and other, more basic parts take over. When this happens, you become a specialized survival machine. Back in the days when we were running around in the tall grass and might easily become lunch for something bigger and hungrier than we were, this was a good design.

This design is not as useful when we're on the way home in commuter traffic and someone cuts us off. Using our higher brain functions might be more optimal when we're driving two tons of steel down the freeway. This survival design also isn't very efficient if we're in a work situation and some unexpected remark triggers our "fight-or-flight" instinct. When that happens, we lose the ability to think rationally and express ourselves persuasively. Again, it's how we interpret our situation with our mind that causes our brain to revert to our flight-or-fight instinct.

So, body connects to brain, and brain to body. And your mind, the part that feels like "you," is a pattern of nerve connections in your brain. You are housed in your brain *and* your body. But if someone were to cut open your body or brain, they wouldn't find a picture of your home, or the taste of chocolate milk, or the sound of birds singing. All that you experience, all that you think, you create in your *mind*.

The bits of data are stored in the brain, in billions of neurons, but to make the connections and to create the experience that make up our lives requires "us." The brain is not a hard drive that can operate on its own. It takes our *conscious* minds to make everything work so that we can ride a bicycle, go shopping, enjoy a meal, or make music.

Different Planets: The Worlds Inside Our Minds

I bet you think you know what's real, right? If we were in the room together, you might assume that the world you live in is the same one I live in. Sorry, Charlie, it just ain't so.

As soon as we're born, we begin noticing things. At first, it's chaos. You can imagine all that stuff flooding in, all those images, all those sounds, smells, tastes, body sensations. What does your mind do with all this stuff? Well, it develops languages, five languages. The only way you can think is to use pictures, sounds, feelings, tastes, and smells; these are the basis of the mind.

For now, maybe you need to take my word for it that the world that *you* see and the world that *you* live in is really IN YOUR HEAD. It's in *your* head and no one else's. Your own mind is creating the world you live in. The relationships that you have, the way you feel about the people around you, and the way you feel about yourself are all filters, and almost all of these filters were created unintentionally.

Because you've chosen to pick up this book, you've probably already done a lot of work on yourself. You've worked on the content of your thoughts. You've worked on what you think. Here's my point: *how* you think can profoundly affect *what* you think. Until now, you've had no tools to deal with how you think and how that affects you. The process that we're going to be immersed in is dealing with the HOW, *not* the WHAT.

Your brain has sight, sound, feeling, taste, and smell, but you don't use them all with the same intensity. Rather than talk about this more, let's play with an example of your own so you can discover your own personal world. Throughout this book, I'm going to ask you questions you've probably never thought about before. Even so, you'll always know the answer, even if you've never heard the question before. So here's one to get started.

Discovery Activity:
Discovering Your Inner World

Think of the clothes you wore yesterday. When you think of them, how are you seeing the clothes? Are they hanging in the closet or do you see them on your body as though you're looking in a mirror? Perhaps they're laid out on the bed before you put them on—or lying on the bathroom floor after you took them off. There are lots of ways you might see yesterday's clothes.

Here's what I'd like you to do next. As you see them, notice how you are really seeing them. After all, it's not like yesterday's clothes magically appeared in front of you.

In your mind's eye, can you actually see the clothes you remember wearing yesterday? Take a good look at the image itself, how you see them. Notice that you actually made a mental picture. This is your brain's way of saying, "Oh yeah. He said yesterday's clothes; here they are."

You automatically went in and retrieved the data. Your brain constructed this image for you. This particular picture probably wasn't filled in the way you're seeing it now. After all, as you went through your day yesterday, you filed countless images of the day's experiences. But you may have been unaware of this particular image until you called it up in response to my question, so notice that.

Here's another example. No matter where you live, there's probably a front door to your home, right? Whether it's a house, an apartment, a room, a tent, or a cave, there's some sort of way to close the entrance. I invite you to notice something.

When I mentioned the entrance to your home, you thought about it, didn't you? And you can think of it now, and when you do you'll notice that you know exactly what it looks like. You can see the color and the form of the door or tent flap, and you know what side has the handle, and exactly how to open it.

How do you know that? You may be thinking, "I just know it, that's all, I live there!" Here's the deal: being able to imagine your front door requires a new awareness on your part. You just have to look inside your mind, and slow your thinking process w-a-y down so you can see your thoughts in slow motion, like watching a movie frame by frame.

Think of your front door again. You see a picture of it in your mind, don't you? Check it out and you'll see I'm right. When you think of your front door, you can see it. You'd have to see it to be able to know what it's like from memory.

So now you see your front door. Let's open it and step inside.

Is there any sound as you open the door? Listen for a moment and notice the sound of the door opening. Perhaps you hear the latch as it releases, a squeaky hinge, the door scraping along the floor, or some other sound as the door opens. Maybe you also noticed how heavy the door was or how cool the knob was when you touched it. What physical sensations did you notice?

Again, it's just your front door. But you have lots of information about it that's stored and automated. You only notice these pictures, sounds, and feelings when you slow down and try to remember them.

Let's explore a very different example that will show you more about how your mind works. I'm going to ask you to think about something that I bet you've never thought about before. Think of being at the beach, and think of using your elbow to scratch something in the sand. If you're right-handed, think of using your left elbow. If you're left-handed, think of using your right elbow. In other words, this is an elbow with no special skills. Now, think of scratching the letter *A* in the sand. Can you imagine doing that? I bet you've never done it before, certainly not with your off-elbow.

Here's an interesting thing. To imagine doing that, you have to see the letter A. Maybe you saw it in the sand, but you began with the shape of the letter A in your mind. You're doing this and you're sitting someplace reading this book. My question to you is, what does that letter A look like in your mind?

We've all seen the letter A printed in lots of different styles and sizes. We've seen it as big as a billboard and as small as directions on a jar. We've seen it in an array of colors, bold script, lit-up letters on neon signs. But when you think of the letter A, what comes to your mind? After all, your mind has a way of producing the letter A for you.

Writing the A in the sand required you to do more than remember something you'd experienced. You had to remember the letter A and how to write it, as well as what sand at the beach is like. And you had to construct an imaginary experience where you combined all these remembered elements—including how to write with your opposite elbow! Your mind can do amazing things.

Okay, let's leave the beach and go back to your door; remember how it sounds and feels when you open it.

Think about other doors in your life, and think about how they sound.

Notice other differences when you enter other places.

Notice not only the sounds associated with the door, but perhaps the smell. When you think of the door to a coffee shop or a bakery, a friend's house when dinner is grilling on the barbecue, the door to the gym, the door to the hospital. Or maybe you might remember a different smell.

Think of other places you might visit in your mind. Let your mind wander to your old school or workplace, or other homes and businesses. Think of parks and outdoor spaces.

As you think of the different places you might visit, you may notice other feelings attached to these memories.

Perhaps you need to walk up steps to a certain place, or pull extra hard on a door. Or maybe your memory took you to a camping spot . . . somewhere wet . . . or somewhere cold.

You might notice that your emotional feelings are different depending on the place you think about visiting. They might range from unpleasant . . . to neutral . . . to excited . . . to happy, depending on the experiences you connect to the place you're thinking about.

Here's the reason. We live inside our bodies and the only way we can know what's outside our bodies is with our senses. We see, hear, feel, taste, and smell the world, and that information has been flowing into our brains since a little while before we were born.

When information first began to enter our awareness, there was no way to make sense of anything, so it must have been pretty confusing for a while. Then our brains began to put the sensations together.

As we learned earlier, our brains figured out how to sort and file this information. It decided what went with what. It stored everything you have ever thought, felt, seen, heard, dreamed, or imagined. Even now, as you read this and check the memories and ideas that I've suggested, you are pulling up old pictures, sounds, feelings, tastes, and smells from your personal storage.

Not Just Basic Cable: "Representational Modalities"

As your thoughts occur, your experience of life is *re-presented* in your mind in words, pictures, taste, smell, and feelings. (Okay, usually just pictures, words, and feelings.) Understanding how this works makes lots of things possible. These phenomena are what we call—here comes the jargon—"Representational Modalities," or "Rep Modes." *Rep modes* is a fancy label for the five senses.

Most of us tend to favor one rep mode over the others. Some of us will favor an image. Some people favor voices. That's me; I'm highly auditory. People like me tend to remember something by the way it sounds rather than how it looks. It's better for me to remember a phone number by hearing it than seeing it. But because now I both hear *and* see the phone number, it's even easier to remember. Other people remember more kinesthetically, which means physical and emotional feelings.

The ways we behave and express ourselves reflect these kinds of thinking. To give you a little preview, here are some broad generalizations. Auditory thinkers tend to have more melodious voices and tend to talk a lot. Visual thinkers, like my wife, Vikki, tend to talk more quickly. Kinesthetic thinkers tend to talk more slowly.

There's a difference in the way they *process*, too. Kinesthetic thinkers tend to process things more slowly and thoroughly. They like to really get a feel for things or have a firm grasp on the situation. They don't get the point until they've wandered all the way around it and have satisfied themselves that they have completely covered the territory.

If someone is auditory, they really need to hear what you're saying. These people march to their own drummer and tend to make their own music. People who prefer visual modes of thinking are people who see your vision, picture themselves driving that new car, or talk something through until they can see eye-to-eye with someone. Someone's rep mode preferences are also evident in their language (which you'll learn more about in a later chapter).

The different ways our minds create thought, using these five senses, touch every part of our lives. The more you think about that and the more time you spend exploring these concepts, the more it will become apparent that these processes affect *every* part of your life.

Most of us have grown up not thinking about the HOW of how we think. So, at first, we may have a hard time doing that. Some of us don't visualize as much because we're feeling people. Some of us are visual people, like "quick take" artists, who get things really fast and then are on to the next thing. There's a big contrast between that kind of thinking and kinesthetic thinking, which is slower and more thorough.

It takes all kinds, so wouldn't it be useful for all of us to become a little more well-rounded? All of us have access to parts of our brains that we just haven't used. You do what you do because it's what you've always done. One of the great benefits of learning about NLP is that you'll have many more choices and ways to think.

When you're focusing on this book, you're doing more than just reading, aren't you? You are adding NEW stuff to your memories and images. You are adding your comments right now, as you read this.

I'm talking to you and you're also talking to yourself. You might be saying "That's interesting" or shaking your head in disagreement. In fact, you're doing it right now!

And the next time you think of your front door or one of the other places you might have thought of during this last Discovery Activity, you will also remember where you were when you read this section of the book. You'll remember what you said to yourself and how you felt about what I'm telling you.

So basically, in your mind, your brain has created a whole model of *your* world, with every viewpoint you have ever seen, sensed, or imagined. When you think of the world, you don't actually think of the real thing; you just *think* you do.

What you actually are thinking of is *your* "model of the world" in your brain, the way that you particularly remember it.

And your emotional reactions are determined by this internal personal reality, not by the outside world. All of the information coming from outside is taken in and blended with all of the information that we generate in reaction to it.

Mind affects body, body affects mind.

When we have an emotional feeling, our blood chemistry changes and affects our brain even further. Round and round . . . mind to body . . . to mind, all becoming part of even more memories stored for later use. All of these images and sensations are stored throughout our lives, just waiting for us to call them up to recall something we once learned, or to mix the information in new ways to make something new and wonderfully possible for us.

What do you think that says about your memories? Did you think that you remembered things just as they happened, as though you captured them with a video recorder?

Actually, you store a highly *customized* version of your past, what may have actually happened and WHAT YOU THOUGHT ABOUT IT AT THE TIME. Every time you revisit a memory, you see what really stood out for you, what made an impression on you, and you don't bother with the rest.

In other words, the foreground of the memory gets sharper with repeated visits. In turn, the "background" gets duller and dimmer each time you remember the important part and ignore the rest, which changes the memory even further.

This means that there are NO accurate and complete memories in a human mind. Basically, your own personal history is a moving target. It shifts each time you call up a memory.

Most people make these shifts unconsciously. They really think that their reality is the same as it is for everyone else. It's one of the main reasons why there are so many disagreements between people about things that have happened, even if both parties were at the same event.

Memories are highly personalized; they change with each new recall.

Mental Sticky Notes: The Power of "Anchors"

There's another way your mind works—I call it mental sticky notes, although the proper term is "Anchors." Here's a quick example to illustrate the profound effect of an anchor. In fact, it's probably one of the main reasons I'm married today.

About fifteen years ago, I was on my way to my favorite bookstore. I'd just had lunch with a dear friend who's an NLP author and trainer. During our time together, I told her I was feeling grumpy about my love life. I'd been dating a lot of women; it felt sort of frantic to me and very tiring. I wasn't getting anywhere and I'd pretty much decided I was just going to stop. She said, "You make commitments too quickly. You don't need to cut off relationships, you just need to go on a commitment fast for a while."

I was musing over what she said as I went up the elevator to this bookstore, and there was a very nice lady in the elevator who smiled at me. I smiled back. It didn't mean anything—there was no "come-on" at all. The elevator opened up, we got out, and I forgot all about her.

I went into the bookstore and was just browsing when I heard a voice behind me asking for help. The clerk said, "Oh, go down to the other end of the store and ask somebody," and I thought, "Oh man, this is my favorite bookstore and that's so unhelpful." So I turned around to uphold the honor of the bookstore and found that the woman with the question was the lady who'd smiled at me in the elevator. When I asked her what she was looking for, she told me she'd just graduated from college (in her forties) and needed a specific book because she was starting grad school to become a psychotherapist. That's when I brought up NLP and we started talking.

She completely forgot about the book she was looking for, and eventually I became embarrassed that we were standing in this aisle in the bookstore talking, so I invited her next door for a cup of coffee. I needed to get back to my office, but I thought I would take a few minutes and do a little missionary work on behalf of my beloved interest in NLP. We went next door and we were having a cup of coffee and we talked about everything: NLP . . . our kids . . . our ex-mates (she was a widow) . . . our work . . . our interests.

It was a very pleasant time and I remember this moment like it was yesterday. She was sitting on my left and as she talked, she would laugh at something she'd said and lean over and gently place her hand on my left forearm. She'd say, "And Tom, that was the funniest thing!" and I just liked her. I wasn't romantic about it. She was too young, too cute, too blond, just not on my radar at all. But she was so natural and enjoyable to be with, I just wanted to talk to her some more. So I made an arrangement to talk to her. The rest is history.

But here's the thing. It's fifteen years later. We've been married for fourteen of those years and I swear I can still feel her hand on my left forearm where she placed it the day we met. *That's* an anchor, a very powerful one.

So anchors—whether they are kinesthetic, auditory, visual, gustatory, or olfactory—that are momentary and out of our awareness can stay with us and influence us for years. We have thousands of them throughout our lives. When you start becoming aware of the phenomena of anchors, you will weave these things into your consciousness and understanding and find little ways to work with them to make your life more convenient or richer—just like you did when you created a "Circle of Excellence" earlier in this chapter.

An anchor is anything that your mind uses to remind you of something else. As an example, we've all probably had the experience, at some point, of smelling a perfume, a cigar, or wood smoke, and instantly being transported to a different time in our lives.

Maybe that smell reminded us of a parent or a teacher or a relative, or that wood smoke reminded us of camping or barbecue, or a disaster. Bottom line, things remind us of other things. The interesting idea here is that this phenomenon, which is called anchoring, can be used deliberately.

Here are some other examples that you might not think of when I talk about anchors. How about doorknobs? A doorknob means egress and ingress, so that's an anchor. Remarks are anchors. People in advertising know this well.

Sometimes the anchor was simply a color. But a powerful anchor might be an image like a flag or a helmet. It might be a slogan that sounded almost like it made sense, but it didn't make sense unless you knew what it was we were selling. All of these are anchors.

Here's a phrase that most men react to as an anchor. A woman says, "We have to talk." That's an anchor. What she means is "I have something I want you to hear," but what we say to ourselves is "Uh-oh." Women have anchors, too. Not being female, I don't know what they are for sure, but maybe it's when a man says, "I'll be a little late from work," or "I'll do that tomorrow," or "I'll get around to it sometime," or "Don't bug me." These are all examples of anchors.

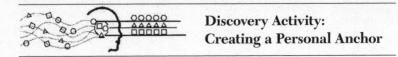

Discovery Activity: Creating a Personal Anchor

When you worked with the "Circle of Excellence," you created a powerful personal *spatial* anchor. Let's experiment with another kind of anchor. You're going to create a kinesthetic anchor, a touch anchor, that you can use on yourself, *for* yourself. How about an anchor that gives you a shot of confidence, enthusiasm, optimism, and self-regard whenever you need it? Would that be handy?

The nice thing about this particular anchor is you can do this anywhere, anytime you need a little lift—whether you're alone or in the middle of a meeting. Now, here's how to get the lift.

Use your nondominant hand for this activity. (If you're left-handed, use your right hand, and if you're right-handed, use your left hand.) With the tip of your thumb, find the spot that's the second knuckle of your middle finger. Practice touching that, because this is going to be an anchor we're going to use in just a minute.

Go back to a time when you actually had an experience when you felt optimistic and happy. It could be anything.

For a guy, it could be a time that your girl said yes to the prom. For a woman, maybe it was a time the right guy asked you out. Maybe it was a spelling bee or a swim meet you won. Maybe it was when you were out walking, where you were just overwhelmed by the good smells of nature and the wonderful feeling you had.

Okay, take a moment to go back and find a memory, a specific experience, that gives you the feeling of being optimistic and confident and happy with yourself. It could even be something from a movie you watched or a book you read.

The next question might be "Well, what do I do with it?" or "I can't find an experience like that." Let's take these one at a time. The answer to "What do I do with it?" is simply to go inside that experience. Remember how old you were at the time, and go inside that experience and relive it and enjoy it.

Take a moment. Give yourself thirty seconds to really enjoy that memory, and when you do, look around you and notice what you were seeing at the time. Notice what you were wearing. Notice how your body felt at that time.

When you're at the peak of feeling good, touch your thumb to that inside knuckle. Just press it once. There isn't much to it, but we're not done yet.

Now what I'd like you to do is to go back to that memory and notice that feeling.

Now find another memory where you felt that good, or even better. Go through your life and find another memory. When you've found that, go inside and imagine that experience.

When you first found the memory, you may have seen yourself as if you were in a photograph or a movie. Now I'd like you to go inside your imagination and actually *be* yourself, and go through that experience. When you're at the peak of good feelings, again touch your thumb to that inside second knuckle of your middle finger.

I have a question for you. What would it feel like if that positive feeling were twice as strong? Just imagine what it would feel like in your body if that good feeling were twice as strong, and again touch your thumb to your middle knuckle.

Wow! Now imagine that it doubled again, and it doubles as you touch the tip of your thumb to that knuckle. Imagine that. That feeling doubles again.

Okay, stop touching the anchor for a minute and take a step backward. If you've done that, you're probably back to your normal state, whatever you were when we started this exercise.

Think of your phone number.

Backward.

Now what I'd like you to do is touch your thumb to that knuckle on your middle finger again and just notice any good feelings that come up. Fascinating, isn't it?

For additional demonstrations and/or examples, go to http://eg.nlpco. com/1-1.

Anchors at Work: Intentional and Unintentional Anchors

As I mentioned, this is a basic kinesthetic (touch) anchor. To strengthen this anchor over the next couple of days, continue to go through your life experiences, finding the ones that gave you great joy and great optimism, and touch this certain spot again and again.

What this does is "stack" the anchors. This just tells your body and your unconscious, "Oh, this is a thing I can do to make myself feel good," and it knows how that is because it's felt good before. It's felt good in the past.

The effectiveness of this technique requires that you do two things. One, it requires that you actually use your imagination to relive a specific experience. Two, it's got to be specific. It can't be theoretical. It can't be general; it has to be concrete.

A recent good feeling for me was when my four-year-old granddaughter came up and said, "I love you, Poppa!" out of the clear blue sky. I melted and I just added that to the thousands of other experiences that I've done this with over the years. You can do it, too.

Here's another anchor just to think about. If somebody's near you and they've put their hand on your shoulder, usually that's a warm feeling. Some of us might feel invaded by that, depending on the relationship or timing, but for most of us that's a warm feeling. And you may notice that good salespeople will do that frequently.

For example, the Cornell School of Hotel Administration teaches hotel management skills. They did research on waitresses and found that waitresses who touched their customers' hands or shoulders (even accidentally, but who managed to make physical contact) earned an average of 25 percent higher tips. That's the advantage of what we call a touch anchor.

There are also other kinds of anchors. For instance, there's a certain tone of voice our loved ones have that we all recognize. Those are anchors. There's probably a tone of voice our parents had or our teachers. Those were anchors. These might not have been positive, but they were definitely anchors; they trigger a memory that has feelings attached to it.

When you're facilitating a meeting or presenting to a small group, those of us who've had presentation training have learned that if you're going to take questions, you move to one part of the stage and take questions from that location. When you're giving information, you move to another part of the stage. Gradually, the audience becomes aware of when they have permission to raise their hands and interrupt you, and when it's not okay. Those are called spatial anchors—like the "Circle of Excellence" you created.

We'll be coming back again and again to how you see and hear things in your mind, and the subject of anchors. This book introduces certain ways the mind works, gives you plenty of personal experience about how *your* mind works, and then shows you ways to use this information, first with yourself and then with others.

So What? How You Can Use This Information

You might be thinking, "So what?" or wondering how you can use this information. Here are a few examples.

If you're haunted by some dark memories, they may be affecting your behavior or limiting your choices. In this book, you will learn to change the way you hold a specific experience, if you wish. Or, suppose you have a habit you want to change. By managing the *process* of your thinking, you can learn how to shift old unwanted habits into new and more useful ones. There may be other behaviors you might want to adjust. Perhaps you're shy, you put things off, or you're hesitating to explore the life of your dreams.

In these first few Discovery Activities, we've begun to develop an understanding of how, by storing elements from our senses combined with some internally generated comments and imaginings, we actually re-create reality inside our minds. In the rest of this book, we'll be looking at the many ways we can shift the pictures, sounds, feelings, tastes, and smells in our memories so that we get better results in our daily lives.

Here's something else that always amazes me when I work with clients. You won't remember who you were when you began reading this book—because you've already begun to change—but your friends and family around you will. In fact, a couple of months from now, somebody is going to comment on the changes they notice in you. They'll see the difference between the way you are and the way you were. They'll notice a single, specific way that you're different—or the cumulative effect of all these things that you're learning and applying—which is why the first chunk of this book is about applying these processes to yourself. When you have successful experiences with these different techniques and ways of thinking, they're *real* to you.

As you integrate these strategies into how you think and the choices you make, they become second nature. What happens as you become more aware and more expert is that you begin to see how they are at work around you in other people, too—which is fascinating in a whole new way.

Because your NLP skills can heighten your awareness and personal effectiveness, you want to keep them handy and sharp. After all, like any tool, it only works when you use it, not when it's stashed in a drawer. Let me tell you a story about my friend Tom Dotz. Even though he's been immersed in the NLP field for years, running a major NLP institute in the United States, he still has moments where he forgets to use his NLP skills.

I was visiting his Colorado office one day and we were about to go out to lunch. Like most people, he felt compelled to check his email one more time before we left. When he did, he suddenly looked much less than happy. "Damn, it's so-and-so *again*. I'm getting to the point where I just hate to look at my in-box."

I couldn't resist responding to such a limiting statement from my friend since it wasn't a reflection of how he usually thinks and behaves. And because Tom and I have had a long and enjoyable friendship, I just laughed out loud. Then, with a big *Gotcha!* smile, I said, "Well, Tom. It's too bad you *can't* do anything about that."

My choice of words was quite intentional. You see, Tom has a leaning toward what, in NLP, we call "Counter-Exampling"—which means that if you give him an absolute statement, he feels almost obliged to point out an exception—or two, or *more*!

So when I jokingly said, "Too bad you can't do anything about that," I *knew* his mind would automatically start feeding him ways he *could*. And it did.

"You're right, Tom. Sometimes I forget to use my own stuff on me. I'm totally congruent about changing this. One thing I can easily do is anchor a *different* more positive response. Or, I could . . ." and on he went to list several more ways he could change his response to his in-box to one that served him better.

The point is that knowledge is power—but only if you use it. After all, positive and negative anchors are everywhere—someone's name in your email in-box, the tone of someone's voice, the way they shake their head or chew their fingernails may stimulate a feeling in response. When you notice a feeling you don't want (or do want) and trace it back to the cause, you will find a trigger—it could be an image, sound, touch, or even a taste or smell—that sets that feeling in motion. Then, you can do something to make your experience better. Once you learn NLP, you always have the power to make positive changes. You just have to remember and use the amazing selection of tools you have right at hand.

An Easy Ride: How This Book Is Structured

I've structured this resource in a way that guides you through your first reading *and* makes it easy to refer to specific things in the future. Although I'd like you to read the chapters in sequence because each chapter builds on the earlier ones, the Contents (in the front) and Index (in the back) will help you look up anything you want to revisit, and the glossary provides definitions of common NLP terms.

The book is divided into two sections. The first one (Chapters 1–4) focuses on *you*—how your mind works and changes you can make to feel even more confident and energized. The second section concentrates on your interactions with others and how these can be easier and more rewarding.

Section 2 *builds* on the first section and enables you to apply what you've learned to other people, not just to yourself. This doesn't mean that you're changing or "fixing" someone else. (After all, it's inadvisable to do that without their permission.) It simply means that the same NLP concepts that helped you understand how *you* "work" can help you understand *other* people. That new understanding enables you to make different choices about interacting with them—hopefully, in a way that's more in line with your desired outcome.

Each chapter is a bit like a conversation where I'll introduce different NLP concepts and share examples that illustrate how these ideas are important. The Discovery Activities give you an opportunity to explore these concepts as they relate to *you* and changes you might like to make. After many of these activities, I've provided an Internet link where you can access a demo of that process or easily get additional information.

At the end of each chapter, there's a quick summary of Key Ideas, as well as a URL link and QR code to access a list of Bonus Activities and additional examples that will help you enhance your understanding and NLP skills. The two blank pages at the very end of each chapter offer you a place to capture your thoughts and list future things you'd like to work on with the concepts you learned during that part of the book.

In the final chapter, I've included highlights from the book and processes you will have learned. To help you determine what next steps you want to take to strengthen your NLP knowledge and skills, I've provided an easy 21-Day Guide and a link to a list of my favorite NLP resources. My goal is to make becoming an NLP power user easy and fun so you can create an even better life.

As I mentioned in the Introduction, *NLP is more important today than ever before* because, in this world of ever-evolving technology, we are *constantly* connecting—with people we work with, people we love, and people who have information and/or access to others. We're so busy responding, that we hardly have time to think.

One final note for this chapter. NLP is a robust and evolving technology, so no book is all-inclusive. This one focuses on key concepts and strategies that lend themselves to a self-study format. It also focuses on *you*! Here's why. Because NLP was initially designed as brief therapy, many available resources target helping *other* people make desired changes.

Yet, after years of working with NLP masters and trainees, it's clear to me that most people really want to use these powerful tools to help *themselves.* Using NLP to become a better you isn't a selfish thing—like putting on your oxygen mask first during an airplane emergency, it's purely practical. There are two reasons. First of all, changing yourself *is* within your control. Second, when you change any variable in an equation, the results change. As you change yourself, you'll notice how—without a word—people around you shift in response. This phenomenon is fascinating and is likely to inspire you to make more changes!

So turn the page, and let's start to explore more about how you think, and the amazing things you can do when you choose to "customize" your thinking.

Key Ideas

- Our brains interpret the sensory input we get, and assign a meaning to it. As soon as a meaning is assigned, it leads to an emotion. This is unconscious, and fast, so that we have the stimulus *and* the emotion. The rest is out of awareness.

- When we learn, we generalize. Because we had some experiences in the past that seem similar, we generalize and automate; it's an efficiency strategy.

- Generalization is also how beliefs get formed; then beliefs filter all the different stimuli coming in. The mind doesn't really get raw information; it no longer gets to choose.

- Deletion is when the mind ignores specific sensory input.

- Distortion is changing an experience from what it *actually* is to some modified form of it.

- Each of us is a blend of body, brain, and mind.

- The world inside someone's mind is based on five languages: sight, sound, smell, taste, and feeling.

- The world each person sees and lives in is really the world *inside* their head.

- People often favor one sense or "rep mode" over the others so they are more visual . . . more auditory . . . or more kinesthetic.

- What people remember is a moving target; it shifts each time someone calls up a memory.

- Our minds can recall what we specifically experienced *and* combine remembered elements to create new imagined experiences and ideas—which are critical to change and innovation.

- Consciously using mental sticky notes (anchors) is a powerful way to strengthen positive mental "states" and diminish negative ones.

- Of the NLP Presuppositions, this book touches on the following ones:

  > Experience has structure. *It consists of sensory impressions. Some are internally generated and others come from the outside world. That blend, plus the meanings we add, makes up our individual experience.*
  > People are like mapmakers. *We make internal representa-*

tions ("maps") of personal experiences. People's maps are made up of pictures, sounds, feelings, smells, and tastes. These are the "languages of the senses" that our brains use to record our experiences.

> The map is not the territory. *Each of us creates a personal map. It's our world, not THE world.*

> People respond to their maps of reality, not to reality itself. *All thought—memories, recall, imaginings, daydreams, fantasies—can be called maps. They're what we respond to.*

> If you change someone's map, their emotional state will change. *To all of us, the map IS the experience. Maps are the source of emotions and beliefs. Our feelings change when our maps do.*

> Some maps are out of awareness. *We are unaware of some of the maps that we have made; it takes language skills and sensory acuity to identify these maps. They are in the unconscious.*

> Behind every behavior is a positive intention. *When we seek the "outcome behind the behavior," we will find a universally shared need, like love, safety, self-respect, etc.*

> There is no such thing as an inner enemy. *Yet there are frequently clumsy or misguided "inner friends" who have positive intentions for us but tend to repeat inappropriate or outdated patterns of behavior.*

> Choice is better than no choice. *No choice means slavery or robotic behavior. Having choices in any situation gives each of us the freedom to change and grow. Choice gives us more "clicks on the dial."*

> People always make the best choices available to them at the time. *We do the best we can in the moment and we might be happier and more effective if we had more choices available to us.*

> A system's most flexible element has the most influence. *When we have more choices, we have more influence and more ways to get our desired outcome.*
> The meaning of any communication is the response it gets. *Communication is not a solo act. It doesn't matter what our intentions are; communication is defined by the reaction it gets.*
> People work perfectly to produce the results they are getting. *If our results are not satisfactory, we can learn to develop more choices so we can get different results.*
> Every behavior is useful in some context. *Every capability exists for some useful reason.*
> Anyone can do anything that anyone else can do. *Since all human nervous systems are similar (except in the case of actual physical or mental limitations), we can model and learn each other's skills and attitudes. "Monkey see, monkey do."*
> Chunking: using small chunks to learn big stuff. *People learn easily by breaking big subjects into small chunks. For example, these presuppositions are easy to learn, if considered a few at a time.*
> People already have all the resources they need. *We either have the experience in our memory banks or we are capable of successfully imagining it. Then we can use it where it's needed.*
> There is no such thing as failure, only feedback. *We are always producing a result; if it's not what we want, we can use the unwanted result as feedback to guide us in experimenting with other choices.*
> The quality of our lives is determined by the quality of our communications. *How we communicate with ourselves creates our personal experience and how we communicate*

*with others determines the way we are treated throughout
our lives.*

> Mind and body are part of the same system and they affect
each other. *What each of us thinks affects our individual
physiology, as well as our health, and what we do to our
bodies affects our feelings and thoughts.*

> Communication is redundant. *People are simultaneously
communicating in all three systems—visual, auditory, kinesthetic.*

> Positive change comes from adding resources. *NLP helps
us add choices; it doesn't delete.*

> If what you are doing isn't working, try anything else. *If
we keep experimenting, we aren't guaranteed success, but
we can sure stack the odds. The only way to fail is to quit
trying!*

 To enhance the skills you learned in this chapter,
check out the recommended Bonus Activities at our
special "Essential Guide" website: http://eg.nlpco
.com/1-4 or use the QR code with your phone.

Discoveries, Questions, Ideas, and Stuff You Want to Work On

Discoveries, Questions, Ideas, and Stuff You Want to Work On

CHAPTER TWO: MANAGING YOUR MIND

Who's driving the bus?

A man who has control over his mind
is able to realize its full potential.
—The Sama Veda

B ecause few of us understand how our brains and minds work, we don't really take charge. We don't really *know* what pictures, sounds, feelings, tastes, and smells are in our brains and minds, let alone how that information is impacting us right now. Here's the deal. The *brain* operates pretty much on its own, doing its job to process information and keep us alive. In contrast, the *mind* is able to focus on more than just survival; it affords us the opportunity to create and choose from a myriad of options.

In this chapter, we're going to explore the way our brains make sense of the world, how to fine-tune that process, and how to deal with things that cause an emotional reaction and pull us off our desired course, so we can better navigate our personal journeys.

Where Do You Want to Go? Outcome Frames

Imagine this. Someone gets into a taxi and the driver asks, "Where to?" and the passenger says, "Don't take me to the airport." It sounds silly and yet it's how many of us navigate our lives. It's hard to get where we want to go when we're not completely clear or congruent about where that is. It's easy to wind up somewhere we don't want to be and wonder how we got there, isn't it?

So first, we need to know what we want: we need an "Outcome." What's an outcome? It's something you desire that's achievable, appropriate, *and* measurable. It's easy to mistake a desire that's a social influence for one that is personal. Maybe you do want a private jet, but maybe what you really want is just to be able to travel more easily. Owning and maintaining a personal jet is pretty expensive, and there are many other easier ways to travel.

One of the most essential NLP processes is the Outcome Frame, because it carefully and thoroughly addresses the elements that make up a worthwhile goal that truly serves *you*. Leslie Cameron, one of the codevelopers of NLP, explains it this way:

> The Outcome Frame is a set of questions that orient your thinking to maximize the possibility of your getting what you want and being glad that you got it. It's actually an orientation, a way of perceiving experience as a set of choices. Rather than addressing the issue of why a problem exists, it organizes experience around what is wanted, and how it is possible to achieve it.
>
> In NLP, there is an ongoing presupposition that if it's possible for one person in the world to do something, it's possible for anyone to do it; it's only a question of *how*.
>
> The "how" orientation of the Outcome Frame makes it possible to turn the inevitable setbacks and stumblings that you experience into valuable feedback. As long as you have a specified outcome that you are holding constant, and know that it is possible to attain, a setback is simply something that happens along the way towards your out-

come. The things you do that take you towards your outcome let you know you are on the right track. Those that are disappointing indicate only that what you are doing to attain your outcome is not useful and that you need to change your tack.

Once I learned to use the Well-Formed Outcome, I wondered how I ever got along without it. It's so simple and effective that you can apply it to anything you want. It's especially helpful when you're planning big changes, find yourself stuck, or when you simply want to fine-tune a goal you have or are pursuing. Let's review the key questions and conditions of a Well-Formed Outcome and then you'll have an opportunity to apply them, using a simple worksheet, to an outcome that you want.

The Well-Formed Outcome involves the following six questions, which we'll explore one at a time, using the sample goal of wanting to feel more persuasive.

- What specifically do you want?

- How will you know when you've achieved what you want?

- Under what circumstances, where, when, and with whom, do you want to have this result?

- What stops you from having your desired outcome already?

- What resources will you need to help you create what you want?

- How are you going to get there—and what's the first step to begin to achieve this result?

1. WHAT SPECIFICALLY DO YOU WANT?

W. Clement Stone said, "All personal achievement starts in the mind of the individual. The first step is to know *exactly* what your problem, goal or desire is." Using the Well-Formed Outcome, a goal must be: stated in positive terms, chosen by you *and* within your control, described in a sensory-specific way, and have a manageable size or scope—which we call "Chunk Size" in NLP. (Common NLP terms are described in the glossary at the back of the book.)

Here we go. Imagine that you wanted to feel more persuasive. Remember, if your goal is to feel more persuasive, you *can't* state it as "I don't want to feel pushy" or "I don't want to seem like a know-it-all." These aren't really goals at all. They're simply a statement of what you *don't* want. It's too vague to ever know if you had attained it. It's also very hard for the brain to work with negatives. How do you *not* think of a purple elephant? First, you *have to* think of it and then try not to think of it. That's just a big waste of energy. So every time you think, "I don't want to be pushy," you first have to think of being pushy. The only way to stop that thought is to think of something else. So why not just go for what you *do* want, directly?

And you have to think, "Even though there might be factors, like a critical boss or spouse, difficult customers, or product problems that may impact my emotions, feeling more persuasive *is* largely within *my* control."

To fine-tune what feeling persuasive is, I'd want to describe what that means to me in specific, sensory terms. To do this, I ask myself, "What will I see, hear, or feel when I am feeling and being more persuasive? Or what might other people notice if I were feeling persuasive?" In response, I might say, "When I'm feeling persuasive, I'll feel like I'm really being helpful, that I'm giving someone what they need to make a good decision. I'll be breathing comfortably, thinking clearly—easily accessing information and materials I need, and expressing myself in a dynamic, helpful way."

Because feeling persuasive is a large outcome, I may want to narrow that down. For example, I might want to narrow the focus a little so my goal becomes: "I want to be feeling more persuasive in my job."

Next, I'd ask myself about the outcome of the outcome (the "Meta-Outcome") so I can try on what *achieving* my goal will do for me. What is essential, and often missed, is that in any outcome or goal, you are unlikely to know how satisfying it really will be until you have actually experienced it. In the case of any large goal, you want to find or create opportunities to sample it before investing what may be years of your life only to be disappointed. For instance, before starting law school, an internship or administrative job in a law office would be a good idea.

To explore my meta-outcomes, I'd ask myself, "What will feeling more persuasive in my job do for me? When I'm thinking clearly, easily accessing information and materials I need, and communicating effectively, what else will *that* do for me that's even more important?" When I think about this, I might say, "My customers will respond more positively and give me more orders. If they give me more orders, I'd make more commission. If I make more commission, I could buy a better car. And, if I could buy a better car, I'd feel more comfortable taking those long road trips my spouse loves." You get the drift—this line of thinking about the "Meta" (next-level) outcomes took me from getting more orders to taking long road trips!

2. How will you know when you have it?

Because I now have refined my goal using the first question and sub-questions, I can more easily address this next one, right? This question requires me to create evidence—so I'll know if I've achieved my goal or at least am making progress. Establishing appropriate and timely evidence invites me to consider how soon, or how frequently, I want to have this outcome. As the saying goes, a goal is a dream with a deadline. Absent a commitment to take action, little is ever accomplished.

So when I ask myself, "How soon do I want to feel more persuasive at work?" I may be tempted to answer, "Right away!" A more realistic approach is to identify a time frame that allows me to take the necessary steps to achieve my goal—but doesn't leave things in a "someday" type of holding pattern. So, I might say, "I'd like to feel more persuasive at work by end of second quarter because I'll get to present my sales numbers at our June meeting—and my results will reflect my increased feeling of persuasiveness." This gives me a *specific* target date. To establish additional evidence, I could determine benchmarks for my current orders and sales dollars.

3. WHERE, WHEN, AND WITH WHOM DO YOU WANT IT?

The objective of this question is to determine if the goal is "Ecological." To give you a silly example of a nonecological goal, there was a man in Indonesia who wanted to get in the *Guinness Book of World Records*. The record he chose was one for which there wasn't much competition. Although that makes good sense, he decided to pursue the record for the longest time buried alive. He survived his first attempt, but fell short of the record. Unfortunately, he didn't survive his second attempt.

Of course, you wouldn't do anything that extreme, yet people frequently find themselves pursuing all sorts of goals from the small (that ideal pair of shoes) to the lifetime ones (a law degree, a marriage) only to realize upon getting them that they weren't worth the sacrifice.

How much better to consider this in advance? How do you make sure you don't choose a goal that might prove to have disastrous effects? Here's how you do that. Try it on. This might be by imagining what it will be like to achieve your goal. If you don't have enough information to make a mental movie, it may be advisable to identify opportunities that would enable you to try it on.

If, for example, your goal is to become a doctor, you might want to volunteer with the Red Cross or try working in a hospital before making a twelve-year commitment to the extensive medical training required. Also, if the goal you're considering is something major like a career goal, assessing elements like income potential and costs are basic and essential ecology checks. So another way to explore ecology is to ask, "How could pursuing and getting this outcome be a problem for me?" You see, ecology checks are there to protect you.

Another ecology-oriented question is "How will my desired outcome affect my life? How will this affect my health, friends and family, finances, and work?" Even though the meta-outcomes I came up with were attractive to me, I didn't consider how the potential ripple effects of getting what I want might affect the people who are important to me. For example, feeling persuasive might change my behavior *and,* consequently, some of the friendships I currently enjoy at work. My coworkers might become more competitive with me. My boss could be happy, but he could also be intimidated. If I really excelled and got promoted, I might be asked to transfer, which I don't think my spouse would like because our children are all nearby. You get the picture.

A twenty-six-year-old client of mine dreamed of being a speech pathologist and was the first woman in her family to earn a college degree. When she got it, she was surprised that her family wasn't more excited. In fact, they treated her as though, all of a sudden, she thought she was too good for them. This potential reaction had never occurred to her. So if you're having trouble anticipating the ripple effects, get some input from people who know you, your situation, and your significant others well. There's no guarantee or threat that what you come up with will actually happen as a result of getting your outcome—but it's important to anticipate these possibilities.

4. WHAT STOPS YOU FROM HAVING YOUR DESIRED OUTCOME ALREADY?

The purpose of this question is twofold. First, it helps you generate a list of action items. Second, it can reveal what you're thinking and feeling.

So when I ask myself what stops me from feeling more persuasive, I might be thinking, "I need a better script for positioning our latest product" or "I need to memorize our latest research data." Whatever answers I come up with simply become tasks on my to-do list.

However, when I ask myself what stops me from feeling persuasive, I might also find myself feeling frustrated and thinking, "In this economy, it's really hard to make appointments with prospects." This limited thinking stops me, and it's not completely true. Other salespeople are getting appointments with prospects. So even though it may be challenging to get appointments and I may need to experiment with different approaches, it is possible. After all, it *isn't* likely that these potential clients won't see *anyone* new, is it? Identifying what's real and what's not makes it possible to create a workable strategy for achieving a goal. Asking questions like these helps you reconsider and refine goals that have been producing mixed feelings.

5. WHAT RESOURCES WILL YOU NEED TO HELP YOU CREATE WHAT YOU WANT?

There are two parts to this step. First, what resources do you *already* have that will contribute to getting your outcome? Second, what *additional* resources will you need in order to get your outcome? (In NLP, "Resources" might include knowledge, time, experience, money, contacts, support, and so on.)

So now I'm wondering, "What resources do I have right *now* that I can use to feel more persuasive at work?" Upon reflection, I might notice that I feel and am most persuasive when my presentation materials are well organized and I can easily put my hands on the right data or collateral. I might recall that I feel more persuasive and helpful when I tell success stories about how this solution has worked for other clients. And I might decide that because I have a proven track record with them, my current customers are often very open to new solutions I recommend. Talking with them to find out what their needs and challenges are helps me understand what's important to them and how I need to share information if I'm going to persuade them. I guess I could even ask them for referrals.

So, what *additional* resources do you need in order to get to your outcome? When I try this on in terms of my goal, I'm thinking that some additional sales training on getting appointments could be useful. I could check out what's offered online or in my community. Maybe my boss could be a resource, too. I could record my phone calls and get coaching on what I could have said or done differently.

Sometimes when we're feeling stuck, it's hard to think of what resources might be useful. Checking out the Internet and online groups, or brainstorming with colleagues or friends, can help loosen up our thinking and open up new possibilities.

6. How are you going to get there?

Without action, a goal is just an idea. In addition to a timeline, a useful plan breaks the who, what, how, when, and where into manageable chunks. Since talking with current customers will move me closer to my goal, part of my plan would include a list of which customers to contact and compiling a list of key questions to ask them. My plan might also include some Internet research and networking on appointment setting so I could strengthen my selling skills and not feel so flustered when someone isn't yet ready to meet with me.

Although chunk and sequence size are critical to a successful plan, having *options* about how to accomplish a goal is also essential. In NLP, we operate on the premise that more choice is better. So a plan whose success depends on just one way of doing something can be a recipe for disappointment. Ideally, a plan is just a road map. You use it to get where you're going, and it includes alternate routes.

That's an overview of the Well-Formed Outcome. So, right now, think of at least three things you want. It might be as simple as "What I want to get out of this book is . . ." or as complex as "I want to travel more." List these "wants" you came up with on the blank pages at the end of this chapter.

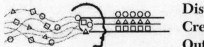 **Discovery Activity:**
Creating a Well-Formed
Outcome

Pick one of the wants you just identified and use it to apply the Well-Formed Outcome, answering the questions using the worksheet on the following two pages.

Well-Formed Outcome Worksheet

1. **What specifically do you want?** *Describe your desired outcome or state in a positive sensory-based way that's an appropriate chunk-size and also addresses WHAT ELSE having or achieving your outcome will do for you (Meta-Outcomes).*

_____

_____

_____

_____

_____

2. **How will you know when you've achieved what you want?** *Determine if the "evidence" you're focused on is appropriate and timely (soon and regular enough).*

_____

_____

_____

_____

3. **Under what circumstances, where, when, and with whom, do you want to have this result?** *Reflect on the context(s) in which you want to have this outcome and evaluate the ecology so you can consider how achieving this result may affect other areas, aspects, or people in your life.*

_____

_____

_____

_____

4. **What stops you from having your desired outcome already?**
   Identify and explore any feelings, thoughts, or circumstances that seem to inhibit movement toward your outcome.

   _____

   _____

   _____

   _____

   _____

5. **What resources will you need to help you create what you want?** *Determine what resources you ALREADY have that will help you (knowledge, money, connections, etc.). Consider additional resources you'll need to move forward.*

   _____

   _____

   _____

   _____

   _____

6. **How are you going to get there?** *Identify manageable steps to help achieve your result, consider multiple options to get where you want to go, and determine the FIRST step you'll take.*

   _____

   _____

   _____

   _____

   _____

To use the Well-Formed Outcome for other goals, go to: http://eg.nlpco.com/2-1 or use the QR code with your phone.

One of the most valuable uses of the Well-Formed Outcome may seem counterintuitive. Updating your goals and throwing out ones that you realize don't fit is every bit as useful as creating ones that do. Maybe they did at one time, or maybe they were just nice to think about. Now, having taking these through the outcome process, the achievement is to *take them off* your list. Good for you. That frees up your energy and time for the outcomes you realize you really do want, that are worth having, and that you are ready to move toward.

Being of Two Minds: Congruence/Incongruence

"Have you ever felt like you wanted to go, but you felt like you wanted to stay?"

That lyric from an old Jimmy Durante song is a great example of something we all experience. It's that sense of an inner conflict, like one part of us wants to do one thing, and another part of us wants to do something else. Or it can seem that we're just uncertain about what we really want to do. NLP calls this "Incongruence": times when you feel conflicted about a goal or a situation.

You can also feel incongruent about a more pleasant conflict, like when part of you wants to go to the mountains and part of you wants to go to the beach. More important is when incongruence reveals a conflict in our values. Imagine, for example, that your boss told you that you need to be more aggressive with a certain customer. Yet, to you, being aggressive means being pushy, and being pushy violates your values and your sense of who you are.

You've also experienced times when you've felt no doubt or conflict, and everything seemed to be going your way. This is frequently referred to as "being in the zone" or being in a flow state. In NLP, we call this being "Congruent." Learning to detect when you are congruent, and when you are not, is a very important life skill. The more you are aware of your personal signals of incongruence, the faster you can identify and resolve the conflict you've uncovered. The faster you resolve any incongruence, the easier things will be for you *and* the more effective you will be because you're not spinning your wheels and unconsciously resisting or debating an issue.

Incongruence is a real source of friction in our lives. It takes a lot of personal energy to overcome a part of you that's really opposed to a certain course of action. The more you try to override that part, the more likely it is that the unwilling part of you will object more strongly. And when you fight with yourself, you tend to lose.

It's far more effective and in the long run simply easier to develop the ability to notice when you're incongruent and resolve it. It's one of the easiest skills to learn and one of the most rewarding. One of the greatest sources of emotional and physical stress is when your mind is trying desperately to override your body's righteous desire to stop you from doing something that violates your integrity. The most effective way to turbocharge your life is to learn to move in harmony with your values.

Here's how. We've all had experiences of being completely congruent about something we wanted. Just think back to when you were a child and you really wanted that special toy for your birthday, or you really wanted that cherry Popsicle on a hot summer afternoon. In your adult life, you've had lots of experiences of being congruent about something you wanted. It could be as simple as knowing you craved Thai food or wanted to see that new movie.

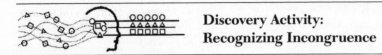

**Discovery Activity:
Recognizing Incongruence**

You've had many recent experiences of being congruent about something you wanted, right? So simply think of the first one of those recent situations that comes to your mind. Now, very specifically remember the time and place where you felt that way. Remember who, if anyone, was around you, where you were, what you saw, what you heard, and what you felt. Remember that experience now as if you were there and looking out from your own eyes. What are you seeing now? What are you hearing? What are you feeling?

Recalling all that is pretty empowering, isn't it? Right now, just pick one aspect of that memory, whether it's a picture or something heard or felt—one aspect that seems most important to you. It's your mind, so whichever element seems most important to you is the one.

Now, set that aside, and consider the opposite experience. Think of a time when you were really uncertain, when you really felt ambivalent about something that you were supposed to do. It's often easier to find a useful example when you think of something that someone else wanted you to do and you didn't really want to.

Think of that experience now, with this difference. Remember it as if it were at a distance, as if you were outside of it watching someone else. Watch that memory from outside, and notice—what's the first thing that let you know it was not something you wanted to do?

Now take that feeling, sound, or image and magnify it, make it louder or larger or brighter or stronger. You want to be sure that you'll recognize it every time it comes up. This is your warning signal. This is the signal that will let you know you need to really pay attention and sort out what's going on. Whenever you get that signal, it's time to stop the action, step back, and thoroughly assess your situation.

This is why I've found that creating a congruent Well-Formed Outcome is such an indispensable tool. When you make it a habit to review your goals and dreams through the Outcome Frame and your Congruence Check, you're less likely to get into situations where you find yourself in conflict with others—or, more important for the moment, with yourself.

Are You In or Out? Being Associated or Disassociated

In the two memories you just recalled, you may have noticed something different about the emotional impact. If you followed the instructions, in the first memory you were "in" the experience. NLP calls this an "Associated" experience. In the second memory you were outside the memory observing yourself, and that's called a "Disassociated" experience.

The technique of associating and disassociating is really useful and here's why: When we associate into an image or an experience, whether it's real or imaginary, it's much more intense for us. When we disassociate from an experience, we are watching ourselves in it and we still get most of the information from that image, but not the emotional impact.

The ability to recall an experience in a disassociated way allows you to observe it more impartially. Think back to the two different experiences you remembered. In the first experience, which was associated, you were *in* your feelings. In the second one, the disassociated experience, your feelings were observed from outside. They were "over there."

If you have a memory that feels yucky, I suggest that you always visit that memory disassociated. There's no reason to feel those old yucky feelings again, even once. You can still access the information by just seeing the movie, if you even want to do that. If a memory is really bad or traumatic, there are powerful ways to deal with it.

It's fascinating to me that some people tend to see all the unpleasant things, whether they're real or imagined worries, as *associated*. In this way, they're doing a lot to make themselves unhappy. Even if they're not doing it deliberately, it's a bad habit that causes them to get in the image and *live* the yucky bits. And, all the pleasant stuff, they view *disassociated*! If you sometimes do this, you can easily turn that around. You could immediately start changing your life outlook by noticing all of your experiences that were pleasant and revisiting them in an associated fashion, so you're actually reliving the experience. Try it; it will enrich you.

Because you're a different person than you were at the time the memory was created, and you know more today than you did then, you'll be able to perceive and understand more things about that past experience. Here's why. All of the data that was available is stored in your brain, so you can look around now and notice things you didn't notice before. This is the same phenomenon that makes hypnosis so effective. In hypnosis, you may have access to information that you ignored simply because it was in the background at the time.

It may be that you would choose to view all of your unpleasant memories, your worries, and even things about the future disassociated. Why live through them again? It was probably bad enough the first time. It's unnecessary roughness to do it again. There's no reason for it. If your brain says to you (or if you've been taught), "Well, that's how we learn," that's not true, it's not. You're really smart. You can learn the first time. You know what you like and don't like, and you know what feels good and what doesn't feel good. There's no necessity for or benefit from *any* continuing punishment.

Subtle Distinctions That Matter: Sub-Modalities

Association and disassociation is just one example of the finer distinctions our sensory systems make. In NLP, we think of the senses as "Modalities," and the unique and subtle qualities *within* each modality are called "Sub-Modalities." Because these distinctions reflect and impact how we feel, we refer to these as "molecules of meaning."

Just as learning to view your memories in a disassociated way can change your experience of that remembrance, discovering how to tinker with the other sub-modalities of your experiences can dramatically change how you feel about something *and* how you integrate it into the way you think about things in the future.

Because exploring sub-modalities is interesting and fun, much has been written about them and we could easily spend a lot of time on each one—but we won't. Instead, you'll have an opportunity to discover the sub-modalities of sight. Later, you can apply these same steps to exploring the sub-modalities of your *other* senses.

 **Discovery Activity: Tinkering with Visual Distinctions**

The process of making these discoveries may be unfamiliar and yet you'll know the answers to the questions I ask. My experience is that you'll have enough information available to you to recognize the differences between generalities about human behavior and the particulars that are very specific to you. In fact, you already successfully did some of this fine-tuning in the last activity.

Let's get started by exploring a specific example where you can compare and contrast a few of your select mental pictures.

Right now, I want you to imagine your favorite food, the one food on the planet that you most enjoy eating, and just imagine a picture of it. When you're seeing that picture, hold on to that in your mind's eye.

Leave that in one place, and now look at the food that you like the least, and observe the differences between the two. They may be in different positions in your imagining. If you really look at the images, you may find them with one slightly to the left and one slightly to the right, or one higher and one lower.

But look at the pictures and notice the differences in brightness. Notice also the differences in nearness. Which one's closer? Notice if there are any other differences in the pictures. As an example, does one have a frame around it? Is it kind of flat? Is one in color and one in black-and-white? Is one smaller than the other? Is one still and the other a motion picture?

The modality of vision is optimal to play with because most people are usually somewhat aware of their pictures or mental movies. We can easily access and reference them and notice that they have a lot of distinctions. These differences make a difference, as you're about to experience. You already know about association and disassociation, so let's try to experiment with that sub-modality and several new ones.

Look back and find a very pleasant memory that you may not have thought of for some time, something that you really enjoyed. Actually go back as if you were having that experience right now, so you're actually "in" it. As you look around, you're seeing what you saw at the time of the original experience. You can see what you saw.

Now, step out of it so you just see it as a movie with yourself in the picture. You can see yourself in that movie wherever you were.

When you were first remembering this pleasant memory, you weren't seeing yourself in a movie, you were "there," right? So when I asked you to step out and see yourself in a movie, that was a brand-new image that your brain just put up there. I have no idea what camera angle it picked or how distant you were, but your brain just automatically selected something.

Many of us experience memories as though they're mental movies. When you step into your mental movies and associate, you find that you can turn your head. You can see all the way around. When you're associated, it's like you're really in the picture. When you're disassociated, it's like you look at it from a slight distance. Most of the information we have in our heads, we see in a disassociated way.

So let's get back to this really pleasant memory of yours. As you're in the picture, go back in and associate into the memory so you're reliving it, and as you relive it, increase the brightness and notice any changes in your emotions about that.

Now don't bring the brightness up to blinding, but if you gradually increase the brightness, most people notice that they feel more attracted to that experience or that picture. It has more impact on them.

Now do this: Decrease the brightness slowly, slowly. Let it dim down until the image is hardly visible and see how that changes your feelings about it. Then brighten it up again. Bring it back to normal or better than normal (if you like that and it was a good experience for you).

There are some exceptions here. For instance, if your really pleasant memory involved candlelight, then increasing the brightness might take the romantic feeling away. Similarly, if you had a yucky feeling about being afraid of the dark and you make it dimmer, that's not going to work because you're even more afraid of the dark because you can't see.

So there are some places where brightness and dimness might work in the opposite way you expect, but you'll quickly discover when that's the case and can readjust the brightness to give you a positive effect. Now that you've experimented with brightness and associating, I'd like you to play with a different memory in these same ways.

Take an unpleasant memory. Now do not associate into this; see it about five to ten feet away from you in your mind's eye, as if it were a movie, and notice how your feeling changes about that memory when you do that, when you push it away from you a little bit and when you're outside it.

Then dim the picture. Slowly turn the brightness down on the picture and notice the change in your feelings. These are new sensations, so I don't expect you to be moaning with ecstasy or shuddering in horror. These are brand-new experiences and you need to get used to this. Your brain has been doing this for you all of your life.

Now let's try another one. From your vast scrapbook of pleasant memories, pick another really good experience that you had in your life. This time, I'd like you to see the memory like a movie. If you had a dozen memories like that, maybe you pick out one. What I'd like you to do with this pleasant memory is increase its size and notice how that changes your feelings about it. Notice how you may be more attracted to it as it gets larger.

And if you decrease its size so it's smaller than other memory photos that you might have lying around, you'll notice it's less noticeable and less attractive. It has less draw for you.

The sub-modalities of vision are fascinating. In addition to brightness, distance, and size (which we played with), there are sub-modalities that involve color. You can have the contrast turned up so it's very harsh light and dark. There can be just a lot of gradations of gray and pastels or the colors can be rich and vivid. An image may also be shifted from two-dimensional to three-dimensional. It can be crystal clear or it can be fuzzy.

A picture can vary in scope; it can even appear with a boundary around it. Usually you don't notice these subtle distinctions.

When you think of a picture of a grandmother, immediately some image pops into your mind. I don't know what that image is, but if you study that image you'll notice whether the image is in a context. Do you see that person actually doing something? Is the picture moving? Is it still? And as you look at the image, does it have a boundary around it? And is the boundary a formal frame or does it kind of fade out or is it sort of irregular?

For additional demonstrations and/or examples, go to: http://eg.nlpco .com/2-4.

To make it easy to play with different adjustments, in the Bonus Activities for this chapter you'll find a chart of sub-modalities for vision, hearing, and feeling. Take notes about your experiments of tinkering so you can identify which subtle distinctions make the biggest difference in your experience.

What's Your Day Going to Be Like?
Sub-Modalities and Your Emotional State

Because you can influence your experience of the past, present, and future by fiddling with your sub-modalities, imagine how much more pleasant and compelling your life could be if tomorrow you started to *consciously* shape your day. This is a self-management process that you can use to make your life easier every day.

Here's an example. When I wake up and I'm just coming to the planet, I ask myself five questions before I let my feet hit the floor. My first question is "What am I looking forward to today?" The second question is "Longer-term, what am I looking forward to?" Having something to look forward to gives me and most people a sense of direction and purpose.

The third question is "Am I doing things that lead directly to my goals?" If the answer is no, then this is an important area to explore because there's no reason why anybody should be doing things that don't lead them to their goals. Some people who find themselves on an unproductive path discover that their goals are unclear or not compelling.

When I ask this third question, I immediately hear the voices that have been in my head for decades saying, "Well, I *have to* do it. I have responsibilities. I have commitments." Right, we all do. Truth be told, almost all of those responsibilities and commitments were voluntary. What you're doing each day should be managing your time and energy, because that's the best thing *you* can do to support your goals.

The fourth question is "Am I being my best friend and supporter right now?" Are you your own cheerleader or your greatest critic? Research has shown that people who cheer themselves on generally do better. They're happier and they're actually physically healthier than people who are constantly criticizing themselves.

The fifth and final question is to scan your five senses and ask yourself, "Am I present in my body, here and now, feeling what I feel, seeing what I see now, hearing what I hear, and am I enjoying the gift of being alive?" Think about that. Are you in your head? Are you in your chest? Are you aware of your whole body? Are you *fully* inhabiting it?

If you're not in your body, you may be experiencing the kinds of negative feelings that hold some of us back or hold all of us back some of the time. Let's talk about when we're not in our bodies. If I'm feeling worried or anxious, I check myself to see if I'm in my body, and I find I'm really not. I'm often in my head probably just thinking about the future and occupying some future space that's unpleasant. That's how I rehearse worry, so the smart thing for me to do is to stop that and come back to being in my body right now.

One way to stop this sort of free-floating is this very simple physical technique you can do almost anywhere. I just take several deep breaths, focus my eyes upward, change my physiology (if I'm sitting down, I stand up; if I'm standing, I sit down or stretch), and all of a sudden I'm back in my body and in the present.

Now, when I look at that future worry, I disassociate from it. I make sure that the picture that I'm seeing is away from me. This way I still have the information, but I can make notes and determine if I need to make some changes or take some action. This physical and mental "reset" enables me to deal with the concern constructively instead of being a victim of the experience.

The phenomenon and impact of sub-modalities is very powerful, and the shifts you make with them can last a long time.

The Way You Do the Things You Do: Understanding Motivation

Another important aspect to understanding how *you* work is to discover how you are motivated. A fun way to explore this that is also sort of counterintuitive is to play with getting *unstuck* from procrastination. Now, you may not have this issue, but many of us (especially entrepreneurs) do, because we always have more on our to-do list than we seem to be able to get done.

When someone is stuck, they usually complain to a friend or walk into the therapist's office saying, "I can't get anything done. I can't do my taxes on time. My boss is yelling at me because I don't turn my expenses in on time. I don't know what's wrong with me, doc. Help. Can you fix me?"

At this point, they're usually seeking help pretty late in the process. After all, by the time they're aware of the problem, which is being stuck, a whole lot of things have happened, right? Let's take a look at how that worked.

The idea is to reel back the movie to *before* the person was stuck. Being stuck is, after all, also a behavior. If a person *doesn't* do something, that's also an activity. (Rosa Parks's refusing to move from her seat on a bus? Pretty profound activity that was.) They have to *intend* to do something and then stop themselves.

Before that behavior, there was a feeling. There was a feeling of motivation to *do* something. It might be to do something bad like eating too much chocolate or smoking too many cigarettes or giving in to unfair demands or it might be to do something good such as doing work on time or being more attentive to a friend.

So, when *you're* exploring motivation and procrastination, go back to the time right *before* the behavior and you'll find a feeling. You may actually find a series of feelings that flicker by so rapidly you're not aware of them until you get stuck; then you get anxious about being stuck. So let's go back *before* you're stuck. How did you *get* stuck?

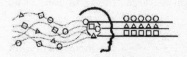

Discovery Activity: Exploring Roots of Procrastination

From my personal experience and the people that I've coached through the years, it's clear that we all generally have some sort of an image in our mind of what we want to do and then, alas, something else comes up. It's either an image or a voice that says, "But don't. Wait. Wait a minute."

The experience is going to be different for all of us, but what I'd like you to do is to find a time when you wanted to do something and you didn't do it right then. You hesitated, and you put it off. Maybe you eventually got it done, but it was difficult for you. You either put it off or you did it by overcoming huge internal resistance. Notice the picture you called up about this experience. Notice any feelings this image brings up for you.

I'm pretty sure you don't like that picture, and that you'd like to make it go away or alter it, so here's how to do that. As you look at that experience, keep going back to *before*. Keep going back before until you get to a place where you fully had the intention to do whatever it was.

Now, if it was your intention to do it, if you wanted to do it, if you're clear and congruent about that, then you can move forward and find out where the block is. Let's say that this task is something you knew you needed to do, maybe you *wanted* to do, even if you were not going to like doing it, for example, taking out the trash or flossing your teeth. After all, we do many things we don't like, but we know we're going to do them because we need to do them. Yet this particular task wasn't getting done. Perhaps it had a deadline and as the deadline was approaching, you were getting more and more nervous.

So go back, and there's a point where your brain produced a cue that said, "I'm not going to do that now." What do you see? What feelings does that image bring up for you?

This picture and the feelings you have will provide you with insight into what's underneath your procrastination. As you are exploring, you may encounter a few cues that other people commonly notice. The most innocent one is a distraction. It acts like an anesthetic. "Oh, I'm just going to do this for a second," and then you find that a couple of hours have flown by. These are just side trips that take you away from your destination.

If that was something that happened for you, if you look very, very closely you'll find that there was a picture or a voice that suggested something distracting, like "Oh yeah, I really need something salty right now. I'm going to go downstairs and make some soup," or "I'm just going to check the Web. There's this one site that I need to check out. I'm going to go look at it now," or there will be somebody you intended to call. The important point is to find the moment that you went from intending to do, to doing something else, and find the sequence of pictures, sounds, and/or feelings that you experienced.

That Damn Report: An Example of Procrastination

Recently, I worked with a forty-three-year-old sales rep who felt that procrastination was becoming a problem for her. She had to produce a report and waited until the very last minute—right before we were scheduled to talk—to get it done. I could relate to her dilemma because putting off a report is something I'm very familiar with. I was an expert at that when I ran my company. In my case, I put it off because I just don't like homework. I didn't like it when I was in school and I don't like it now. The picture in my mind was a picture from the eighth grade of me doing fractions, which I hated. I didn't have much of a choice then, but I do now, so I sometimes find myself procrastinating.

When I asked my client what came up for her when she thought about putting off a report or a phone call, she said, "If it hadn't been for the deadline of talking with you, I probably wouldn't have gotten it done yet. One of the things is that I had to have money to go with it, so I had to make sure I had the money. That's always stressful. I guess it's like you; it's just this boring detail that I don't like to do."

Accepting her explanation would have been the easy path, but we persisted until she realized that she saw a picture of an administrative assistant who used to do these reports. Now she feels frustrated and resentful about not having someone to help her. She was stunned to find this clue to her procrastination.

Two for the Road:
Tips for Uncovering Roots of Procrastination

Of course, determining a solution is a separate step, but identifying the clue to what's at the root of procrastination is the first thing. You want to find the image that's linked to this behavior. And it's not always easy because the mind automates tasks. We've been doing certain things for years and no longer notice them. We have to be patient and thorough to understand what's *underneath* a behavior.

Here are two tips to keep in mind when you're trying to identify what's at the root of something you're procrastinating about.

Tip #1: Slow Down, Way Down

When you work on one of your issues, what I'd like you to do is to stretch out the point where you procrastinate. Slow down the mental movie and run it in slow motion. Go from the point where you *intend* to do something because it's on your list to do, to the point where you *put it off.* In my client's case, this report was being done at the last moment. There was probably an earlier time when she could have done it and it would have been easier and much more convenient for her, right?

So when you're looking for that image or voice that stops you, put the movie in slow motion. Look for the image first; then listen for "Not now. I don't want to do it now." Don't think about the thought, because the thought comes *after* the image. The image is being presented by the unconscious. In a moment, I'm going to give you some ways to blast through that, but first I'd like to explore why looking inside ourselves and finding the pictures and sounds in our heads is essential.

You have a right to do this exploration and adjustment. It's your brain. There's no reason why you shouldn't get in there and look around. It's just a new skill. Just be patient and take your time. If you examine anything in your life that you've been putting off, it's likely that the reason you put it off is that your brain is trying to protect you.

Now, it may be trying to protect you from something that bothered you when you were five, ten, or fifteen years old or from something recent that was traumatic for you. Here's the thing: when people are doing this, it's *not* because they're broken; it's because they're working perfectly. When you put something off, that's perfect. You're doing something very well. You're doing it so well you can't change it by effort of will. That's pretty impressive. So the solution is "Okay, let's not fight anymore. Let's study the process and then find the detour point."

Imagine for a moment that you had a paperwork task that you were putting off. I've had clients in this situation, who once they saw the image, realized, "Oh, this is a cartoon. I'm sitting at this desk and this pile of papers is like ten feet over my head. That's ridiculous." Or they saw an image like a movie image, but it was right in front of them and it was larger than life and it was all this work they had to do. Or they saw a piece of paper or stack of papers that was all messed up with scratch marks on it and staples in the wrong place and pages torn, and it was really scandalous to turn in to anybody because it was very poorly done. There are lots of ways that we have of making ourselves afraid to do something and we're not even aware we're doing it.

Tip #2: Recognize Confusion for What It Really Is

In your process of trying to uncover the root of your procrastination, you may have moments where you feel confused. What you need to know is that feeling confused is code. Confused usually means either afraid or angry. It's code; it's protecting you. When you feel confused about something, if you look around you'll find there's a feeling under there that's probably even less pleasant than confused.

I invite you to, in your head, start running your movie in slow motion. Define the points of decisions, and the points of decision are *not* where the feelings are. They're *before* the feelings came up. Remember, the structure goes like this: you have a thought, you make a meaning out of it, then you have an emotion, and then you do the behavior.

For now, let's not worry about changing behavior. That's the wrong end of the lever. We need to work backward, because the easiest thing to manipulate is the image or *trigger* itself; there's no feeling attached there. There's no risk. I want to give you a couple images that you can play with right now that could make things easier without all this kind of archaeology.

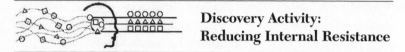

**Discovery Activity:
Reducing Internal Resistance**

Procrastination is a form of resistance. Here's another effective strategy that works well with resistance. It's called the "Godiva Chocolate Pattern" and it doesn't really have to do with Godiva chocolate (unless that's your favorite thing). Here's how to work with this process.

I want you to make two images. The first image I want you to make is of your favorite thing to do. I would say not sex, because that involves somebody else, so make this something that you might do on your own—whether it's eating Godiva chocolate, being in a boat fishing, playing solitaire on your smartphone—something that you really enjoy doing. Remember what it was like to do that and what it will be like to do that again. Actually be in that image so you have the feeling of what that's like.

Once you've got it, put that image out in front of you a ways. Then, between that image and you put the image of the task you've been putting off, only see that task disassociated. In other words, that it's just a picture. It's a still picture of the task, however you represent it—whether you see yourself doing it or whether you just see the task itself as a pile of papers, a cluttered garage, a tax form to be completed, a dirty cat box, or a phone call that needs to be made—whatever it is. Just see the task itself.

Now, right in the center of your picture of the task, make a little pinhole so you can see your favorite thing that's behind the task. Notice how the picture is brighter. You can see through it. Open the pinhole a little bit so you can see that really good thing. Open it until you get the feeling of the really good activity. As soon as you get that feeling, hold on to that feeling and start closing that pinhole. If the feeling starts to go away, open it up again until the good feeling gets strong.

This is a simple but very powerful motivation process well worth practicing repeatedly so you can more easily accomplish whatever you want. Review the step-by-step process at a time when you're alone and can get in touch with your feelings without being interrupted.

For now, here's a quick summary of the process. The strategy is based on the picture that's behind the task. The task is between you and the thing you want to do. You just open up a little window in the task so you can see through it to the thing you *want* to do, a thing you love doing. This window becomes your iris that opens until you begin to get the emotional connection to the thing you like to do, then you very slowly close it down. What will happen is your motivation will blast you through that task. It'll change your relationship to the task. Guaranteed.

For additional demonstrations and/or examples, go to: http://eg.nlpco .com/2-7.

As I said earlier, these techniques are a technology, not voodoo; so you should test them ruthlessly. Do this process and then set it aside and ask yourself, "How do I feel now about that dirty cat box, cluttered garage, report, phone call, or whatever it is. Do I feel any better about it? Am I more likely to do it?" If you don't feel better, go back and try this process again.

Been Down Too Long?
The Power of Inner Voices and the "Auditory Swish"

Based on hundreds of clients that I've personally worked with and thousands of clients that my trainers have described, we've learned that anxiety, jealousy, fear, and irritation (those energizing emotions) are frequently *visually* oriented. Yet when we feel depressed or discouraged, these downbeat feelings are generally from an *auditory* cue, a voice in our head. Here's a way to notice that and deal with it.

Discovery Activity:
Removing Negative
Auditory Cues

I'd like you to listen for an internal voice, a voice that maybe crops up and discourages you from doing something, or robs you of your self-confidence. It's completely arbitrary and automatic. These are artifacts from our early lives that we've generally outgrown, but the voices are still hanging in there. They're just echoing away because we never turned them off.

So go inside and notice what voice you hear. Here's an easy way to find it. Take the feeling that you have that's a downbeat feeling: discouragement, shame, sorrow, or even some negative self-talk, like "I can't do this," or "Nothing good ever happens to me." If you listen very carefully, you may hear somebody else's voice talking to you.

One thing to notice is what direction it's coming from. We have two ears because humans are designed to localize sound; so it's going to be coming to you from above and behind you or from one side or from the other side. You may start out thinking that it's coming from inside of you. But even if you're talking to yourself, the voice is coming from someplace and it's interesting to notice where it is.

When we talk to ourselves, the voice is generally coming straight at us. (In a moment, you'll learn how to change that.) If it's somebody else's voice—a father's, teacher's, or coach's (as it was in my case)—then it's typically coming in from one side or the other, and generally behind you and above you, because these voices were recorded when you were small.

In many cases, what you hear is something that was or has been re-peated. It could be an unkind comment, like "You're lazy." It may have been repeated over and over or said only once, but it just rattled on in your head. Any time you need to move out a voice that isn't working on your behalf, follow these steps. Let's go through the high-lights so you can do it. Although detailed instructions are provided as part of a link at the end of this chapter, try it now if you want to.

First, get your brain to hear that voice, and as soon as it hears it, as soon as the first sound starts, press the volume control so it quickly fades out; it doesn't even complete the first word. You can't even un-derstand the first word. It just fades out completely. That's Step 1.

Step 2 is fun. You know how in a restaurant or an airport or movie theater, you've looked up and just glanced in someone's eyes as they walked past and you have an idea about that person. "That person has a good sense of humor, that's nice," or "I wouldn't want to make that person mad," but you get some knowledge or impression of that person.

What I'd like you to do is to create an image of yourself, the you that's reading this book, just a half step ahead of this moment. Have this person, this future you, facing you. When you look into this person's eyes, into this "you," the only difference is you see that this person doesn't have that voice. You can just look at them and know that. Now note that they are saying something to you.

They're either saying, "I feel good about myself," or "I feel safe." You choose the statement, one or the other, and that comes right at you but it doesn't go into your head. It sort of rings around your head.

You know how when you run a wet finger around the lip of a crystal glass, it makes the sound of a bell ringing? Well, this is like a crystal bell that's upside down over your head, maybe at eye level, so the rim is at eye level and this sound is ringing around and around and around your head. Hear it now: "I feel safe. I feel safe. I feel safe," or "I feel good about myself. I feel good about myself. I feel good about myself." This is the future you. This is the wonderful you who no longer has that negative voice in your head. That's Step 2.

Step 3 is the sound of the surf to wash it all away. As you listen now, you can hear it just like the waves sizzling on the sand, and then it repeats. As soon as the voice starts, that first yucky word, it just fades out and turns into "I feel safe. I feel safe," or "I feel good about myself," and then the sound of the surf, and then the steps repeat. This easy and effective process is called the "Auditory Swish," which was originally developed by Richard Bandler.

As the CEO of a manufacturing firm, I learned that frustration, irritation, and anxiety were my occupational hazards. I always seemed to feel one of these emotions (which, as you might imagine, is not ideal for someone with employees). Because I was signing people's paychecks, it made them feel uneasy when I was difficult or short with them or someone else. When I noticed these feelings or behaviors, I tapped on the brakes and checked in with myself to see what was going on. If it was an image that cued up some negative emotions, then I shifted my experience by playing with my visual submodalities. If I was hearing a negative or critical voice, I'd use the "Auditory Swish Process."

Emotions as Passengers, Not Drivers: Choosing and Changing Your State

---

Feelings really are just options and I've seen people make important shifts when they treat their feelings as options instead of as things they have to endure. As you learn and experiment with the information in this book, you will gain significant influence over how you feel from day to day or moment to moment. *You* get to make choices here. How much of a difference that will make for you depends on how much time and energy you put into using these skills.

As you get more and more tuned in to how you feel, it will become easier to go back behind the feeling to notice the image or the sound that triggered the emotion, or the body feeling. During the next couple of days, I encourage you to notice the emotions you're having and to immediately explore what's behind them. Ask yourself: "When did that start? What was I thinking just *before* that started?" First, you'll find the thinking you're aware of, then look beneath *that*. "Was there any image in there or was there any sound that teed up the feeling? Was I making a comment to myself that sort of biased me . . . flavored things . . . and took the energy out of something . . . or made me particularly happy?"

You're likely to find that you're talking to yourself all the time and so are *other* voices. I don't know about you, but I've got a whole Greek chorus of voices in my head that are chiming in, spontaneously noticing things and commenting, in some way, on everything. You'll also find there are lots of images flashing that you largely ignore. After all, if we pay too much attention to these movies in our heads, we'll never get anything done. But they are, in fact, going on all the time. As you become aware of them, you can make changes. The good news is that, given a better choice, your brain will *continue* to choose that better option.

Curiosity: A Preferred State

Once I learned NLP, here's what I did to address my personal frustrations, irritations, and anxieties. I call it the "Curiosity Shunt Installation." (Refer to the link at the end of this chapter to access a detailed summary of this process.) I did some research on emotions and I found that the emotion of curiosity is really a curious emotion. It's a very neutral and engaging emotion that affords you greater flexibility.

All parts of the body like curiosity. Curiosity actually helps grow T cells! It helps grow new synapses in the brain so the immune system gets stronger. People function better when they're engaged and curious.

When you're curious about something, a lot of the blocking self-talk and images go away. Once you're curiously exploring the answer to something, it's amazing how a lot of negative stuff just disappears and how this state of information-gathering opens people to new possibilities.

Here's what used to happen for me when I was managing a manufacturing company. When I got frustrated, I would think of what was frustrating me. A vendor didn't ship a part on time so we couldn't meet our manufacturing deadline, so we were going to be late shipping stuff. We were going to get a bad reputation. Then I'd start all over again. "Well, the vendor wouldn't ship on time, so yada yada yada," and it was a loop.

The more I did the loop, the more frustrated I got. As you might imagine, I did the same thing with feeling irritated or feeling anxious. "Suppose this goes wrong. Then this would happen and this would happen. Then suppose this goes wrong. This would happen and this would happen." Same damn loop. You get the picture.

I thought it would be really nice for me if, as soon as I became aware that I was stirring up one of these negative, unresourceful, and unproductive states, I would remind myself that I could be curious instead.

So immediately I'd think, "That would be really nice. As soon as I start feeling irritated, I'm going to get curious about the cause of this irritation."

Well, that put me in a whole different frame because then I was curious about the cause of the irritation rather than mad at it. And I'd want to know what caused that irritation. Was it me? Was it the other guy? Was it something I missed somewhere? Could I have done it better? How could I change it? How could I make peace? What curiosity did was kick my brain onto a completely different track.

Sound good to you? I hope it does. Because it resonated for me, I studied how frustration, irritation, and anxiety worked in me. I began to notice exactly how each of these feelings began. Then I looked at what happened *just before* that.

You may be surprised to discover that it's *not* different experiences that create these familiar feelings. It's not "Well, it was *this* vendor, it was *that* guy." No, no, no. It's not that. It's actually what you said to yourself about that or it's the picture you made about that. The emotions are triggered by a cue. The cue is going to be the same even though the stimulus is going to be completely different because the *cue* leads you to the emotion. It's so well rehearsed, it happens really fast. It's a flash just like greased lightning.

Because it's a fast, automated process, it's sometimes difficult to find what's driving us. The only way to do it is to slow things down, take a few deep breaths, and run the mental movie at half speed, quarter speed, or 10 percent speed really slowly, back before you had the feeling. And to discover, just *before* you had the feeling, what happened.

You'll be amazed and amused. You'll find there will be an image or a phrase that will trigger you, so here's what you want to do. If it's a phrase, as soon as it comes up, press the volume control on the machine so the voice quickly fades out. If it's an image, you can use a Visual Swish. Go to http://eg.nlpco.com/2-5.

In both cases, here's what you want to see: Right in front of you is the wonderful you. Here's you *without* this problem. This you is perfect.

He or she is dressed just like you are at the time, but this you is curious. "Hmm, I wonder what started that? That's very interesting." This you has a look of curiosity on his face. The facial expression *this* you has is one of sincere curiosity.

What this other you says is "Wow, I wonder what started that?" Then you have either the sound of a wave to interrupt the old pattern or, if you can actually see this other you, you can have a flash of white appear, like what happens when the film breaks in the movie theater. You need a blank screen. You need a break before the cycle starts again. So try that.

Again, the step-by-step directions for the "Curiosity Shunt Installation" can be found by following the link at the end of the chapter. And, to quickly summarize, it's three steps. You find the cue for the emotion, you start to destroy the cue, and you immediately replace it with a future you who doesn't have this issue and who's curious. Play with this process and you'll experience a profound shift.

Depression: Auditory Cues That Hold the Story

Earlier in this chapter, I mentioned that negative feelings are often linked to an auditory cue. Before I give you some tips to deal with depression, let me start by saying that I've really shifted my attitude about it. I've lived with people who have clinical depression and I've suggested they see a doctor and get a psychoreactive drug, because depression can result from a physical ailment. If depression is long-lasting, take it seriously whether it's in you or in a friend, and seek professional help. Before I learned about depression, I used to think, "Well, just tough it out." Now that I see how painful and debilitating depression is, I'm much more sympathetic to how difficult it is to cope with.

With depression, it's also important to reframe its purpose, and here's what I mean by that. Depression is illogical. To become depressed, we have to take a problem or bad news and we have to make it personal (it's only happening to us); we have to make it pervasive (it happens no matter where we are, no matter what); and it happens forever (it's permanent).

We call these conditions the 3 P's: personal, pervasive, and permanent. They're the way someone achieves depression. Depression is when a person takes discouragement and makes a habit out of it, which is a really painful way to go through life.

If you're feeling down, that the world is against you, or that nothing is ever going to work out, go inside and explore what's happening. As you do this, remember there is *no* inner enemy. Even if you're feeling lousy and you don't know why you're feeling lousy, it's wise to assume that there's a positive reason for that. Something inside is trying to do you some good, even though you feel lousy.

Listen to the inner voice. If the inner voice is a broken record that's just going over and over and over again, there are two things you can do. One is to disassociate: stop being in the picture and get outside the picture so you can see yourself in it. If it's a voice, let the voice talk to you from across the room. Make the voice more seductive or make it sleepy. Make it a child's voice that yawns. Maybe it's time for it to take a nap.

Your objective is to find out what's going on in your head to produce the emotion, and then to interfere with that sequence. Now you can experiment with different changes to your sub-modalities until you experience some relief to heaviness, darkness, weighty silence, or whatever stored information you discovered.

Shaping Your Experience:
The Habit of Fine-Tuning Sub-Modalities

We've covered a lot of ground in this chapter, but you can reread it or review the key points and/or follow the link at the end of this chapter to get detailed summaries of the processes. What we've been doing here is exploring the pictures, sounds, and feelings in our own brains. Finding them is sometimes the tricky part. But once you begin to find them, you'll start looking and listening more intently. You'll notice the difference in location, the difference in size, the difference in brightness, intensity, and all the aspects of pictures, sounds, or feelings.

As you examine these different representations and tinker with one of the qualities, you'll discover that your responses and emotions will change. As I said earlier in this chapter, sub-modalities are called the "molecules of meaning" because they're what give us the meaning. It's a little weird how you get a meaning from a picture that's bright or a picture that's dull, but part of you says, "Good. That's the way I like it." This is the way your brain has bookmarked everything!

You can enhance or reduce the impact any picture, sound, or feeling has on your experience. If, for example, you have a positive emotion and you look inside and realize, "Yeah, I've just looked at my kids and they're playing by the pool," or "I'm at a family barbecue," or "I'm with buddies playing cards," or "I'm with the girls out having coffee," or whatever it is, if it feels good, make it brighter. See if you can make it *even better*.

If it feels bad, then get disassociated from the picture. Make it small, push it away from you, and notice how that reduces your negative state.

Over the next several days, step into your own mind, and pay attention to the positive and negative states you experience. Explore what goes on in your head when you have these feelings. Notice the images, sounds, and feelings, then use the tools you've learned in this chapter to change them. It's fun and the results are amazing.

Ready to learn more about living in the zone? Then, read on.

Key Ideas

- The *brain* operates pretty much on its own, and its focus is survival. The *mind* is able to focus on more than just survival; it affords us the opportunity to create and choose from a myriad of options.

- The Well-Formed Outcome process is a deceptively simple set of six key questions that enables its users to flesh out and evaluate a goal before committing to it and a course of action.

- Feeling uncertain or conflicted can be an internal signal called incongruence. If the conflict is about something unpleasant or something that goes against someone's values, incongruence can be like a smoke alarm. There may not actually be a fire, but it's prudent to determine what set it off.

- The structure of experience is based on five representational systems called modalities: pictures, sounds, feelings, tastes, and smells.

- Each modality has different qualities, subtle distinctions that are called sub-modalities. For example, some sub-modalities of vision are: location, brightness, and size.

- Sub-modalities impact how someone experiences a memory. By changing a sub-modality, a person can alter their experience, making it more positive, neutral, or negative.

- Associating into the picture usually makes the impact of seeing the image more intense (either positive or negative) for the person. Recalling difficult memories in a disassociated way reduces the emotional charge and makes it easier to get the information related to that situation.

- Feeling an emotion is just an *option*.

- Most of our emotions, interpretations, and reactions are so well rehearsed that they're automatic and the initial "cause" is out of our awareness. To understand what's going on with you, slow down the mental movie so you can more easily discover the "cue" (picture, sound, feeling, taste, or smell) that produced a feeling.

- When striving to discover a specific "cue," some people may discover they are distracted or confused. Often, these reactions are just detours taking you away from the real destination.

- To improve your focus and productivity, consider asking yourself the following questions at the beginning of every day.

  1. What am I looking forward to today?
  2. Longer term, what am I looking forward to?
  3. Am I doing things that lead directly to my goals?
  4. Am I being my best friend and supporter?
  5. Am I in my body and enjoying the gift of being alive?

- Someone can feel depressed when the three P's are at work: personal, pervasive, and permanent. Depressed people may benefit from exploring related auditory cues and tinkering with those sub-modalities.

 To enhance the skills you learned in this chapter, check out the recommended Bonus Activities at our special "Essential Guide" website: http://eg.nlpco .com/2-10 or use the QR code with your phone. This link includes a summary of the "Curiosity Shunt Installation."

Discoveries, Questions, Ideas, and Stuff You Want to Work On

_____

_____

_____

_____

_____

_____

_____

_____

_____

_____

_____

_____

_____

_____

_____

_____

_____

_____

_____

_____

_____

_____

Discoveries, Questions, Ideas, and Stuff You Want to Work On

Whoa, is my brake on?

Just as your car runs more smoothly and requires less energy
to go faster and farther when the wheels are in perfect
alignment, you perform better when your thoughts, feelings,
emotions, goals, and values are in balance.
—Brian Tracy

Some conversations, some projects, some relationships, and some days seem effortless—and most of us prefer to operate in that optimal zone. So in this chapter, you'll learn how to improve your energy, confidence, focus, and productivity. You'll discover how to remove energy obstacles, increase your ability to persevere, amp up your enthusiasm and optimism, and much more.

High or Low? How Expectations Impact Performance

The expectations we have shape our experiences. They can make us feel as though something is a piece of cake, a worthwhile challenge, or an impossible dream, right?

Let's say, for example, that you'd like to change jobs. You might say to yourself, "I could easily change jobs because it's never been a problem to do that before." Or "It will be interesting to see what attractive opportunities are out there and how I can use my connections to help me find what I'm looking for." Or you might feel discouraged before you even begin because it took your best friend, a talented professional in your field, eight months to find a decent job. Notice how these *very* different perspectives and expectations would influence what it's like to explore various employment opportunities.

This dynamic is at work in our lives all the time. Yet quite often our expectations are out of our awareness—*and* they may not even be accurate! Even so, they can be very powerful. So, how can we make expectations work to our advantage? Let's play with a simple example.

 **Discovery Activity:**
Exploring Your Expectations

This activity will show you that your expectations are imaginary. Please stand up. For this exercise, choose an area where you have the space and privacy to move freely. (If you are reading this where you have an audience, either go someplace where you can do this alone, or wait until later.)

Stand with your feet stationary—about shoulder width apart. Now, extend your right arm straight out from the right side of your body, then rotate your torso gradually to the left. Bring your arm around to the left as far as it can go. Using the hand and arm that's now across your body, point to the farthest place in your rotation—and notice where that is. Then come back around.

This is a very simple but helpful exercise because it teaches your body something important. An old Maori wisdom says that knowledge is only rumor unless it's in the muscle. This honors the difference between seeing and doing.

Now, as you're standing still—relaxed and breathing easily—just *imagine* that you can simply rotate your torso and arm farther to the left than you did just a moment ago. Just imagine what it would feel like if you were able to loosen up your torso and your shoulders so your right arm came much farther around to the left.

Now actually extend your right arm—and swing it around slowly to the left. Just for fun, find out how far you can go this time. Don't bend your elbow. No cheating. Just notice that because you *imagined* going farther, you probably did go farther. It might not have been 50 percent farther, but it was certainly farther than you went the first time—even though the first time I asked you to turn as far as you could and I believe that you consciously intended to do that.

In the Mind's Eye: The Power of Mental Rehearsal

What's important to take away from this is that whenever something takes place in the mind first, you're likely to have a better performance—simply because you've already tested the reality of it. In fact, top athletes visually rehearse their performance as part of their workouts and preparation. To test the power of this phenomenon, Professor L. V. Clark of Wayne State University conducted a study in the 1960s to determine the effects of visualization on the free-throw performance of basketball players.

In the study, first the athletes were tested to determine their free-throw proficiency. Next, they were randomly assigned to one of three experimental groups. The first group went to the gym every day and practiced doing free-throws for one hour. The second group also went to the gym, but instead of physically practicing, they laid down and simply visualized successfully shooting free-throws. The third group did nothing. In fact, they were instructed to forget about basketball and told, "Don't touch a basketball—don't even think about it!"

What happened was interesting. At the end of thirty days, the three groups were tested again to determine their *current* free-throw proficiency. The players who hadn't practiced at all showed no improvement in performance; many in that group actually exhibited a decline in performance. Those who had physically practiced one hour each day showed a performance increase of 24 percent. And the visualization group, by merely *imagining* themselves successfully shooting free-throws, improved 23 percent!

Researchers concluded that visualization enhanced motor coordination *and* intrinsic motivation. Bottom line? You can improve your performance by mentally and/or physically rehearsing a task or interaction to expand and refine your expectations.

In Sync: The Link Between Physiology and Energy

The first thing I want you to consider about energy is that the mind, the body, and the brain work together—they're in concert. So it's important to use the body in a *conscious* way because it will affect the mind. Let's work on enhancing your physiology right now because it will help you feel more energetic and get more out of the rest of this chapter.

Tip #1: Breathe into It

If you straighten your spine, even in this moment as you're reading— straighten your spine, bring your chin up slightly, and breathe deeply and slowly—two things will happen. First, the rhythms in your brain will begin to deepen. You'll start to relax, and oddly enough, you will also increase the level of your intention. This is an example of energetic physiology.

Just as conscious breathing is a technique to enhance the harmony of brain and physiology, there are other ways to minimize the impact of energy obstacles. In addition to deep breathing, here are a few things you can easily do that will raise your energy level and keep you living in the zone.

Tip #2: *Hydrate Your System and Your Brain*

The second simple energy improvement tip is to drink plenty of water. Today, most Americans and Europeans are dehydrated. In previous eras, in which we were outside and our lives were more physical, we would drink water every time we had a chance. Now we confuse our bodies with coffee, tea, and sodas, which are all diuretics. Drinking pure water hydrates the brain and that actually increases the speed with which you can transfer nerve impulses. It also keeps your energy up, smooths out your digestion, and helps your skin. Like exercise, this is a simple practice that will pay immediate and long-term dividends.

Tip #3: *Break Tasks into Small Bites*

The third strategy, based on the Pomodoro Technique, is to take a physical and mental break. About every twenty minutes, change your posture and get out of your seat. If you work sitting down, get up. If you work walking around, sit down. Take a brief break about every twenty minutes—and a longer one about every two hours. The positive effect on productivity is so apparent that many people set a timer to remind them to shift their physiology—and avoid the temptation of "Oh, just another ten minutes . . ." which can easily turn into an hour or more!

This technique has such a good track record of increasing energy and productivity that many management consulting firms have adopted this approach. Basically, all you need is a timer, your list of to-dos, and your appointment schedule so you can divide your work into twenty-minute segments with breaks in between. This way, you're working in thirty-minute blocks. That's more manageable, right?

This method increases productivity by guaranteeing that you take some kind of break to refresh. By committing to shorter, focused work states, you'll find you can stay at it. If you don't challenge yourself to be hard at it for hours on end—and you instead *truly* focus for a short time—you'll discover that you can be even more productive.

Tip #4: Notice and Reduce Resistance

In the last chapter, you began to explore how incongruence and resistance affect you. Resistance and coping with it can take a toll on your energy and really slow you down. It's like driving with the parking brake on. You use a lot of extra gas and rubber getting around this way. You wouldn't consciously choose to do this, would you? However, all too often, we do this physically, emotionally, and energetically.

Imagine for a moment that there's a task you need to do—and every time you think about it you just feel sapped. This used to happen to me a lot. I left high school because I couldn't stand doing homework. It's an irony that I now make a living writing—it's actually something I've come to really relish. Here's what's funny. Even though I enjoy the process of writing, I don't enjoy *contemplating* it. When I contemplate a task that requires me to sit down in front of a computer, part of me says, "I don't want to come in. I don't want to stop playing. I don't want to come indoors yet"—just like a little kid. Perhaps something like this happens internally for you, too.

Roadblock Removal: "Eye Movement Integration"

When an energy drop like this occurs, it's your system saying that some part of you isn't completely on board with doing that task, making that call, meeting with that person, exercising, or whatever it is. Your emotion about the task ahead may feel like a roadblock that you can't figure out how to get around. "Eye Movement Integration" is a quick and easy nonverbal way to handle this kind of challenge.

Here's the way it works: Your brain is processing and storing huge amounts of information quickly; it does this by divvying it up and storing different types of information in different places. In fact, it "files" things into six different sections. For now, it's just important to know that as you move your eyes into these different sections, you're actually accessing the parts of the brain where various memories and details are stored. The fundamental version of the process you're about to learn is derived from Steve and Connirae Andreas's "Eye Movement Integration" model.

 **Discovery Activity: Decreasing Resistance or Trauma**

To get started, you'll need a pen or pencil that has a tip that is a different color from the shaft—or the end with the eraser can also work well. Once you have this pen or pencil, keep it handy because you'll need it in a minute.

Now think of something that you need to do, but when you imagine doing whatever it is, you feel your energy drop. Using a 1–10 scale, with 10 being really resistant, how strong is your resistance to doing this task? Just make a mental note of that.

Now pick up that pencil and hold it out in front of your face about twelve to fourteen inches away from your eyes. You can easily see the tip, right? And recall that task you need to do—but also don't want to do. It could be making a presentation . . . paying bills . . . confronting a friend . . . exercising . . . whatever it is that you're not particularly keen about doing. Imagine that you can simply put that feeling of resistance right on the tip of the pencil that's out in front of you.

Now look at that point and keep your head very still. In a moment, using the pencil, you're going to slowly draw a sideways figure 8 in the air so it looks something like this.

As you're doing this, you're going to keep your head very still and allow *just* your eyes to follow the tip of the pencil.

Start now and move your hand—slowly drawing that sideways figure 8. So as you're making the first right hand loop, you're moving the tip around and down. And as you are approaching the middle part where the center lines would intersect, make this movement an upward sweep. As the tip with that feeling on it comes in front of the tip of your nose, just go up and then continue the left-hand loop—going around to the outside and down—and then back up through the middle as you make the next right-hand loop.

As you make the next loops, gradually raise the figure 8 higher and bring it down lower, so the loops you're making are at the edge of what your eyes can see comfortably, and bring it back to the center. Make at least five complete figure 8 loops.

Once you've completed at least five figure 8s, stop and notice how you're feeling now. Using a 1–10 rating, how does the feeling of resistance you have now compare to the one you had at the beginning? How much has it improved? Make a mental note of that.

If the feeling is not as bothersome, but you'd like it to be even less so, put that feeling on the tip of the pencil and make five additional figure 8s. Again keeping your head still, allowing your eyes to simply follow the movement of the tip as you go around each outer loop and down . . . and then up through the middle. Once you've completed these additional figure 8s, check and see how the bothersome feeling has been reduced.

You should notice an immediate change. This is not something that takes days, weeks, or months to shift. Because brains move fast and generally prefer comfort, they're quick to adopt things that are more comfortable and more efficient—and the changes are literally instantaneous!

Now, do the same process, this time using a circle instead of a figure 8. This is a kind of a double-check or cleanup version. Do it three or four times, paying particular attention to whether there are any points in the circle where your movement seems to hesitate or stutter. If you notice any kind of hesitation like this, do the pattern a few more times until the movement is smooth and symmetrical through the whole pattern.

This process can be used to reduce minor resistance or to take the sharp edges off a physical or emotional trauma. Although you can easily and beneficially do this process with yourself, you may want to do this to help someone else. If you were talking with a friend who was feeling irritated or dreading an upcoming task, you could just say, "Let's try something and see if it works." Simply follow these same steps and see what kind of positive shift they make.

Just remember, the key is to move slowly. And make sure that when you cross the center you're always moving in an upstroke, *not* a downstroke. Don't move any faster than the other person's eyes can go. As you do this and watch their eyes, you'll probably notice that they're following your pen smoothly, but at some point in the figure 8 pattern, their eyes may skip. They may just sort of jump to the next point. That's where the person's "glitch" is—where they've stored the troubling information. Your goal is to do this and help them smooth out that rough point—so they can follow the lines of your figure 8 smoothly, without interruption.

Here's the theory. By moving a person's eyes through all six sections of where the brain stores information, the information that's troubling them (which has been stored in one spot and perhaps is stored in a distorted way) gets mainstreamed by holding that event in mind. And as their eyes move through all the areas of the brain where data can be stored, it seems to smooth out the glitch and reduce the emotional charge of whatever was troubling them. This technique is used quite successfully with people who've been victims of crime or abuse and with veterans suffering post-traumatic stress disorder.

For additional demonstrations and/or examples, go to: http://eg.nlpco .com/3-4.

Getting in the habit of noticing and adjusting your physiology and internal resistance allows you to maximize your physical and emotional energy.

Not Just Pollyanna:
How Energy, Enthusiasm, and Optimism Act as Drivers

Energy, enthusiasm, and optimism are important drivers; they influence how we feel—and are responsible for how we actually get moving.

As you have become more proficient at going inside yourself, you've been noticing various feelings . . . then going back behind those feelings to find what triggered them . . . and asking yourself, "What triggered that—was it an image—was it a word or tone . . . ?" You've learned to slow down your personal mental movies and explore what your process has been.

To help you apply your new understandings to enhance your optimism and enthusiasm, I invite you to set up an inner barometer that will regularly assess, "What's my level of optimism today? How am I feeling about this? Am I enthusiastic? Am I looking forward to things? Am I happy? Am I grateful?" Get creative and give yourself some kind of scale so you easily notice these positive drivers. You can also choose, if you wish, to play with your sub-modalities, as described in the last chapter, to feel even more enthusiastic.

Motivation in Action

Motivation is a close relative of enthusiasm. Let's say that you have something to do—like organizing your financial records to do your taxes—and you don't know how to *make* yourself do it. People typically motivate themselves one of two ways. They do it either by creating anxiety or imagining a positive experience. These are pretty different strategies, aren't they?

So, if you're someone who uses anxiety to get into gear, you might imagine not getting everything done by the deadline, not being able to find a specific receipt, having your accountant tell you you've missed the extension date, or getting an audit letter from the IRS. All of these negative imaginings produce anxiety—and adrenaline. However, some people get so anxious that they kind of just freeze up and they can't get anything done.

Fortunately, there is a simple alternative to stirring ourselves into a negative (or even frozen) state, and that is to hold a positive expectation. How do you motivate yourself most of the time? Here's a way you can find out.

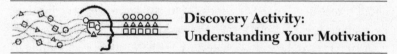 **Discovery Activity: Understanding Your Motivation**

Think for a moment. Consider how you got yourself up this morning. What did you actually do to get up? What did you say to yourself upon first awakening that kept you from rolling over and going back to sleep? What did you say to yourself—or imagine—to get out of bed and begin your day? Just take a look at that and see what comes up for you. What motivators were at work with you? Make a note of these.

Getting out of bed may seem like a mundane example of motivation. Yet it's an important one because each of us has to do it every day. Understanding how you do that can provide you with insight into how you motivate yourself in other situations.

For most of my life, I wasn't much of a morning person. And yet I was almost always expected to be somewhere in the morning. So I'd hear the alarm, open one eye, and see what time it was. Then I'd usually say to myself, "Ugh, I better get up. I don't want to get stuck in traffic and end up being late." As you can see, I used negative pictures to keep from hitting the snooze alarm.

In contrast, a thirty-four-year-old client of mine, who's an artist, described her experience of waking up like this: "When I open my eyes in the morning, I first look for the dog. When she looks at me and we connect visually, it gives me energy to reach out and pet her. Then, after a couple of minutes, I get up and go to the bathroom. Then I'm up and awake . . . everything is fine . . . and I'm ready to begin my day. When I see my dog, that connection—the love and affection she has for me—gives me energy to do anything when I wake up in the morning." My client, Ellie, gets started by a positive see-feel strategy.

Even though I'm still not a morning person, I've changed my getting-up strategy since I learned NLP. When I fall asleep, I'm telling myself about something I'm looking forward to doing the next day. It might be making breakfast with my wife, working with a specific client, going for a leisurely walk—whatever it is, there's always something to look forward to.

If you find that you are currently using a stressful strategy for getting out of bed, I recommend that you not abandon it until you have something that works *equally* well. It's usually safest to start playing with a pleasure-based strategy for waking up on weekends or doing nonessential projects. Then you can see how you can also create a more positive set of feelings to get you up and out of bed on workdays or ready to tackle more critical projects. To get the best results from your experiments, use what you've learned about sub-modalities to enhance your feelings.

Generally, when people look ahead to something pleasant, the folks that do it effectively do it in an associated fashion. They actually can feel themselves *doing* that thing. So when I get up in the morning and I can feel what it's like to be sitting at the kitchen table watching my wife make her tea, I feel happy and pleasantly energized. When I imagine taking a walk, seeing the trees along the path, running into neighbors who are walking their dogs, I'm sure to do this in an associated fashion so I can feel the movement of my feet, the sun on my face, the dog's fur against my palm, and I am beginning to feel energized.

Unfortunately, sometimes people get it sort of backward. For example, if they have something unpleasant planned, like going to the doctor or the tax guy, they do that associated, and anything pleasant they do disassociated. Sounds painful, doesn't it? And it's probably unnecessarily so.

Here's what I recommend. Instead of imagining, in an *associated* fashion, the penalty of something possibly going badly, imagine (again in an *associated* fashion) the payoff of a potentially positive result. For example, you can do this two ways. You can focus on having gotten *something* done. And even if it's something that might be yucky or tedious for you, you can still imagine how good it will feel. Or imagine how good you'll feel about yourself when you've made some progress, or completed your task, right?

You can also notice the little sort of substeps involved in getting something completely done, and what pleasure you can find in each of these. Oddly enough, as in the case of preparing your tax information, there can be satisfaction in finding and organizing the receipts and bank statements . . . in coming up with an accurate total for a set of expenses . . . in filling out a whole section of the tax worksheet. You get the picture—in every task, there are lots of potential little victories on the way to the finish line.

And as you're performing a difficult task, imagine how good it's going to be to get it done. Be sure to cheer yourself on while you're doing it. "Look, I'm under way. This isn't as bad as I thought. This is actually getting pretty easy. Dang, I'm good at this." Positive inner dialogue will help increase your energy, optimism, and enthusiasm and keep you rolling forward because you'll have more brain cells available. So give this a try on any project.

A Case in Point: How to Generate Energy

So far, we've explored how to improve the conditions to accessing energy. Now let's talk about how you can *generate* energy. I've had tremendous personal success with this. All my life, I was a slow riser (even though I've been in many occupations where I was either up for twenty-four to thirty-six hours or had to get up at all hours of the night). I just always liked to ease into my day—and sometimes that wasn't possible.

When I learned NLP, I thought, "Since I can picture these images and I can do what I want with these images, I wonder if I can energize myself on my way to work in the morning."

Here's what I did. I created a process that kicks in as soon as I leave the house. As I step out onto the front porch, I hear the sound of violins beginning the "Ride of the Valkyries" (which is a powerful and uptempo piece that opens the third act of Wagner's third Ring opera and has been used in many movie sound tracks, including *Apocalypse Now*).

Then, as I get out to the garage, into my car, and start driving down this small suburban street, imaginary loudspeakers pop out on either side of the car—they're about eight feet tall and capable of the volume you'd experience at a rock concert.

And then the song begins to crescendo—and all the way down the street, the symphony horns are blaring. I can actually feel the car vibrate as the sound waves hit it. It's an amazing experience. I usually let that stay with me for the first two miles of my trip, until I get out of the car to go into a coffee shop, where I get my second cup and am ready for the rest of the ride to work.

The amazing thing is, on the mornings that I do this, as I walk into the coffee shop, heads turn. It's like I'm radiating energy. Understanding how I'm motivated enabled me to create this internal process that has had a profound effect on my energy, enthusiasm, and optimism. This is another use of anchors that you can easily set up for yourself. Just choose a favorite piece of music and anchor it to a place you touch every morning. Practice it consciously for a week or so, and you'll find yourself doing it automatically from then on. Nice, isn't it?

Optimism and Confidence in Concert

Helen Keller said, "Optimism is the faith that leads to achievement. Nothing can be done without hope and confidence." So let's focus on confidence for a moment.

From my experience coaching other people, I've learned that feeling more confident seems to be a universal desire. Before we experiment with ways to do that, I want to be clear about this: confidence is *not* based on truth. Confidence is based on choice—and I'm happy to be a beneficiary of this discovery.

One of the things that used to run in my mind was "Well, it's not reasonable to be confident. You're a screw-up. You dropped the ball. You did this and that." Of course, the part of my mind that was devoted to keeping me hesitant would just select and bring up the experiences where I'd been less than stellar . . . I'd really screwed up somehow . . . dropped the ball . . . not lived up to myself . . . not lived up to my rules . . . or not lived up to somebody else's rules. It seemed unreasonable to feel confidence in the face of these examples.

When you want to feel confident, it's better to be unreasonable. This is about *choice*, not judgment. After all, you can't judge yourself fairly anyway—you'll either be too favorable or too unfavorable. In this case, it's better to err on the side of too favorable.

A long time ago, I was just coming off a crushing failure and about to build a success. One day, the lady I was dating came to me and she was very troubled; she said, "You know, I just had lunch with your ex-wife. She said you say that these failures are always just glitches, that you always just explain these away." My girlfriend was concerned that this was a problem.

In response, I said, "No, it's absolutely right. All entrepreneurs need to be neurotic enough to ignore their failures. They can take the information from it, but it's only feedback. You take the information so you'll do better next time, but you can't internalize it."

So what I did instead was to consciously and conscientiously rehearse my triumphs. I recommend that you keep score so you can remember your victories and the many ways you've improved. Literally write them down—little victories and big ones.

I have a list of about thirty of the things that I've done that make me feel good about myself. They're not earthshaking by any means. For example, I bought my kid brother a bicycle with money that I earned on my paper route. In fact, I bought both of us bikes—and that made me feel pretty good. Another time when I was little, I remembered another guy's Bible verses at church. I did mine and then I did his, too, because he had stage fright and couldn't remember them at all. Your list can be anything that makes you feel good about yourself, but write down those examples. A friend of mine calls these her "greatest hits."

During periods when I'm going through a down time in life, I am very deliberate about reading that victory list *every* morning. This helps to remind me that I've done a number of things right in my life. Again, it doesn't have to include only big achievements—like winning a Nobel Prize—just things you've done that make you feel good about yourself. You can note times when you were generous or tolerant or brave or courageous—whatever reflects your value system and gives you reason to be proud of yourself.

I think of tuning up my confidence as a kind of mental hygiene. Sometimes when I get a sore place on my gums, I'm a little more attentive with the Waterpik than I am at other times. It's the same way here. When you're feeling a little down or you need to build up your confidence, it's useful to revisit that list.

So, what does a "greatest hits" list have to do with NLP? *Here's* what: If you just read that list like you're sleepwalking or like you're glancing through a magazine article, it's not going to have much of an impact. The way to read that list is to go through each of those experiences in an *associated* fashion—quickly step into each experience and remember it. Be "in" the movie and revisit once again how wonderful you felt. Recalling your "greatest hits" this way will actually change your neurology and your blood chemistry.

**Discovery Activity:
Amping Up Your Confidence**

Let's experiment with a technique to deliberately increase your confidence. This activity will change your mind and what your reference images are. First, though, there are some serious things to consider whenever you come to the issue of confidence. A lot of people have said, "Can you give me more confidence? I just want more confidence all the time."

This is like wishing for eternal sunshine and permanent happiness. It's a silly idea, and if you *had* it, you'd probably soon *regret* it. Permanent anything *eliminates* choice, and without choice we're simply robots, right? If, for example, you automated confidence so you had it *all* the time, you could get yourself in some hot water pretty easily. Imagine being so confident that you carelessly walk down a dark alley in the wrong part of town. Think that would be such a great experience? Sure might poke a hole in your permanent happiness.

There is a mythical (I hope) story about a man at one of those "be all you can be" seminars who got himself so jacked up with confidence he tried to swim Hawaii's Molokai Channel—and was never heard from again. Naturally, you can enjoy a solid sense of confidence in situations where you know you have what it takes to perform. That's an appropriate place to use this process to rev up your confidence so it's really strong.

That said, there is a confidence you can have in all situations. Regardless of the context, and whether you have even been there before, there's one ability that you have everywhere. That's your ability *to learn*. You can learn from any and *every* situation, from every event that touches your life. At an absolute minimum, your learning might be "I sure don't want to do that again," right? And that *is* learning.

It may be that you just needed that one last repetition. The bottom line is that it's realistic to have a strong sense of confidence in your ability to learn in any situation you face. This gives you a positive attitude that will build and sustain your energy. You'll be able to profit from any feedback you get, discoveries you make, and use that information to do even better in the next opportunity.

So think of a situation where you have full confidence in your abilities, any situation where you're pretty sure that you know exactly how to manage whatever it is that comes up. It could be anything— making breakfast, changing a tire, teaching a group of people—just something you know you can do. Now, here we go again with submodalities. Notice what comes up for you when you think of that situation. Do you see a picture? You do? Do you hear anything? What?

I suggest that you step into that situation in your mind so you're associated. This is important for two reasons. First, you'll get more information. Now you can probably hear what's going on and you can even hear your self-talk. Notice that.

When you're actually in that situation, how do you feel physically? Take a moment and write down these details so you can use them as a model to make positive changes. Notice where that feeling resides in your body? What's it feel like? Is it warm? Is it tingly? Does it move around? Does it make your muscles swell up? Do you breathe more deeply?

What you want to develop here is a list of the specific sensations you have when you're in an associated experience of being confident.

Once you've specified that, it's important to change your focus of attention, so just for a moment think of your zip code backward, the five digits in reverse order.

Now think of a situation that you need to tackle, but where you're a bit doubtful about yourself. You're doubtful that you'll handle it as well as you'd like to.

If you've got one, go into that situation and notice the differences. Notice any images (size, color, distance, etc.) and sounds (volume, tone, location, etc.) and feelings (warm, tingly, moving, etc.). How are these images, sounds, and feelings different from the confident experience that you reviewed a moment ago? Notice where in your body the nonconfident feelings are.

Now start changing those feelings. Start replacing them with the qualities of the confident specification. Change the qualities of the image that you're in to match the qualities of the image when you were confident. Change what you were hearing in your mind's ear, what self-talk there was, to the same kind of self-talk as when you were confident, and change the body feelings, too.

When I'm feeling confident, I notice I have more mental energy and am actually thinking more clearly than when I'm overly self-conscious or caught up with self-doubt. This is a process that you can easily practice. I recommend doing it every day for at least a week or two if you really want to build your ability to achieve a more confident state of mind.

Mission Critical:
Motivation Tips from Navy SEALs Training

Another way to build confidence is to develop an inner knowing that you can do almost anything. Navy SEALs, as you've probably heard, have the most difficult military training on earth—and many people come to the United States to learn about it. This training was originally modeled on the methods the British Special Air Services used with their commandos. But the demands on Navy SEALs are even greater because they do so much work in the water—where being constantly cold and wet is a huge disincentive to forging ahead.

Let me give you a little background first—and then we'll explore how *you* can benefit from SEAL training. The first training that SEALs are put through is really just a six-week sorting-out process that concludes with something called hell week, where they get four hours of sleep over a sixty-hour period of time, and they spend a lot of time being cold and wet.

In this phase of training, here's what the Navy discovered. They selected candidates who had high IQs—and were, of course, great physical specimens. These people were able to perform all of the activities the job required them to perform. But what the Navy noticed was that, in this six-week period of time, 76 percent of these carefully selected candidates were dropping out of the program.

This dropout rate represents a huge loss not only in terms of recruiting and training investments, but also in terms of this division's readiness and capability to deliver when called upon. Because both of these issues became a real concern to them, a few years ago they hired Eric Potterat, a psychologist, who became the command master psychologist for the U.S. Navy SEALs. He was instructed to review the mental toughness training and find out what the Navy could do to increase the abilities of these candidates to force themselves to do things that the Navy estimated they could physically do, but instead resulted in the candidates quitting.

Potterat came up with what he called the Big 4 and he trained SEAL candidates intensively in these four habits. As a result, the graduation of candidates increased by 50 percent! This improvement was particularly impressive because the Navy was *starting* with a group of exceptional candidates, and then studying these people to find out what made the difference between quitting and persevering. In NLP, we call that "the difference that makes the difference."

In a nutshell, here are the four critical habits that may mean the difference between life and death—and a successful or failed mission. Although these are presented in a sequential way, they can be used simultaneously.

Habit 1: Focus on Right Now

The first habit involves a special kind of goal-setting thinking. There are all sorts of ways to set goals. You may have learned them in school or on the job, but this is different. This is short-term goal setting.

The major way to combat stress when you're doing something very difficult is to narrow your focus. Narrow it down to the immediate future. Navy SEALs focus on just getting to the end of the twenty-mile run. They don't think about *anything* after that. They do *not* think about the next meal. They do not think about the inspection coming after that. They would not think about any further tests.

This first habit reminds me of the advice I got when I was bicycle touring: "Don't look at the top of the hill" when you're slogging up a hill. Just turn the pedal over, crank it over again (and again and again), so each rotation moves you further along.

So one of the things the Navy SEALs were trained to do was to just do the job directly in front of them and focus on that. That's Habit 1.

Habit 2: Imagine How Good It Will Feel

This one's related to rehearsing past successes. And, as you know, when you go through a victory list in an associated way, by the time you're done with twenty or thirty of those successes, you'll be very familiar with the body feeling that tells you, "I'm pleased with myself. I'm on top of this. I'm doing this. It's working."

So then, you would take that feeling of success and *imagine* what it will be like when you successfully do the thing you're doing right now. The trick to that is to transfer those wonderful feelings. What you're actually doing in this step is utilizing *your* most positive sub-modalities. In this step, transfer these positive feelings to any task you're doing and tell yourself how good its feels to be making progress—how good it feels to be almost done—how good it feels to be completing this task.

Break down the task into smaller pieces so that every little step feels good and moves you forward—just as every revolution of the pedal on my bicycle felt good. Every time you finish a little set of tasks in a project, you check it off—and that feels good. So make a habit of noticing that.

You can do this over and over again. And as you do, you're providing your brain with *extra* experiences of success, which will further deepen the feelings and make them easier for you to access when you need them.

Habit 3: When All Else Fails, Breathe Deeply

There often comes a time in the process of being discouraged, demotivated, or physically drained when there's sort of an inner collapse and a panic reaction. "Oh, I can't do it! I can't do it. I can't hold on! I can't hold on! It's slipping . . . it's slipping . . . it's gone! Oh, no!"

That's when two little parts of your brain about the size of a pair of thumbnails take over your life. As you may recall, this part of the brain is called the amygdala. It determines when you're safe and when you're not. So when you feel yourself failing, the amygdala decides that everything has gone to hell in a handbasket; then you're likely to have a panic reaction of some kind.

The way to beat this primal reaction is by flooding your body with oxygen. You actually change your blood chemistry—and when you do, it calms down the amygdala. So here's a special kind of breathing the Navy SEALs were taught to do—and you can try it right now.

Inhale deeply for a count of six. Hold it for a count of two. Then exhale for a count of six—completely emptying your lungs. Do this three times, just three times anytime during the day. Do these three deep breaths, in for a count of six, hold for a count of two, exhale for a count of six.

When you do this kind of breathing, you'll find that several things happen. You lower your blood pressure. You flood your brain with oxygen and it increases your ability to think and react thoughtfully— instead of out of panic or emotion. Being able to breathe easily and think makes using the other habits possible!

Habit 4: Cheer Yourself On

This habit is related to something we talked about in the last chapter— hearing voices in our heads that are discouraging or critical. What the Navy SEALs are taught to do is to create their own cheering section—to be their personal encouraging chorus.

They mentally have their own voice say, "You can do it! This is easy. Forget that mistake. Focus on the next shot and on getting it better." They constantly cheer themselves on *while* they're in the process of doing it—instead of saying, "This is terrible. This is exhausting. I wonder if my ankle is going to hold up. I've got a blister. My pack is loose and shifting around."

Instead of listing their troubles, they list everything that feels good. As I said, this isn't about being reasonable; this is about being suc- cessful. This methodology is working for people who are in the most challenging situations that humans can invent. So that's Habit 4.

Try these steps the next time you feel anxious about an upcoming event or are feeling sort of freaked out in the moment. Six-two-six- count breathing will help you regain some equilibrium and enable you to put your focus on the task at hand, tap into past successes, and cheer yourself on.

Messing with Hecklers:
How to Silence Critical Inner Voices

In Chapter 2, we talked about the voices in our heads—our own and those of others, who are or *were* important to us. A moment ago, I mentioned the benefit of having a cheering section—in your own voice—that you can have at your immediate access to encourage yourself whenever you need it.

But sometimes we have negative voices, too. What about the hecklers in your mind? "Oh, this is all a bunch of hokum. This doesn't really work. This is just a bunch of feel-good crap. I can't do this. It's not going to change reality. The reality is I'm failing. You can't do this. You're not good enough," or whatever the negative voices are.

I had one that stayed with me for years. It was a little voice that said, "Screwed up again, Hoobyar." I didn't realize until my mid-fifties that it was the voice of Coach Marshall, the gym teacher who'd been in charge of the high school track team. At one point, I was a really good runner, and then I started smoking—which definitely impacted my performance.

When Coach Marshall saw my running times begin to slip, he would shout that out at me when I was puffing around the track. "Screwed up again, Hoobyar." That voice went in because I totally admired the guy and was very ashamed of my behavior. Coach Marshall's voice went into my mind's eye and ear and stayed there—for years.

After a while, my mind just began applying poor old Coach Marshall's voice to everything. Every time I forgot a thank-you note, every time I was less than gracious, every time I was late anywhere, any time I dropped the ball anywhere, I heard that comment. I felt like I could actually hear him.

Well, those kinds of comments can become predictive. They *could* convince you that you're just so crummy, you'll never do it. Because they lower your expectations of yourself, they degrade your performance. That's why it's so important to interrupt those critical voices. They are not going to help you. Period.

These voices just sort of take the fun out of life and take the energy out of our commitment, out of our actions, and out of our will to succeed.

When that happens, here's what you can do: First, sort of set a trap for it. Notice it. Be an attentive audience for your own inner talk, and listen for any negatives, any self-sabotage. When you hear a negative voice, immediately obliterate it. Immediately change it.

Once you notice it, you have choices. Let the critical voice say whatever it's saying, and as it's talking, gradually change its tonality from whatever it is to something really pleasant—or funny. Change it from that tone that communicates, "You're not worth it. You don't have what it takes." Change the tone to something sexy or a voice that sounds like a cartoon character—making it faster and higher until it sounds more like one of the famous Chipmunks.

In either event, the critical voice will stop. Notice how changing the tone changes your feelings about what you're doing—and about yourself. That's the quick fix. The longer-term way is the "Auditory Swish," which you practiced in the last chapter.

More Than Maintenance:
How to Increase Energy and Productivity

So far in this chapter, you've learned about the importance of expectations and mental rehearsal, the link between physiology and energy, ways to fine-tune your focus in the moment, how to reduce the impact of resistance and negative inner voices, as well as the importance of enthusiasm and confidence. As you integrate these concepts and techniques into the way you think and operate each day, you'll be able to more easily maintain your positive energy. But how do you *increase* it?

Franz Kafka said, "Productivity is being able to do things that you were never able to do before." So, here are a few additional tips to help you maximize your focus and productivity.

Tip #1: Rehearse Positive Mental States

Energy, motivation, enthusiasm, and optimism all feed on each other. After all, it's easier to feel optimistic when you're confident that the outcome is going to be positive. Each of us can elicit enthusiasm and optimism by practicing certain mental states. To start changing your blood chemistry, regularly rehearse the energy-generating physical interventions we explored at the beginning of this chapter. This neurological energy will improve the mental processes that generate your motivation.

As I mentioned, I used to motivate myself by just putting my head down and slogging through it. I figured, "If I bang my head against this wall, either the wall's going to cave in or I'll die, and if I die I don't have the problem anymore, so either way . . ." At the time, it seemed to be a good way to solve the problem. But, as I look back on it now, I'm painfully aware that I was operating from a limited set of choices.

Now it seems easier to motivate myself by saying, "As I begin on this, the wall begins to dissolve, because as soon as I start, I'm immediately learning more about my energy, my abilities, the task—I'm immediately making it easier because I'm taking the first step."

Basically, when my motivation kicks in, my optimism says, "I'm going to get started and it's going to be easier than I thought, and I'm going to do better than I thought. And guess what? Next time, I'll do better than this and the fiftieth time out, I'll do *even* better than I'll do this next time." So I have a positive expectation.

Because of the way I experience time, I have an expectation that in the present moment, I'm in the middle of my personal timeline. So I'm going to do the best I can today and *that* combined with the experience of taking action—noticing what I might have done better or how it could have been more enjoyable—will make me even better at it the next time.

After you review how a recent or long-ago experience happened, just look at the sub-modalities of that situation. Once you re-create and fine-tune those sub-modalities, it will put you in a more constructive frame of mind. All the pieces go together.

Tip #2: Update and Relive Greatest Hits

As you enhance your NLP skills and self-awareness, you'll experience many more successes. Be sure to add these to your list of greatest hits. To enhance your in-the-moment work, athletic, or interpersonal performance, *before* you get started, access earlier times of success, earlier feelings of success, and, as you feel them, anchor that to your performance spot on that joint of your finger (which you first worked with in Chapter 1). So now you've got energy, you've got self-satisfaction, you've got pride, and you continually anchor that.

Tip #3: Strengthen Your Positive Anchor

The kinesthetic anchor you created in Chapter 1 is sometimes referred to as a sliding anchor. Simply sliding your thumb up along that spot on your middle finger—just like turning up the volume on your TV—will increase the positive feelings. Let's try that now and see how much more energized you'll feel.

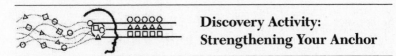 **Discovery Activity:**
Strengthening Your Anchor

Right now, go back to a time when you felt full of energy. Perhaps it was when you just landed an appointment with an important prospect you'd been pursuing. Maybe it was when you just came off a workout and you had that jazzed, tired, pumped feeling. Or maybe you just came back from a concert and you felt all revved up from music. Whatever it is that really gets you going and feeling "up"—set up into that experience and feeling—breathe into it—maybe even turn it up a little so you have more of that feeling. And when you have that, then touch that spot and anchor this energy to the same place where you've anchored your self-approval and confidence.

Here's an interesting thing: When you touch that spot, you can slide your thumb tip a little bit, and every time you slide it, the energy doubles. That feeling can actually double. You can imagine the way to do that is to touch that spot with that feeling, and then say, "Wow, what it would be like if the feeling were even twice as strong as I slide my thumb along my finger?" and it becomes twice as strong. Wow!

Then go back and say, "What would it be like if it were stronger yet?" and you bring it up to a really pleasurable level. Don't take it past your threshold, and I doubt that you will. Just bring it up to your pleasurable level.

When I'm writing or when I'm talking, I often find myself absently tapping that spot on the second knuckle of my middle finger. Because I use this anchor so often, it's like my system *knows* what I need— and I don't have to consciously remember. After a lot of practice, this will most likely happen automatically for you, too.

Tip #4: Celebrate Small "Wins"

Sometimes as I work with clients, I find that they get overwhelmed with a lot of these different ideas. It may feel like it's difficult (or even impossible) to learn these NLP concepts and skills—or *any* new things. But here's what's true: learning easily is something the human brain is designed to do.

Despite this fact, we sometimes say to ourselves, "Oh, I could never learn languages" . . . "I'm no good at numbers" . . . "I can't dance." I went for years thinking that I was some sort of dummy because I had left school when I failed at algebra. I just couldn't hack algebra. Well, I couldn't hack algebra because I was in a hormone toxicity state and other things were going on in my life, but I blamed it all on algebra.

Then, in my thirties, I went back to junior college and took all the algebra classes—as well as Boolean algebra and trigonometry—just to kill that old belief. Why did I think I could do that? Because I did believe that I could *learn*. Unless you have some kind of actual disability, you can learn anything you want.

Remember, everything that you do well today was impossible, or at least poorly done, the first time you tried it. Whenever I watch my one-year-old grandson while he's eating, I notice how he alternates between getting the spoon into his mouth . . . onto his cheek . . . into his nose . . . or flipping stuff on the floor. I notice how he's learning.

It reminds me that every time we try something new, we're all a little like my grandson. In the course of our lives, we've mastered many new things—so we should be comfortable with that process, right? Absolutely! And yet, our expectations are often out of sync with this "knowing."

So I invite you to relax and ease up on yourself in terms of your expectations about how fast you can do something or how good you can be at something. And while you're doing that, *raise* your expectations of how easy and fun it's going to be to get there—because the process can be known. By making this mind-set adjustment and using submodality distinctions, you'll find your actual abilities changing even more quickly. And celebrating small "wins" will contribute to the momentum you're creating.

There's no limit to how you use your imagination. Because each of us is so uniquely individual, it's up to each of us to discover on our own what works best. Finding ways to optimize experience helps us make life sweeter. So play with the different ideas you've explored in this chapter to understand what draws you forward and makes you feel even more energized, confident, and enthusiastic.

Next, we're going to move beyond just "self-esteem" and learn how you can remodel your whole self-concept.

Key Ideas

- The expectations we have shape our experience. People can limit or expand what's possible for them by changing their expectations.

- Mental rehearsal, like visualization, can enable someone to increase their actual performance.

- Our energy levels are linked to our physiology. Someone can improve how their brain, body, and mind work together by changing their body position, breathing deeply, drinking enough water to be well hydrated, and breaking large tasks into smaller ones of where they focus for twenty minutes and then take a break. (For more details on the Pomodoro Technique, visit http://www.pomodorotechnique.com.)

- "Eye Movement Integration" can help reduce resistance to doing specific tasks that seem almost too energy-draining to even contemplate.

- Someone's get-out-of-bed strategy is a sample of a motivation strategy that works for them. Once someone identifies a motivation strategy that works well, they can apply those insights and sub-modalities to motivating themselves in other situations.

- Energy, enthusiasm, and confidence work together to shape motivation and build momentum.

- Navy SEALs training uses four key practices to strengthen confidence, productivity, and tenacity.

- Critical voices can be internalized and active for years. These bullies can be silenced with a quick fix like making the voice sound like a cartoon character or doing the "Auditory Swish" process, which is outlined in Chapter 2.

- Someone can increase areas of current competence by rehearsing positive mental states, reliving their greatest hits, tinkering with sub-modalities, strengthening existing positive anchors, and celebrating small "wins."

 To enhance the skills you learned in this chapter, check out the recommended Bonus Activities at our special "Essential Guide" website: http://eg.nlpco .com/3-10 or use the QR code with your phone.

Discoveries, Questions, Ideas, and Stuff You Want to Work On

Discoveries, Questions, Ideas, and Stuff You Want to Work On

CHAPTER FOUR: UPGRADING YOUR SELF-CONCEPT

How'd things get this way?

It's never too late to be the person you might have been.
—George Eliot

Whether you're twenty-five, forty-five, or sixty-five, it's not too late to make the changes in yourself that you'd like to make. To understand how this is possible, in this chapter we're going to be looking at ourselves—how we're built, who we think we are, and how we got to be this way. And we're going to explore options for changing that. Ready?

Life Vest First: How to Prevent and Reduce Stress

Before we talk about self-change, which is really kind of profound work, you have to get in condition. To prepare for dealing with your unconscious to make this sort of change, it's important to know how to manage your stress reactions and practice stress reduction.

In Chapter 2, you learned how to explore and fine-tune what you want, as well as how to recognize and resolve internal conflicts so that you're congruent about whatever you're doing. These new skills will help you significantly prevent and reduce the friction and stress in your life. And yet, no matter how much you do to improve your choices in life, some things are beyond your choosing. There will still be red lights, rudeness, and bad weather. Some amount of stress is a perfectly natural response.

The problem with stress is that it generates some pretty nasty chemicals in your brain—and those chemicals can do some long-term damage. They also actually degrade your performance—at work, at home, and in virtually all areas of life. They preoccupy parts of your neurology that would be better utilized by thinking creatively. To help you be in control of your response to stressors, it's important to have an emergency protocol *and* a daily practice. Let's explore these one at a time.

911: PANIC MANAGEMENT

There's something called a panic reaction—the "fight-or-flight" (or freeze) reaction we touched on at the very beginning of the book. As you may recall from the last chapter, the amygdala determines whether or not you feel safe. It's a very primitive part of the brain that can trigger a cascade of reactions and hormones in your blood stream. It shuts down critical and deliberate thought, so all your energy can be dedicated to move into fight-or-flight. Once all that starts, it's pretty much a stampede.

Rather than get run over by this rush, you can employ the four practices you learned about in Chapter 3, the ones that Navy SEALs use. Here's a brief refresher. (1) Be only in the *exact* moment; don't think about the *next* thing; (2) break a task/activity into small, achievable steps and celebrate your progress; (3) at the point of discouragement, do six-two-six-count breathing to oxygenate your brain; (4) create a cheering section (in your own voice) that's encouraging and supportive.

LETTING THE AIR OUT: PREVENTING STRESS

Stress also accumulates over time. It's a little bit like blowing up a balloon. If there's too much air in it, it will explode. So it's important to monitor your stress level; then, regularly and proactively, let a little air out of the balloon. A powerful way to raise your level of stress endurance is a daily practice of meditation. There's an abundance of research going back to the 1970s that enumerates the physiological, neurological, emotional, and psychological benefits of meditation.

Much of this research was done by Herbert Benson at Harvard University, who wrote *The Relaxation Response*. What he found was that a daily practice of meditation—even fifteen minutes just once a day—creates long-term benefits in people's health, sense of reality, and even manual dexterity. Blood pressure lowers, the alpha relaxation rhythm in the brain deepens, and both halves of the brain synchronize. There are numerous significant long-term health benefits. Best of all, these begin within two weeks of regularly meditating.

In fact, when I began meditating, I noticed a change within a week. I felt more relaxed and moved a little more easily in the world. By the second week, my friends noticed and were commenting about the changes they saw.

Meditation is also a great way to just slow down your brain so you can observe your thoughts—where they come from, how they form, what comes up for you as you notice them. This is a very valuable way to make using NLP easier, too.

If you don't already have a form of meditation that works for you, here's an easy sort of plain-vanilla process to play that only requires that you find twenty minutes away from the world. Start by picking a quiet place that feels soothing to you, where you can relax without interruption. Then set a timer for twenty minutes so your conscious mind doesn't get distracted wondering what time it is. You can just let go and rest easy knowing that the bell will go off when the time you've allotted is up.

Here's how I do it. I just sit, take a few deep breaths, and relax my body—beginning with my feet, up through my calves, my thighs, my hips, my lower belly, my chest. I make sure my breathing is easy and regular. I feel my arms relax on the arms of the chair or in my lap, and finally I relax the muscles in my neck and my face. I'm just paying attention to my body and letting my unconscious know that I intend to relax myself. This part of the process takes about two minutes.

As I do that, I notice my breathing is getting deeper and more regular, and I allow myself to just let my breathing go and I try not to think of anything specific. My experience is that random thoughts tend to pop up. Often, I notice that my brain wants to reengage with whatever I tore myself away from. Once I'm relaxed, I find myself remembering things I forgot to do or I wanted to do. The trick here, in terms of not getting hooked into this inner dialogue, is just to allow those thoughts to go on their own.

If I notice that I'm kind of getting caught up in the inner chatter— "Did I turn the gas off? Why didn't I pick that up at the store yesterday? Now it's three more miles . . ."—I start repeating the word *one* to myself very softly. The word *one* suggests unity. It's actually the word they used in the relaxation response research at Harvard. This single-syllable sound works well for me—it's easy to make and doesn't have a lot of meaning. It actually sounds quite a lot like *om*, which is the Sanskrit word a lot of meditators use.

The only things you *need* to pay attention to are that your body remains relaxed, your breathing remains steady and deep, and the sound in your head that you're doing deliberately is just the sound of the word *one*—"one, one, one, one," just like that.

Take a moment and try it right now. Breathe deeply and let any tension in your body melt away. Say "one, one, one" in your mind and just let your conscious thoughts drift away. If you're not already doing it, give it a try now just for a few minutes.

I predict that if you try it for even five minutes today, tomorrow, and the next day, you will have a different week next week. You might even choose to continue meditating—and make it a daily practice.

I find that when I take time to relax this way, I feel refreshed when I return to my other activities—and I'm more resourceful. A lot of the daily events that had normally bothered or kind of paralyzed me—didn't. I feel like "This is small potatoes," or "You know, I can see several different ways this could be handled."

In the beginning, for me, meditation had all the earmarks of being a *discipline*—rather than relaxation. I sometimes found myself thinking, "This is a reward? This is like a time-out. This is like a punishment." But I persevered and over time, it's amazing how meditation has become something I look forward to. Because some people really struggle with sitting still, they enjoy the benefits meditation offers by doing something like qigong, yoga, running, or dancing instead.

When you meditate or follow a discipline that allows you to relax, it relieves stress, and your immune system likes you better. Studies show that cancer rates drop, heart disease drops, the quality of life improves—and it doesn't cost anything! Utilizing a preventative daily practice and an emergency protocol to manage stress enables you to create an inner environment that makes it possible to become a happier, better you.

A Look in the Mirror:
Who You Are Today and How You Got to Be This Way

Before exploring additional changes you may want to make, it helps to consider who you are right now and how you got to be this way.

If I asked you who you are, you could come up with lots of different ways to respond. You could tell me what you do for a living, what roles you play in your life—like mate, parent, friend, sibling—what your goals are—almost anything that has to do with who you are right now. Today's you is a product of all your experiences—of the gifts you were born with, the things you learned at home, at school, at work, in relationships, in your community, and in your travels, right?

It's like each of us is an onion that has lots of layers. Our outside layer is what other people most often see—what we look like, where we live, and how we behave. As the layers are peeled away, we learn more about our core selves. Beneath the papery onion skin, we'd find our capabilities, beliefs, values, and perhaps even spirituality.

You might look like one of your siblings or one of your parents and you may be similar in many ways. And yet you are uniquely you. How you process information, what you believe, and what you value drive your decisions and actions. In earlier chapters, you discovered how sub-modalities and your motivation strategies affect your experience. And you learned how you can tinker with those two things to improve your experience. So let's expand your understanding of how you work by *briefly* exploring beliefs, the Meta Model, predicates, and meta-programs. Okay, I know that's some scary lingo, but don't let this run you off. Stay with me a moment. I promise you'll find it really interesting.

Clues to Beliefs:
The Deep Structure of Language and the Meta Model

In Chapter 1, we learned a bit about how our minds use a linguistic shorthand to allow us to make sense of our world. There are several other specific ways that we filter our experience in order to make our unique world possible; these are called "Meta Models."

Many Meta Model filters are useful. For instance, generalizations save you from having to learn how to tie your shoes every time you put them on. A little of this is a good thing. However, too much of this good thing can be quite limiting. Here's why.

Many of our generalizations are unconscious and this is especially so in the case of beliefs. Many of these "rules" that we've created for ourselves come from an earlier time in our lives. Some of these actually come from someone else and are not really *our* choices at all.

A lot of the generalizations that take the form of beliefs were formed when we were very, very young and another large group were formed when we were adolescents. Beliefs formed in early childhood are generally the result of learning from our parents and our environment how to survive in the world. That's a very useful thing. It's just that now that we're adults we *can* make better choices for ourselves because we have learned an awful lot since we were five years old.

Likewise, in adolescence, in high school, we formed a lot of other beliefs. A lot of those were based on the extensive wisdom of our fourteen, fifteen, and even eighteen-year-old friends. I don't know about you, but I remember that when I was seventeen, I was amazed at how little my dad knew. What really surprised me, though, was how much he had learned just five short years later!

Tips to Notice and Identify Beliefs

To notice your beliefs and discover how they got there, here are some important warning signs to watch for and listen for in yourself. An easy one to notice is when you find yourself thinking "I really *should* do (that)." "It's something that really *ought* to be done." "I really have to take care of that now." Terms like *should, ought to, must, can,* and *may* are called words of necessity. And that is what they imply: that there is an absolute necessity to the statement that contains that word. It can be really useful to simply ask yourself, "Who says?" or "According to whom?" And then listen for an answer. You might be surprised to discover how much of your life is being run by the incredible wisdom of a fifteen-year-old, or your crazy aunt Sally.

This phenomenon isn't limited to words; it can also easily be linked to images that are triggered by an event or a time of day. I have a friend who used to wonder why it was that he found himself washing his car every Saturday morning, whether it needed it or not. After paying attention for a while, he realized that when he got up and walked out to pick up the newspaper, if the dateline said "Saturday" an image flashed through his mind, faster than he could see it. It was an image of his father getting up and washing the car every Saturday morning. It was something he remembered from when he was a very young child. That very young child wanted to be exactly like his father, and wasn't able to know what was important about that and what wasn't. That sequence of events, seeing that the date was Saturday and the image of his father flitting through his mind, and the feeling of affection and respect for his father triggered his motivation. Without his conscious awareness, this resulted in what was almost an obsession with washing his car every Saturday morning.

Well, it was nice to have a clean car. His wife appreciated it. But it probably would have been even nicer if he had some choice about it, and to have been able to do something else on Saturday, like take his wife out for brunch.

Other warning words to listen for are words that you'll recognize are massive overgeneralizations. These are words like *all, always, every,* and *never.* Listen for them when you're talking and even when you're talking to yourself. You'll also hear them when other people speak.

When you find yourself thinking or saying one of those thoughts, like "Oh, I never get to X," or "That always happens to me," it's useful to sort out where the generalization came from. Does this really happen *all* the time? *Everywhere?* In *every* situation with *everyone?* Poking gently at overgeneralizations like that will usually give you some counter-examples to those generalizations. The contrast and comparisons of counter-examples can help you to open up to considering more ways of dealing with those very situations. After all, if you accept that you will never get X, you'll be right. It's like Henry Ford said: "Whether you think you can, or you think you can't—you're right."

The examples you just reviewed illustrate different Meta Model violations. You don't have to concern yourself with the terminology, but if you'd like to explore additional examples and this fascinating deep structure of language, follow this link: http://eg.nlpco.com/4-1.

You'll have an opportunity to explore beliefs in greater detail in Section 2. For now, start noticing how your beliefs are influencing you—either limiting or empowering you. Set your inner antenna to notice what you're thinking and, without judging those thoughts, decide if that's what you want to be thinking. If not, find a preferred thought to focus on, one that feels better.

Like *That*: How Our Language and Behavior Reveal Individual Preferences

---

In addition to beliefs, each of us uses "Meta-Programs" to navigate our lives.

A QUICK META-PROGRAM PRIMER

Joseph O'Connor and John Seymour, trainers and authors of multiple NLP resources, describe meta-programs as:

> perceptual filters that we habitually act on . . . patterns we use to determine what information gets through. For example, think of a glass full of water. Now imagine drinking half of it. Is the glass half full or half empty? Both, of course; it's a matter of viewpoint. Some people notice what is positive about a situation, what is actually there, others notice what is missing. Both ways are useful and each person will favor one view or the other.
>
> Meta-programs are systematic and habitual, and we do not usually question them if they serve us reasonably well . . . Meta-programs are important in key areas of motivation and decision making.
>
> Because meta-programs filter experience and we pass on our experience with language, certain patterns of language are typical of certain meta-programs. . . . For example, one meta-program is about action. The *proactive* person initiates, he jumps in and gets on with it. He does not wait for others to initiate action. A proactive person will tend to use complete sentences, e.g.: "I am going to meet with the managing director." A *reactive* person waits for others to initiate an action or bides her time before acting. She may take a long time to decide or never actually take action at all. A reactive person will tend to use passive verbs, incomplete sentences, and qualifying phrases, e.g.: "Is there any chance that it might be possible to arrange a meeting with the managing director?"

Notice the difference. Again, neither is wrong or right—just different. Which one is more like you? Let's play with a few more examples.

The meta-program called options/procedures is one that's easy to notice in language *and* behavior. Think about this for a moment. Are you someone who likes to have an established, proven way of doing things—or someone who's always doing things a little differently? If you like a "right way," you're probably procedures-oriented. If you feel hemmed in by having to do something the same way over and over, you're options-oriented. Neither is better; it's just indicative of your personal preference.

Here's another to try on. Imagine that you're getting ready to do your taxes. Are you motivated to do them by April 14 because you'll be glad to wrap up your accounting for the year and maybe even get a refund? Or are you more likely to do them on time because you're concerned that you might incur a penalty or that your return may be flagged for an audit if it's late? If your thought pattern is more like the first situation, your motivation strategy is "toward" because you're moving toward a positive outcome. If your strategy is more like the second situation, you're more "away-from" oriented because you're moving away from a potentially negative consequence.

Keep in mind that meta-programs are a framework of thought; each one operates more like a continuum rather than as "either/or." Where you or someone else falls on the continuum often depends on the context, on what's going on. After all, most of us are different in our personal lives from what we are in our professional lives—or when we're relaxed rather than operating under pressure.

Of the more than forty recognized meta-programs, it helps to be aware of these:

Meta-Program	Answers the Question
Options/Procedures	Is it more important for you to do something the "right way" than it is to have alternative ways of doing it?
Toward/Away-From	Are you more motivated by moving toward something that has a potentially positive outcome, or away from a potentially negative consequence?
Proactive/Reactive	Are you more likely to take the initiative to act, or wait for someone else to do it—or for something else to happen?
Internal/External	When you evaluate something, are you more likely to use an internal personal standard or to ask for someone else's feedback?
General/Specific	Do you most often deal in the "big picture"—or the details?
Match/Mismatch	When making comparisons, do you notice how things are alike or where there are differences/discrepancies?

It's not critical that you identify which ones fit you. It does, however, help to be aware that the thought patterns you're working with filter your experience. As you slow down your thoughts and begin to notice more about how you operate, you'll become more in tune with how you motivate yourself and make decisions.

To receive a brief profile of *your* meta-programs, visit the following link to take a fun, quick assessment. Go to: http://eg.nlpco.com/4-4 or use the QR code with your phone.

PREFERRED REPRESENTATIONAL CHANNELS: PREDICATES

Because we use language to communicate our thoughts, our choice of words will reveal our thought patterns and preferences. A "Predicate," for example, reflects the representational system being used. In Chapter 1, you learned about representational modalities. As a refresher, we all operate in all three channels—visual, auditory, or kinesthetic—*and* each of us has an unconscious preferred way of processing. For example, I'm highly auditory, so when I'm learning something, I'd rather listen to a CD or have someone tell me what I need to know. Someone who's visual might prefer to read a manual or look at how-to illustrations.

Since I'm highly auditory, my language will reflect that, too. I'm likely to say, "That sounds good to me . . . I hear you loud and clear . . ." or "That rings true in my experience." These sensory-based words are called "Predicates." Again, it's not important that you recall the terminology, only that you begin to listen to the language you use and notice what *your* preferences are.

The purpose of this brief introduction to beliefs, the Meta Model, Meta-Programs, and representational preferences is to help you understand that how you've become the you who you are today is not random; it's not a mystery. There's a structure to how you take in information, how you make decisions, how you motivate yourself, and how you communicate. And, as you discover your unique structure, you can more easily make changes.

In the rest of this chapter, you'll have an opportunity to take a look at yourself through some NLP filters *and* then make choices to either strengthen the qualities that you like—or reduce the qualities that you don't like as much. You can actually change your self-concept.

Today's You and the Desired You: The Impact of Self-Concept

Here's a story: After completing an NLP seminar with Steve Andreas, a brilliant teacher and innovator, I remember sitting on the plane and writing in my notebook all the characteristics I was going to instill in myself. Well, as you might imagine, I got sidetracked by the immediacies of life and never did that. It wasn't until quite a while later, when I felt a crisis in my identity and self-concept, that I got around to making these changes.

For me, this crisis came with retirement, but it can happen to anyone who experiences a significant life change. Such a change can be positive or negative—graduation, marriage, childbirth, a new career or the loss of one—all of these life transitions can provoke real self-examination. Although I loved the leisure and sudden relief of responsibility that came with retirement, I suddenly wasn't certain what I ought to be doing . . . who I was . . . or what I could do.

It was probably pretty tiresome for my wife until I realized that I needed to take a look at who I thought I was and find out who I wanted to become for the next phase of my life. So here's how you can do that—*without* having a crisis!

The first step is to find out how you build your self-concept. As we get into this, you'll find that there's a structure made up of sub-modalities and generalizations and all the things that we've been talking about. So here's how to find out about that for each of you.

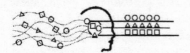

Discovery Activity:
Identifying Something You
Like About Yourself

Go inside yourself and pick something that you know to be true about yourself that you like. Something you like about yourself that you know to be true. Just take a moment. There's no need to overthink it—just find something you know to be so, and write it down.

Now, here's an interesting thing about this process. First, when you think about something that you know to be true about yourself and you can say, "I love to garden," "I've got a good sense of humor," "I'm really generous," "I'm very picky about keeping my car clean," "I'm very truthful," "I'm a great storyteller," "I have a special way with animals," or whatever it happens to be. When you say that, immediately you get some sort of representation about that quality or behavior, don't you? So notice that. This is where you take a look and see.

Details are important here—so notice, is it a symbol? Is it a picture of you doing something? Is it a picture of somebody else doing the thing that you do? Is it saying what you say or feeling how you feel?

It's very important that you learn the qualities of this, so let's follow this down. This is something you've accepted about yourself for some time, and you like about yourself. How has your brain got this information filed? We know it's using the language of the five senses—so is it an image? Maybe more than one, but there will be one sort of representation that's kind of like the generality of this characteristic for you.

Now, notice a couple of things. If it's a visual picture, notice where it is—and notice, is it a movie or is it a still? Is it color or black-and-white? Is it brighter than daylight, not as bright as daylight, or darker? Is it life-size, larger than life-size, or smaller than life-size? These are very important, because whatever characteristics this image has, it's your brain signaling to you that "this is something that's true about me," so note that.

Here's what I know is true. Whatever it is you believe about yourself that you like is probably a good thing. I've never met anybody who bragged about being cruel or flaky or sloppy or lazy or selfish or dishonest, so what you like about yourself is probably something good.

The way that belief came about was the same way you learned about doorknobs and politics. Over the course of your life, you had enough experiences or enough people commented on this thing you like about yourself that you have evidence—so you generalized from that. That's undeniable; that's certainly happened.

My question is, as you look back to see the evidence that supports the trait or way of being that you have—as you see that, I'm curious, how many examples do you have? How many bits of evidence or how many memories do you have that you are that way?

I did this experiment with my wife as we were driving to visit friends and she said, "I have thousands of examples of how I'm friendly and easy to talk to." Then I asked her to go look for them—and initially it was really hard to find them. But then all kinds of examples just sort of popped up, because that characteristic is such a part of her everyday experience.

The important thing to note is that you can list a few, several, hundreds, or thousands of examples—you can write down however many bits of evidence you have in your database that show you are this certain way . . . that you have this trait that you like about yourself . . . and you've noted if it's an image, where it is.

If it wasn't an image, what was it? You say, "Well, I just have a feeling about this." Okay, you have a feeling. Does that feeling include some sort of a visual representation? It almost always does, and it certainly does when you're looking for evidence.

Here's another quality of the evidence I'd like you to note. The first thing we're going to do is to make this thing you like about yourself even stronger.

Whatever it is about yourself that you like, if you would like that to be stronger, then do this: Notice the representation of that characteristic or way of being that you have—and notice whether it's a feeling or a voice in your head telling you that you're that way. And notice if it's somebody else's voice telling you you're that way—or notice if it's an image. By combining this initial representation, whatever it is, AND the other two senses, you will have a remembered experience that's visual, auditory, and kinesthetic. Take a moment and do that now.

Next, look at the evidence in your database, the memories you have where you exhibited that characteristic or way of being—and notice the quality of these examples. What do you see? Are you seeing yourself doing whatever it is—and you're outside that? Can you "go into" each picture so you can relive those experiences at will? Being associated strengthens the experience.

When you look at those bits of evidence that you are this certain way, are they scattered pretty evenly back through your childhood or whenever you developed this trait? Maybe it's something you developed later in life. That's okay. Just notice.

Now, here's a really important step. Check to see if there's any evidence in your future that you are this way. In other words, are there places where you expect to be this way in the future? As you look to the future, if you don't see evidence that you are this way, I suggest you put some in there.

You can put these expectations on little index cards that contain blank movies that just haven't run yet. They can be photographs of you in the future, and you can see yourself from behind as you're moving toward them—because this is in your future. You can see that "future you" doing those things, or you can pop in and imagine you'll be doing them when you're old and saintly. Any of these possibilities will also strengthen this trait or way of being.

Now, here's an interesting thing about self-concept—it's got staying power. Some people are very durable in their self-concept—they're solid—and the more relaxed they are, the more they are who they are. Some people's self-concept is more fluid.

Here's an interesting thing that happens. If there's something you like about yourself that you know to be true, you also know that you haven't been perfect your entire life. Holding these contrasting reflections at the same time can be challenging.

Let me give you an example. I like that I'm honest—and I know that it's true that I am honest. But I shoplifted when I was a kid. In my life, I've lied on occasion. I've even cheated. I've had some earlier experiences that are what we call counter-examples. In the scope of things, they were trivial—but they taught me how bad it was to be dishonest. So, I have old evidence that I'm not honest and more current evidence that I am. What good does that do me? Does it keep me truthful? Yeah, it helps, as long as I keep these counter-examples in perspective. Otherwise, they could also weaken my self-concept.

You see, having a self-concept that I'm honest means that's my first choice—and that honesty is my instinct, without exception, in every situation. I find it's easier, it's more convenient, and I don't have to remember a line of BS, so there are a lot of reasons why it's useful. I make sure that my wife and I are on the same page because I'm not hiding or living a separate reality from her, so there are a lot of reasons why I like this. But I don't wear it like a badge of honor, because I know I'm flawed.

However, if I were to bring those old counter-examples forward and put them in my face so I couldn't even say I'm honest or that I want to be honest, it would undermine my self-concept. It would create incongruity and it would weaken me.

Now, here's what to do. I don't think that you should deny the truth. I think that's unrealistic and psychologically unhealthy. What you do instead is to turn any recollection of a behavioral counter-example into just a statement on a piece of paper in your memory.

Do not go back and relive the time when you didn't measure up. In other words, screen out negative examples—you can do this by choice. You've learned how we can edit things and how we can strengthen things—so you can do this a lot of different ways.

You can actually convert the memory. For instance, I can remember stealing a Baby Ruth candy bar from the corner grocery store in our neighborhood, and then my dad marched me back in. I cried and apologized and got chewed out for it. But I remember doing it—so I know I'm not honest. I remember that little crime when I was a kid. My dad made sure I'd remember it—but I no longer see myself doing that, other than hauling it up now to tell you about it.

Normally when I go back to this experience, it's a little index card in my memory that says, "Yeah, that was one of your learning experiences. That is one of the reasons that you're honest now," so I converted the experience to a reason. And now that reason strengthens my instinct to be honest.

To strengthen the thing you like about yourself, convert a counter-example from something that says, "Oh no you're not," to "Oh, and this learning experience makes you even more that way now."

So again, focus on the trait that you like about yourself, which you should like and appreciate even more now, because you're strengthening it, and then sweep back through your files. If you found counter-examples that made you a little uncomfortable or a little incongruent about having this trait or characteristic—or you felt less than entitled to it because there were exceptions—just change those counter-examples so that they're learning experiences that make you even more this way now.

That's right, it's a little job to do and may take a little reflection. Take your time.

To strengthen self-concept, here's something I do that you might also consider doing. When I come out of my morning meditation, the first thing I do is to thank my Maker for the way I'm feeling and for the life I have. The second thing I do is to just sort of flood my body with gratitude that it's all functioning. I don't even think about it, and the cells are dividing and the blood's moving and everything seems to be working pretty good even after all these years of abuse.

The next thing I do is sort of just be glad that I am who I am. I say, "I'm not perfect, but life's not over yet." I have the sense that I'm learning and that I'll be better tomorrow than I am today and that I keep trying. This just gives me a sense of real strength and ease as I move back into my day.

So you can tie some of this self-concept work, in terms of self-regard, to that little private time. Take thirty seconds to just appreciate yourself and your life as you come out of meditation. Just make that a habit. Your brain will love you for it. Your unconscious will love you.

For additional demonstrations and/or examples, go to: http://eg.nlpco .com/4-7.

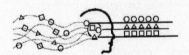 **Discovery Activity:
Adding Elements to
Your Self-Concept**

Now I want to start to make use of some of the groundwork that you did earlier in this chapter. Let's look at adding elements to your self-concept. How would you do that? The same way you built your original self-concept—by generalizing from certain experiences.

I propose that you have many more experiences that you haven't generalized that are positive. So one of the ways to do this is to pick a trait that you would like to strengthen in yourself.

As an example, about a month ago, I picked a way of being that I thought would be useful to me for the next phase of my life. I picked calm, well organized, and highly productive. I've had six years now of being out of a regular responsibility for running a company and the structure it imposed. Some weeks I've written, some weeks I've led seminars, other weeks I've consulted in companies. Sometimes I've just spent time down at the river or at the pool. There wasn't any sort of normal structure and I found I wanted one; I just wasn't satisfied with my productivity.

As I imposed this new structure, part of me said, "Oh no you don't. I've worked for decades for this. I'm not giving this up. Do that Thursday. Do that next week," and this resistance was inhibiting my progress on some of my projects.

So I thought, "Well, I'd like to be motivated to be more naturally procedural in a calm, nonfrantic way, and just plow ahead." I have to tell you, I did this work about a month ago—and my productivity has skyrocketed. It's probably up 60 percent, and here's how you can do it, too.

Before we begin, remember the sub-modalities of the first thing you picked that you like about yourself and know to be true. Refresh your memory about these sub-modalities now.

Next, pick a trait that you would like to have—or that you do have that you would like to strengthen. It can be any way of being that you want. As you identify it and see it now, immediately see some sort of image or see yourself being a certain way. Make sure that the sub-modalities of this new image match those of the image of the *first* characteristic you picked, in every way—location, size, color, lightness and brightness, motion or not—exactly the same. Put it in the same place.

Then, second, do the same thing that you did with that quality or characteristic, which is to take it and make sure that you can see it, you can hear it, and you can feel it. Then, once you have that image just right, step into it so you're actually doing it, and see if it feels okay to be that kind of a person. Does that feel all right?

Again, your choice of a new trait should be realistic: one that you know you could do and would really be pleased to find yourself doing. It's not like you're suddenly a high-fashion model or astronaut or anything like that. This is something that's realistic and it has to do with a characteristic or way of being that you would like to add to your description of yourself—or that you would like to strengthen.

If that feels as good as it ought to, that's fine. Now go back to your memory and notice the many times that you have been that person or that you have been that way. You might not have noticed it before. You certainly didn't treat it the way I'm asking you to treat it now.

Take those memories and make sure they look and feel and sound like the memories of that first trait you chose that you like about yourself. The example should match in terms of the filing system that you let your brain use. What's happening now is you're gradually realizing that you are that way. That it's part of you.

If I hear a little voice in my head saying, "Yeah, but . . ." I address that, saying, "Yeah, but I wasn't always that way. That's why I want to strengthen it," or "I'm not really that way. I want to become that way."

That voice is a voice that's looking at the counter-examples. "Look here. You weren't that way there. You weren't that way here." It's like one of those little shoplifting things. Yes, that may also be true, and those are the reasons you want to become that way.

Again, take those examples—if they're examples of behavior that didn't demonstrate this preferred way of being—and turn them into little index cards with a note on it that says, "This experience makes me want to be this way even more." Allow those notes to drop into the places where those memories are.

So now you've got two sets of filed experiences. One set is the one that we worked with earlier, which has to do with something that you know you like about yourself. The other set of filed experiences includes the experiences for this additional way of being that you either want to add to or use to strengthen your self-concept. Look at them both and make sure that they look the same and that they're stored in the same place.

Now test this out. Imagine this new trait added to your self-concept—and it's true and accurate because you've done it in the past. As it becomes part of you, consider something coming up in the future—perhaps later today, perhaps tomorrow, perhaps the next day, where you'll be exhibiting this new characteristic. Notice how it feels to have this trait. Notice how it is when this is just part of who you are, notice how things look to you, notice how you feel about yourself. Feel this in your body.

What has changed? In terms of how it feels to be you—and this is pretty significant—notice what has changed with this new characteristic added to your self-concept.

Over the next several days, invest a few minutes and do this imagining of how you feel when you exhibit this new trait that's in your subconscious; just do that every morning. Do it for at least three days.

The Archaeological Dig: An Example
of Self-Concept Work

Before moving on, I'd like to share an example from working with a thirty-two-year-old intensive care nurse who wanted to enhance her self-concept by adding the trait of *being energetic*. She was careful to tell me that she didn't want to be *so* energetic that she couldn't easily unwind at the end of the night. (That's ecology, right?)

After exploring her motivation, she told me that if she were *more* energetic, she'd be willing to go out more often at night. When I asked her, "What will being more energetic and going out at night do for you that's even more important?" her meta-outcome was that she'd feel less lonely because she'd have the opportunity to connect more with other people.

By talking through past examples of when she did—or didn't—go out at night, she learned about some of her meta-programs and beliefs that were automatically shaping her perceptions of how things could be different. When she thought about taking the initiative to plan an evening with someone, she experienced a sense of deep sadness—and even some physical symptoms like tiredness and low level of anxiety.

When we explored how she knew to feel like this (what the cue was that automated that response), she found an image of herself when she was a little girl. When her current self asked the little girl (her younger self) what she was trying to do for her, Denise learned that girls were supposed to be nice and that if they were, they'd be invited lots of places. So the meaning that she was making of her current situation was that the lack of invitations or changes in plans meant she wasn't nice enough, wasn't liked enough for people to be with her.

Long story short, by accepting that her younger self was actually trying to advocate for her, Denise's current self was able to stop resisting and begin negotiating with the little girl. Together we explored alternatives that would satisfy both of them.

Ripple Effects:
How One Change Often Creates More Change

When deciding to add being "more energetic" to her self-concept, Denise got more than she bargained for, didn't she? Today, in addition to being more energetic, she's more comfortable being proactive, she's more congruent, and she's less likely to interpret a change of plans as meaning there's something wrong with her.

So that's just one example of strengthening self-concept. There are thousands of others. And if you're the kind of person who really wants to gain more influence over yourself, the way you behave, how you think, and what you know, if you want to be that kind of person, you're on the road to doing that now.

You have the raw material to look inside yourself and to never again become a victim of rage, panic, or long-term depression that runs away with itself. And you have the tools.

I believe that having this kind of familiarity with your own inner processes gives you a chance to work on yourself—and to have a more understanding attitude about other people. Here's an example of what I mean.

Earlier this morning, I was driving in the San Francisco Bay area at rush hour. It continues to amaze me that I lived down here in the middle of five million people because it's so busy compared to where we live in the mountains today. I'm driving along and some young lady who was on her way to work—anxious, busy, distracted—jumps in front of me in traffic and flips me off in the rearview mirror. I was moving too slow. "Here's this old guy . . ." I actually have no idea what she was saying to herself, but it certainly seemed like I ticked her off.

It was kind of funny because I saw her watching me, flipping me off, and then reaching down, taking out some lipstick, and looking in the same rearview mirror to adjust her makeup—all this, just before she slammed on her brakes and almost hit the guy in front of her as we came to the next signal.

I didn't get mad at her. Instead, I reminded myself she's in her twenties, she's got six things on her mind—maybe a date tonight, probably running a little bit late for work, all these people are in her way, including me—so she wasn't having as good a morning as I was. I had a great morning! I just felt humane. I felt compassionate toward her, just because she's so busy and so rushing around and so lost in her own situation and not "getting" it.

Well, everybody's like that. Everybody's in their own situation doing the best they can. If you look at the NLP presuppositions now with your understanding of how you operate inside—if you look at these operating principles (listed at the end of Chapter 1) and really test those statements—you can see that they are not clichés. They reflect the best thinking that there is on how human beings actually operate and why.

In the next chapter, you'll discover how what you've learned about how your brain works can be used to give you insight into how *other* people experience things. This will help you to become more patient, resilient, and relaxed. You'll be more confident, too, because you'll understand that everyone is doing the best they can, and that most of them are reacting to inputs and filters that are out of their awareness. They don't know that they're having pictures, sounds, and feelings in their head. They don't know it's constantly going on and triggering them. But you do now—and this understanding will serve you well.

Key Ideas

- Stress can create a cascade of negative reactions. Having stress-management strategies for dealing with emergencies and preventing the buildup of stress enhances someone's options for positive behaviors and outcomes.

- Each of us is a product of our experiences—and the thought patterns and conclusions we've created in response to those experiences.

- Beliefs are generalized thoughts that act as automated filters that determine what information we "let in."

- Beliefs can be empowering or limiting in the way they shape our experience.

- The deep structure of what we mean is not always clearly communicated by what we say. Our linguistic shorthand often reflects an overgeneralization. These are called Meta Model violations and may "signal" us that we are acting from an old belief, and not current reality.

- Meta-programs are thought patterns, based on generalizations (an efficiency strategy that the brain uses) because we don't have time to relearn everything. These patterns act as automatic filters that help us make decisions; they tell us what's okay for someone and what's not. They also filter out any evidence that's contrary to the belief. Someone's meta-programs are reflected in how they speak and behave.

- Although there are more than forty meta-programs, six key ones to focus on are:

  > Options/Procedures   > Internal/External
  > Toward/Away-From   > General/Specific
  > Proactive/Reactive   > Match/Mismatch

- Predicates are sensory-based words that telegraph someone's preferred representational channel—visual, auditory, or kinesthetic. For example, "That sounds good to me," "I hear you loud and clear," or "That rings true in my experience" are phrases usually indicating an auditory representation of experience.

- Your self-concept is a generalization about your behavior that is based on selecting examples of events that demonstrate your qualities, collecting them together into a database, and then using one example as a sort of summary—what cognitive linguists call a prototype.

- When counter-examples are integrated into your database of examples, as examples of learning, they strengthen the self-concept. Too many counter-examples, or counter-examples that are too large or prominent, can threaten or destroy the self-concept.

- When making changes to their self-concept, someone may discover more about how they "work" and need to negotiate internal changes to get the best possible result (as Denise did).

 To enhance the skills you learned in this chapter, check out the recommended Bonus Activities at our special "Essential Guide" website: http://eg.nlpco .com/4-10 or use the QR code with your phone.

Discoveries, Questions, Ideas, and Stuff You Want to Work On

Discoveries, Questions, Ideas, and Stuff You Want to Work On

_____

_____

_____

_____

_____

_____

_____

_____

_____

_____

_____

_____

_____

_____

_____

_____

_____

_____

_____

_____

_____

_____

_____

Section Two: It's All About Relationship

CHAPTER FIVE: MAKING COMFORTABLE CONNECTIONS

How come we don't connect?

> When we get too caught up in the busy-ness of the world, we lose
> connection with one another and ourselves.
> —Jack Kornfield

This quote is a great snapshot of how many people feel today. Section 1 was all about understanding and making connections with yourself. This section focuses on making connections with *others*.

In this era of ever-evolving technology, experts say we communicate more than ever before because we can so easily connect to information, to other people, to places all over the world. Others say that these instantaneous, fleeting "touches" don't really satisfy our need for human connection. And some educators and business leaders fear that our reliance on electronic technologies will limit our ability to communicate and connect in face-to-face situations.

What you'll learn in this chapter will help you make positive first impressions and create rapport with anyone you choose to—simply by making them feel safe and interesting. That may sound pretty fundamental, and it is. Yet it's not what most of us do when we initially meet and try to connect with someone.

Internal Systems:
How You Work Is Similar to How Others Work

In the first section of this book, you discovered a lot about how your brain works and how you can make changes so you function even more effectively. Everything you learned that goes on inside you also goes on inside other people. We all have the same *structure* of experience. We receive some kind of stimuli, either a memory or something coming in from outside; then the brain assigns a meaning to it . . . that triggers emotions . . . and those emotions trigger a behavior:

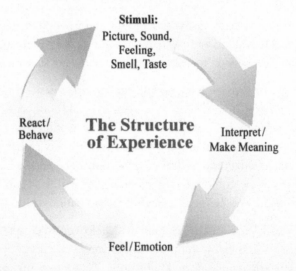

Stimuli:
Picture, Sound,
Feeling,
Smell, Taste

React/
Behave

The Structure of Experience

Interpret/
Make Meaning

Feel/Emotion

To oversimplify things, this "process" is how we create our inner worlds, our personal "Maps." *Now* we're moving into dealing with someone else, too—someone who has their *own* unique map! We're all processing, all the time, right? But here's the thing. When we see other people, all this goes on so fast that we just make assumptions about who they are. We stereotype: the person says this or does that, therefore they're a certain kind of person. Frequently, our judgments about another person, which are really more like first impressions, are really nothing more than a reflection of our own internal filters. *That's* often where the problem starts.

What do we have to do inside ourselves *before* we can cleanly and effectively deal with this other person? If you really want to "get" another person, it helps to drop your filters and find a way to be aware of what you're thinking. In fact, people who are really wonderful with others make it a point to *consciously* check their own thinking. This helps them set aside their personal filters or mental prejudices so they can get the real information as it comes in; they get what's *actually* happening past their personal filters. People who do this effectively are truly able to focus on the *other* person. Because of this, they are considered "good company" and other folks enjoy being with them.

Inside Out:
How to Adjust Your Inner World to Be Better Company

As you learned in the last chapter, there are many experiences that have shaped the way you are today. And now you know that you can change your experience, your responses, and even your self-concept. Here's a hard fact: *Being the way you are is a choice.* I'm not talking about things like being tall or being Swedish. I'm talking about how you think, feel, and act. It may not always seem true, but it is. As you're aware, how we rewire ourselves is also a choice.

If you suddenly came into a lot of money and wanted to renovate and add on to your house, how might you begin that process? You'd probably start by thinking of houses that you really liked. And, most likely, you'd also give some thought to places you've lived, or seen, that you *didn't* like, right? You'd talk with trusted friends who know you well to get their recommendations, and you might even involve them in the project.

Rewiring yourself is a lot like the process of designing and building a house. You start with the foundation of who you are now. You evaluate the advantages and disadvantages of how you are today; then you begin to imagine and integrate new possibilities, right? You could rewire your health-related habits, the way you manage your financial decisions, or how you take care of your home. You can change almost anything. For now, let's focus on how you interact with others.

 **Discovery Activity:
Identifying Ways That You're
Good Company**

Imagine looking into a virtual mirror where you can see movie clips of how you look, sound, and behave when you're with other people. What do you like best about how you interact with people? Perhaps you're a patient listener. Maybe you bring a lot of energy and laughter to conversations. Maybe you're well informed and interesting. What is it that makes you good company?

Take a moment now and think of a time when you felt good about yourself after a conversation. What specifically do you like about what you did, how you behaved, what you said? Note these things.

Consider a few other situations where you felt good about how you interacted with someone, and include specific behaviors or ways of being on the list you're making.

These examples show you in the best light, don't they?

Now it's time to take a look at yourself in the harsh light of day; maybe it's your bathroom mirror that seems to age you ten years. Yikes! Based on this glimpse, identify at least two ways you could be *better* company. These insights may come from things others have told you or you might find memories of interactions where you were kind of whiny, bossy, aggressive, or not really present.

Reflecting back on these times might be uncomfortable, so it can be tempting to dismiss these as exceptions. But wouldn't you be relieved if you could do something so that there were no, or at least very few, repeat performances? You can. And it's *your* choice.

Maybe you're a real sweetheart and you never create any friction. But perhaps, on the odd occasion when you're under stress, weary, or hungry, maybe that's when these less desirable traits or behaviors come out. Yours may be few, but most of us have them. If you sincerely want to become as good as possible in dealing with others, it's time to think about really exploring the ways you could be even more enjoyable to be or communicate with. What are these? *Add these opportunities to your list.*

If you're really committed, or at least brave, get feedback from people you live or work with. You might say, "I'd like to get better at how I connect with people and I'm hoping you can help me by candidly answering three quick questions." Once you get their agreement, start by asking, "When you think of interacting or spending time with me, what do you like best about that? What's one thing you'd like me to *keep* doing?"

They might say that they like how you really look at them when they're telling you something, that they feel like you're not judging them, or that you always have good advice. Whatever they say, make sure you understand it; you may even want to ask them to share a specific example so you can tap into the memory or feeling they're sharing with you. If you don't understand it, it's hard not to *keep* doing it or do it more often.

Thank them for that feedback and ask them the next question. "If you could change *one* thing about how I interact with you, what would that be? You're important to me and I really want to know. What would you like me to *stop* doing?" This may not be easy for you to ask, or for them to answer. Remember, you're looking for something that you can improve. They might say, "You're always so busy and rushed, I feel like I'm not important." Or they may say, "I hate it when you check email or accept phone calls when I'm trying to tell you something." The reflection they show you may not be welcome or pretty.

You might be thinking, "Wow, that was harsh" or "I only do that once in a while." Breathe. Of course, you don't *intend* to be bossy, negligent, or condescending. But if the meaning of the communication is the response that you're getting back, then you want to change your approach so you get a different response back, right?

When you ask these three questions, really try to hear the response. Remember, this person is entrusting you with something that's uncomfortable, something they wish were different. It's important to avoid being defensive and to make sure you understand what they mean. Acknowledge what they said: "So, what I heard you say is that you'd like me to give you my full attention when we're talking and if something happens that I have to attend to right away, you'd like me to commit to a time when we can pick up where we left off. Is that right? Thank you for telling me that. It's very useful feedback—and it's something I'm very willing to work on."

Asking this question can generate some emotional sparks and the other person may see this discussion as an opportunity to get some other things off their chest. If so, you'll have to decide how to handle that in the moment or schedule a time to fully address their concerns. Later in this chapter, you'll learn some tips to help cool down emotional situations.

The final question is "If you could wave a magic wand to change how I interact with you, what's one thing you'd like me to *start* doing?"

The answers to this question usually surprise me. The answers don't feel like criticism and they provide me with insight into what's really important to that person. This has been a blessing to me in personal and professional relationships.

Three simple questions—keep, stop, start. When asked with intention and sincerity, they can help you immensely. Right now you're probably already thinking about people you want to ask for feedback. I recommend starting with easy situations first; perhaps it's your favorite client, a friend who's usually complimentary, or a teacher who's given you good advice in the past. Whomever you ask, thank them for sharing their impressions with you. By responding, they're taking a risk and making an investment in your relationship.

Of course, the feedback you get reflects what the other person makes up in *their* mind, but again, we're the ones who are striving to be the most flexible because we want the most influence. Therefore, it's not about right or wrong, it's simply about who's going to be the most flexible.

Once you get feedback from others, add their input to your list. Knowing the ways you are good company *and* the ways you can be easier to be around is a gift. If you act on the information people share with you, you *will* be easier to be around. Happily, I'm proof of that.

Friction on the Line?
How the Three Parts of Your Brain Work Together

If you've reflected on your past experiences, you know what behaviors or ways of being you have that you want to improve. Even with this awareness of your habits, your brain and your state of mind affect how you radiate and what kind of vibe you're sending out.

Here's why. The brain has different parts—and these parts have different jobs. A *New York Times* article titled "Inside the Mind of Worry" by David Ropeik explains this well.

> Work on the neural roots of fear by the neuroscientist Joseph LeDoux of New York University, and others, has found that in the complex interplay of slower, conscious reason and quicker, subconscious emotion and instinct, the basic architecture of the brain ensures that we *feel* first and think second. The part of the brain where the instinctive "fight or flight" signal is first triggered—the amygdala—is situated such that it receives incoming stimuli *before* the parts of the brain that think things over. Then, in our ongoing response to potential peril, the way the brain is built and operates assures that we are likely to feel more and think less.

This instinctive part of the brain is at work almost every time we meet someone. In fact, it's probably operating when you walk into a dark room. At some level, the amygdala is sort of saying to the higher brain, "Pay attention. Look around. Make sure everything's okay."

This situation is kind of like a pan of water that's set on simmer. As long as the water is warming and on simmer, there's no problem. The amygdala communicates with the higher brain, and the higher brain can analyze and solve problems and reduce danger. That's fine.

However, when it boils over, then that's it. Now the thinking brain shuts off because the amygdala is saying "Run! Run!" or "Get ready to fight!" At that point, you're not going to be very successful in managing yourself to deal with others. And if you're dealing with somebody who's in that state, you're not going to be able to talk to their higher brain, either.

People are being driven by different aspects of their brain at different times. So it's important to be aware of where they are and how resourceful they might be in their *current* state of mind. When we encounter somebody in traffic, they may be driving with raw emotion, like anger. It's really dangerous and I see it a lot. When you're the passenger where the driver is flipping people off, honking their horn, or cutting other cars off in traffic, there's no real way to have a conversation with them that's going to be at a higher level, or to have any sort of reasonable interaction.

I want to mention the multifaceted brain because we're always shifting back and forth between its different parts. When we're in conversation with someone else, we want to be able to move from the feeling parts of the brain to the thinking parts so that we can actually talk. That means that we want to reduce the possibility of amygdala hijack, ours *and* theirs. We want to calm this part down. We want to make the other person feel safe, and then we can have a conversation with them.

Too Much of a Good Thing? The Role of Empathy

One of my clients, a twenty-nine-year-old social worker, asked me if it was possible to have *too much* empathy. She went on to explain that she was worried that she was sometimes so empathetic that she felt like she lost herself a little.

As we talked about this concern, my thought was—and this is a generalization—"This is something I hear from my other female clients and friends." Like my wife, Laura often wrestles with her early conditioning of being a good little girl—struggling to balance the childhood messages she got with her present-day experiences and needs.

Because being empathetic with others is a good skill to have, I wanted to make sure Laura decided to develop *additional* resources, rather than "bench" this one. So I encouraged her to intentionally notice throughout the day what perceptual position she was in, and to experiment with each of the three different perceptual positions. I advised her that whenever she felt too deeply involved with another person's feelings to step outside herself and ask, "Am I going too far? How am I feeling inside? What are *my* feelings?"

You might be wondering what perceptual positions are. We played in this neighborhood during Chapter 2 when we explored association and disassociation—the sub-modalities of being "in" the picture or mental movie or outside it. Let's talk briefly about the three perceptual positions because understanding this will really help you when interacting with other people.

When we're really mentally healthy, we flicker around between first, second, and third positions, as appropriate. And we can go too far with *any* of the positions.

First Position

First position is where you're in your own body. You see everything through your eyes and you know exactly how you feel. You know what you want, and that's a position of great authenticity. It can also be a kind of infantile position. After all, it's the perceptual position we had when we were babies, right? At that point, we really knew what we wanted. "I'm hungry. I'm cold. I'm wet." That's all we knew then and we yelled until we got it addressed. You probably know some adults who still operate like this. When people get stuck in first position, we describe them as narcissistic or immature. In NLP, some people also refer to this position as *self*.

Second Position

Second position is what my client was talking about. That's the position where you're very, very simpatico to another person. You feel someone else's pain. If you're in second position, you might get someone a glass of water before they even know they're thirsty. It's a position of great solicitation and understanding of others. When we go too far with second position, we tend to be oversolicitous and overdependent, and that's often referred to as codependency. In NLP, some people refer to this position as *other*.

Third Position

In NLP, the third position is often called the *observer* position. That's where you're *outside* a situation and you just sort of record what's happening. You see what's going on, completely separate from yourself, like an objective reporter might. It's a position where you can evaluate yourself and options. (That's what you did when you played with stepping out of your picture or mental movie in Chapter 2.)

Scientists frequently operate from third position, as do surgeons, engineers, and professional performers. People who work in these professions benefit from stepping outside themselves to judge what's going on. And because there's not a lot of emotion in third position, they can effectively determine what's working and what changes might be helpful. What's the drawback? Well, if someone gets stuck in third position, they're sort of habitually detached, and people feel like they can't ever really connect with them.

Again, the goal is to take advantage of these different options. Go into first position to get clarity about how you feel. To try something on from someone else's point of view, briefly go into second position. To evaluate a situation and solutions, go into third position for objectivity.

A *Case in Point: Intentional Use of Perceptual Positions*

Let's take an example of something that happened to me during the early days of studying NLP that beautifully illustrates the usefulness of shifting between perceptual positions.

Back then, I had a girlfriend who wasn't sure what to make of NLP, how it was changing me, and how passionate I was about it. In an effort to put her at ease and maybe even get her excited about it, I said, "I'd really like you to come to this introductory talk about NLP and just hear about it. In my enthusiasm, I don't think I've done a good job describing it to you. Maybe my favorite teacher, Robert McDonald, will."

She agreed to come. And, during the activities, we got separated. It was quite a large room and we were all engaged in activities with other people. I thought it would be useful to her to see several processes without having her experience influenced or contaminated by me.

At the lunch break, she came over to me and said, "I'm going home. I feel terrible."

I said, "Wow, what happened?"

She said, "Oh, I went up to talk to the trainer. I just asked him a simple question and he bit my head off."

I thought, "That doesn't sound likely to me." But I gave her the car keys and told her to head on home and I would get a ride from somebody at the end of the day.

Later that afternoon, I went up to the trainer and discussed it with him. I said, "I brought a guest and you kind of fried her. She was feeling bad enough that she actually left."

He said, "Oh, I remember. She did come up and ask me a question," and then he did an interesting thing. He went through his memory of the interaction with my girlfriend, using all three perceptual positions. He went through it first as himself and said, "Let's see, I was in the middle of talking with somebody else and she came up and asked a question. I said, 'Hang on a moment. I want to answer that, but I need to finish this process.'"

I said, "You know, she's really shy and it wasn't easy to even get her to join me today. It probably took a hell of a lot for her to come and approach you." Then he went into second position. He became her, and he thought, "Well, yeah, I can see if I were shy, and hesitant about being here, if I came up to the trainer and he put me off like that, it might have felt a little abrupt to me."

Then he went to third position and, from outside, he saw the two of them interacting and thought, "You know, that really wasn't beyond the pale. I asked her very kindly if she would just wait a moment, but I understand how she might have taken it the wrong way. Can I apologize to her?" I said, "I don't know. I don't think she's ever coming back. I just don't know."

He asked for her phone number and he called her that afternoon to apologize. It was very interesting how he did it. He apologized for any part he might have played in how she was feeling, but he made clear to her that her feelings were her creation and not his.

He let her know that it was not his intent to make her uncomfortable, and that he was not angry with her or irritated. He told her that he just needed to complete a conversation he was having with the first person who had approached him with a question. He explained that he was treating that first person the way my girlfriend wanted to be treated. I think she got it, because she came back the next day.

This story shows the value of each perceptual position. If you're feeling a little too sucked into somebody or into a situation, get back in to *your* body. The anchor that you created in Chapter 1 can help you do that, because it's an anchor of power, *and* it's a first position anchor. When you touch that place on your middle finger, it should return you to yourself.

In industrialized societies, we are not encouraged to stay in first position. We're encouraged to get out of it. Girls are taught not to be selfish; they're pushed into second position. They hear "Be polite, be nice, be helpful, don't be outspoken."

And boys are taught not to cry. They're kicked out of first position into third: "Don't be a baby; this is the way things are. Be a man." In business and in sports, even though there's a lot of emotion, males are taught not to take it personally. It's like the Mafia. A guy shoots his friend and he says, "It's just business."

I remember when I was in sixth grade, I was playing football with a friend of mine for the first time. He actually hit me below the waist. He said he was sorry and that it wasn't personal. What he did took me out of the lineup and I was kind of brokenhearted that my friend would deliberately hurt me just to get past me in a game. But I learned the code, "It's nothing personal, buddy. It's just business or it's just a game."

I know how I feel when I'm in my body. I know exactly how I feel. I have no clue about how you feel because I'm in *my* body. I know how I do it. But I don't know how *you* do it. How can I find out how *you* do it? I can find out how you do it by stepping outside myself and empathizing with *you*.

As we go into opportunities of dealing with another person, I want to be clear that many of these activities encourage the second position. It's a useful place to visit, but you can't really live there. You go there to gain information; you don't *stay* there. It's only your place to gather information about how other people really are. You want to live in first position—and briefly visit the other two.

Instant Processing: What Your Filters Process *First*

When we first meet someone, our brains begin to *instantly* process information about what we see, hear, and feel. To help people understand and remember this process, Rick Middleton, the founder of Executive Expression in Los Angeles, created an acronym—GGNEE. In a first meeting, here's what we'd initially notice about someone. *In this order*, we notice that person's:

Gender. It's not because of how they're dressed, it's because we're biological critters that come in two versions, so the first thing we notice is what version the other person is.

Generation or age. Are they children? Are they of reproductive age? Are they older? Are they wise? Are they a dependent?

Nationality or ethnicity. Basically what color, what type of person they are.

Educational level. As we talk to them or as we see how they're dressed, we'll draw some conclusions about their educational level, which is sort of socioeconomic.

Emotions. After taking in and processing these other details, then we sort of fantasize about their emotions. What do they seem to be feeling?

This processing happens incredibly quickly—bam! It's so fast that our receiver turns off and now we're no longer open to receiving any *real* or original information from these people. We're just stuck in the efficiency of generalization.

So how do people geniuses handle it?

Although people who are masterful at understanding and connecting with others also have these filters, *they* understand and are aware of how their brain works. When they notice they're getting stereotypes or generalized impressions, they set those filters aside. They don't go there anymore; they open themselves up to another person. Instead of being self-concerned, they manage to turn down the inner noise and focus on the other person.

This conscious habit is one I'm hoping you'll practice and master. If we're going to be really good with other people, we need to rewire ourselves so that we don't let *our* judgments, opinions, or beliefs, our dissonance or uneasiness, take the attention away from the other person.

If we don't have peace of mind, if we're not comfortable with ourselves, if we're feeling the slightest bit insecure or incongruent, guess what happens? The other person begins to feel insecure. They feel like we're uneasy—so *they* get uneasy. They get distrustful.

Managing your inner state is important. What you learned about yourself from the discovery activities in the last few chapters will contribute to positive preconditioning that will enable you to be even better company.

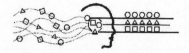

Discovery Activity: Identifying Ways *Other* People Are Good Company

When you look inside your own mind and your own memories now, think of the people whom you consider good company, people that you like being around and who make you feel good.

When I think of the most entertaining people I know, I think of the life-of-the-party types. But they're not the people who make me feel good. Frankly, they make me feel kind of inadequate. The people who make me feel good are the people who are at peace inside and who seem to genuinely be interested in me and to care about me. Is that true for you, too?

When you think about the qualities of companionship that attract you, that make you feel safe, make you feel valuable, you get a really good idea about the qualities that you want to build in yourself.

So, right now, think of someone you like being around, someone that, when you're with them, you feel good. What is it about them that contributes to these good feelings? Make note of special traits, behaviors, or ways of being.

Now think of another person who's good company for you. What are their special traits, behaviors, or ways of being? Compare this list to the first one you made (earlier in this chapter) so you have a robust list of desired behaviors that you want to include as you make changes to your patterns. Note any that are qualities you want to build or strengthen in yourself. Keep in mind that you can repeat this process whenever you notice yourself enjoying someone's company, or witness someone who's masterful at building rapport and relationships.

When you compare these discoveries with the list you made a few minutes ago. you'll notice items on the list that echo something you *already* identified. These repeated things might be the ones offering the greatest leverage to make a significant change. Also note any new traits or behaviors that you'd like to integrate into how you interact with others.

An Inside Job: How to Help Other People Feel Safe

We said earlier that making the other person feel safe is key to creating a connection. To accomplish this, you must control your own incongruence, nervousness, or feelings of insecurity. That's not about other people; that's an inside job.

Some of us, who have an issue with doing this, talk about being shy. When, in fact, it's the way we're thinking that makes us shy. That shyness is going to set off an alert in other people's brains because it's going to make them very uneasy. Basically, it communicates that we're so self-involved that we're not really paying attention. We're nervous, our eyes are darting around, we're shifting our weight or fidgeting, you get the picture. These behaviors are not conducive to comfort. To make someone else comfortable, we have to be comfortable within ourselves. This inside work must be done *before* we can put someone at ease when interacting with us.

The interesting thing is, one way to get comfortable is to focus on the other person instead of on you. Instead of being stuck, you stay in first position, but you focus on the other person from within your first position. You operate from an intention to make the other person feel safe.

Not Just Imitation:
How Mirroring and Matching Help You Make Connections

Here's how you do that. You use your second position to sense how they're doing and you allow yourself to *subtly* match someone's physical movements, doing what they do with their body. Although the content and quality of conversations can determine how our bodies match or mismatch each other, the way our bodies, gestures, and tones match or mismatch can influence the actual conversation.

The difference between matching and mimicking is that mimicking is really overt and it can tick people off or make them very suspicious. If someone experiences your mirroring as mimicking, it'll create dissonance, not harmony. What you really want to do is *subtly* match the way they're seated, the position of their hands, how fast they're talking, or their rate of breathing.

An Example: Natural Rapport in Action

Here's a story about natural rapport from my early NLP training. I walked into the room after a break and discovered that the chairs had been rearranged. I looked at the room and saw pairs of chairs that had been placed back-to-back. I noticed that a lady I'd been seated near earlier was now sitting in one chair and a friend of mine was standing near her, and he invited me to sit in the other chair. As I began to sit in the open chair with my back to Ruth, she said, "We have to talk."

Her tone was intentionally a bit nasty, knowing that it's a rare man who could hear those words from a woman without getting a little chill down his spine. I felt a little uneasy and asked, "What's this about?" She laughed and said she was just kidding me.

Then the instructor directed us to have a conversation with each other, without seeing each other, simply sitting back-to-back. He told us to have a discussion about anything *and* that we were supposed to agree with each other. That's all we needed to do.

As the observer, Steve, who was the third person in our group, was told to just watch us and notice whatever he noticed. They didn't give us any information about what to expect at all, so we began a conversation—what a nice day it was, how much we were enjoying the training, how interesting some of these discoveries were, and so forth.

This went on for a while and then the instructor stopped us and said, "Okay, now I would like you to have a conversation where you disagree." So I decided to get even with Ruth and started immediately by saying, "Well, I think women have way too many rights in this society. It was a lot better when they were just stuck in the bedroom."

Ruth was a ship's captain in a fishing fleet, a very, very smart, tough woman. I knew this comment would send her up like a rocket. So she came back at me and we had a pretty lively conversation for a few minutes. Then the trainer interrupted us again.

He told us to turn our chairs around and face him. Next, instead of asking us anything, he asked the assigned observers to share what they noticed, and it was amazing. One after another, the observers said that when the partners were having an agreeable conversation, no matter how we had been sitting when the exercise began, our posture actually changed and mirrored the person whose back was to us. Steve reported that Ruth and I not only had our legs crossed the same way and our heads tilted in the same direction, but we were also gesturing in synchrony.

When you hear something two or three times, you may think it's a coincidence, but we were hearing the same remarks a couple dozen times. All the observers were saying the same thing. It was really strange to me. I had no personal awareness of this, since I was sitting with my back to Ruth, and I wasn't watching the other pairs.

Then the instructor asked what happened when the partners were engaged in a conversation where they disagreed. You're probably not surprised at the punch line. We went completely out of sync with each other. In no case, and there were probably two dozen pairs of chairs doing this particular experiment, were the parties matching up. Even if they were in synchrony earlier, the mirroring disappeared. Body positions were more closed, and different from one another. Their gestures and facial expressions were out of tune with each other.

This experience was really instructive and I recommend that you notice how these indicators of harmony and discord are at work as you experience or observe conversations that are agreeable—and those that are more conflict-oriented. The process of being in or out of synchrony with someone is called "Mirroring" in NLP.

So, like the story I just shared, when we really want to be in rapport with somebody, we naturally mirror and match them. This is not complicated. You don't have to remember too many things here. You have to have an intention to be in rapport with another person. How do you do that? A great way is to be very curious about their emotional state and "try on" whatever you imagine that to be.

As you get into synchrony with them in terms of their body language, you'll notice there are space requirements. You don't want to crowd people *and* you don't want to be too far away, either. You're probably aware that people from different cultures have different space requirements. I'm half Irish and half Assyrian. So the Assyrian part of me would want to get right up in someone's face, where I can smell someone's breath; that's the Middle Eastern way. The Irish part of me would lean toward the traditional European way, which favors more distance.

Despite my heritage, I grew up in suburban Los Angeles and was raised with the distance requirements that are typically accepted here. I find that if I'm talking with somebody from another culture who gets close to me, I'm aware of it but it no longer makes me uncomfortable. It used to—and with some people it will create a subliminal dislike. And, if you're too far away, it will create a subliminal dislike because they'll feel that you don't want to be near them or you don't like them.

You'll find that eighteen to thirty-six inches apart is generally a reasonable space for most conversations, close enough to reach out and touch someone, but not so close that you're right *in* their personal space.

A Focus on Them, Not You:
How to Create a Sense of Being Felt

A key element of safety and acceptance is feeling felt. To do that, shift your focus from you to them. Here are three easy ways to do that.

Just One Look: Eye Contact and "the Gaze"

To help someone feel seen, you need to make eye contact with them, right? Probably as a kid, you glared at somebody in anger. You might have even been able to get away with that with your parents when you couldn't talk back to them. I couldn't get away with what we called the "hairy eyeball" with my dad because my dad was way too sensitive about that kind of behavior. But as kids, my brother and I would glare at each other in anger and in threat.

And yet, a gaze can also be inviting, can't it? As adults, when we feel flirtatious and want to make a kind of romantic connection with somebody, we might look at them a little longer, too.

Through unconscious teaching, we've all learned the amount of time that it's polite to look at a person's eyes. You *can*, of course, look at them longer when they're talking to you. And when you do it with positive intention, it gives them the feeling they're really being seen and heard. This eye contact has to do with the length of time that you lock eyes with a person. I call this "the gaze."

Holding someone's gaze is fun to experiment with. It's something you can easily do and you'll be delighted with the internal and external results. For example, you can look at a person when they're talking to you, then look away, and then look back at them. What you might not be aware of is the amount of awareness that the other person has about this kind of attention. It actually changes the way they feel about themselves, the way they feel about you, and the way they gauge the value of what they're saying.

So try this. Look directly at a person whom you might ordinarily dismiss, like a waiter, a toll taker, or a store clerk who answers a question you've asked. Normally we don't look at these people for very long. We glance away because we're on a mission. We're anxious. But if you look at them half a second longer, what happens is you make a direct human connection with them. That's all you need to do. It acknowledges them as an individual.

It also is important to look directly into a person's eyes when you say "Thank you" or "Please." Even if you're just asking for more ketchup, you'll get better service if you meet the server's eyes directly, instead of just looking at your plate or your dinner companion and saying, "Can I have more ketchup, please?"

If you stop and look at the waitress and say, "Can I have more ketchup, please?" and she says, "Sure," hold her eyes and say, "Thanks a lot." It's surprising—all of a sudden, you jump up in priority. It's a tiny change, but it's like nuclear power. Remember, people need to feel safe and at ease. So if your interest is too intense, it can feel carnivorous. It has to be enjoyable. Try this subtle, longer gaze and notice how your interactions shift.

To make a person feel felt, you'll want to subtly mirror them and get into sync with them. But you also need to sincerely make them feel seen and interesting. Lots of people feel that they have not been recognized by the world. And you may not be aware of this, but *most* people don't feel okay. Many people don't feel understood. They feel like they're being treated like they're objects.

If, for example, someone is your customer, then you want to be careful to remember that they're a person, too, and that they have value to you *beyond* a business transaction. They're human beings, no matter what their role.

Tell Me More: Questions That Get Them Talking

It doesn't matter if someone is a police officer, doctor, CEO, janitor, or thirteen-year-old soccer player. Everyone is a human being first, so they have feelings. They will be aware of their own feelings first when they're dealing with another person. It's amazing how feelings drive our behaviors—whether we're aware of those feelings or not.

The thing to do here is to get in sync with another person body language–wise, and then instead of talking, ask questions and listen. This is huge. Experts say, "Be interested, not *interesting*." So how do you make the other person feel felt? Simple: you relax, back off, and allow your attention to rest on *them*.

What many of us do when we get together with another person, especially when we're nervous or keyed up, is to increase our intensity. We persuade, encourage, argue, push, entertain, tell them a lot about ourselves, and that overburdens people. What people really are good at is knowing how *they're* doing.

So if you listen, ask questions, and reflect back, it's an easier, softer, less demanding way to engage with somebody. Rather than lead with "So tell me a little bit about yourself," think of it as a detective game where you want to learn as much about them as you can without subjecting them to an interrogation. What works well for me is to ask, "How'd you get into what you do?" And usually, the person will tell me things that I find pretty informative, and that's only the beginning. I want to keep the conversation flowing, so I don't say, "Okay, thanks." Instead, I say, "That's interesting. What do you like best about what you do?"

These are just a couple examples. You can ask, "What are you trying to accomplish that's important to you in your business or in your life?" You don't phrase it that way if you're dealing with somebody with a different vocabulary. You might say, "What's most important to you?" "What do you like the most?" or "What are your plans for the summer or the holiday?"

If they say, "I'm going camping with my family," say, "That's interesting. What do you like most about that?"

The reason I ask this is that someone might say, "The thing I like most about camping is the people you might meet," or they may tell you, "What I like most about camping is the food," or "The thing I like most about it is the smells." Another person may explain that it's the activities—it's hiking, rafting, or it's seeing their kids when the damn television isn't on. You'll discover *their* reasons, and this will give you more information about who these people are.

Then, when they've told you something, say, "Oh, that's fascinating. Why is that important to you?" It's a little like a tennis volley—your goal is to keep the ball in play, not hit a smash return or place the ball so far out of range that they cannot easily make the next move.

In addition to asking good follow-up questions to demonstrate that you're listening, you want to *reflect back*. When someone feels that you heard and understood them, they'll let you know, and often they open the door to talking with you longer or more deeply.

So, pursuing the example we've been playing with, you could reflect back by saying, "So, the most important thing to you about going camping is that you spend time with your family and you have better connection?"

"Yeah!"

"Well, what's it like at home?"

"Well, you know, we hardly ever see each other. We rarely even sit down to dinner together."

"Oh, it must be really busy for you at home."

And they might say, "Yeah, it is."

"Do you work long hours? What's your job? What do you do?"

Or, in response to it must be really busy for you, they say: "Well, I've got this project and I'm really active in the local radio club, so we do rescue work."

If you're genuinely interested when you're talking with someone, you'll find as you begin asking questions that they will be more disclosing. You'll notice that they begin leaning forward or toward you. We'll explore nonverbal behaviors more in the next chapter.

Basically, what we're talking about now is how to make a good first impression, which is very simple. To summarize, make sure that you're okay and *then* look at making the other person feel okay. A good first impression is 50 percent an inside job of managing yourself so the other person feels safe, and then 50 percent of managing the conversation so the *other* person feels interesting and appreciated.

I Get It: Questions That Show You Care How They Feel

In addition to asking questions that show you're interested in them, you can ask questions that let them know that you care how they feel. Again, instead of giving them a lot of information, you *get* a lot of information.

If you hit a nerve or if they come up with something they feel strongly about, you can attach emotion to it. You can say, "I'm trying to get a sense of what you're feeling, and I think it's this. That thing really irritates you, is that correct? And if it's not, what are you feeling?" They will confirm what you said or share more information. People are not always accustomed to someone caring about how they feel, let alone talking about that. Yet we can explore these things in a way where they feel safe and validated.

Your goal is to demonstrate that you care more about how *they* feel than about *making them* feel any certain way.

The most important thing about NLP, and the reason I organized the book the way I have, is to give us power over ourselves, and our automated, sometimes unconscious patterns. As we gain this kind of inner influence and do the change work on ourselves, we will become better company, which enables us to have more enjoyable interactions and relationships.

Changing Lights: Warnings That Signal a Disconnect

I want to underscore two things we talked about earlier—attention-direction and intensity—and how important it is to notice the response our efforts to engage someone are getting. For example, my wife is a very energetic and outgoing person. Early in our relationship, I noticed that when she was eager to tell a story, she'd say, "And . . . and . . . so . . ." and pretty soon she'd lose her audience. Because they didn't get it or they were preoccupied, she pushed a little harder to make her point. She hardly ever does this now, but she used to, especially with her sons. Now, when she talks with them, she looks for warning signals that they're disengaging.

We call this "zooming out"; it's a little like going into the third perceptual position. And this is particularly useful when we get intense. When we're excited or feeling a bit desperate, we sometimes find ourselves trying to encourage, trying to persuade, trying to assert. These intense behaviors push people away. It's that old foot-in-the-door salesman or telemarketer who continues long after you politely said no. To avoid this, pay attention to how someone is responding to you. When you notice someone's lack of interest or a change of being in sync, step back, stop talking, and let them lead.

I had an opportunity to do this at a family brunch just the other day in the Bay Area. I was talking about NLP to the young husband of a cousin of my wife's. Because he'd asked me about it, I thought he was interested.

As soon as I began talking about this passion of mine, I saw him look away. That was my cue, so I said, "Well, let's leave this for another time when we're not in the middle of a family brunch. So tell me about your new car," and he immediately brightened up. I just dropped my topic. I just recognized and respected his lack of interest at that time and moved into something else.

Boy, if years ago I'd known how marvelous this flexibility is, it would have saved me so much hassle. But I know now. And when I look back and see people in my life who were gracious and clever with other people, I realize, "Oh yeah, somehow they knew this early on."

More Choice Is Better:
How Being Versatile Helps You Connect

Earlier, you learned the NLP presupposition that the most flexible element in a system has the most influence. As you change yourself, become more peaceful inside your head . . . more intrigued by the changes you make . . . less subject to involuntary emotions . . . and more flexible in how you communicate, the people around you will change, too. You'll find that the way they respond to the new you is somehow different. So the easiest way to change our experience of other people is to change ourselves.

As you do that and as you look at other people, you begin to realize, "Oh, if I'm moving into this interaction and I'm concerned about how the other person thinks about me, or I'm concerned about making my point, or I'm concerned about being well liked, that's going to be counterproductive."

Sometimes when you make changes that you think everyone around you will be thrilled about, you're in for a surprise. For example, a forty-eight-year-old friend of mine who was an IT guy had been overweight for years—and so had his sister. Somehow he got into running and eventually even did a marathon. He told me that the thinner he became, the more it upset his sister. He said, "I think she takes it as a criticism, when I just want to feel better. I just want to be able to take care of my family and not be a burden." He was clear that this was more important than his sister's being a bit upset, jealous, or scared that she was now alone in her problem. Remember, you, too, may experience this kind of ripple effect.

The most important thing that I can do is to approach another person with a sense of curiosity, expectation, optimism, and interest. "There's going to be something fascinating about this other individual—I wonder what that will be. Because everyone is unique and knows something special, I'm going to learn something by talking with them. And I don't know what that is. This is going to be cool!"

As you may recall from discussions in Section 1, our expectations shape our experience, right? When you have that sort of curious and positive expectation, you can become sort of magnetic. Just think about it in your own life. People like that seem to magically draw others to them, don't they?

As you well know, some people are easier to talk with than others. You may call these folks difficult, moody, closed, or prickly; how you refer to them doesn't matter. What does matter is what you do with the feelings you have about them, or about interacting with them.

A Case in Point: The Importance of Versatility in Difficult Situations

Here's a story that illustrates how the wheels can come off in a conversation, maybe even kind of derail a relationship, and what you can do about it. When I asked my client, Terry, a thirty-six-year-old accountant, to give me an example of people with whom she has a difficult time communicating, she said, "It's hard for me to communicate with people who are accusatory in what they say or how they say it."

When I asked for a "for instance," she told me her son said, "You left the lights on!" Now, this was specific, but I didn't immediately understand why she felt it was accusatory. Frustrated with me, she said, "He was just being passive-aggressive. It's not because the light was on, it's because he was *already* angry about something." She went on to explain that when her son bought a new house and showed it to her with pride, she simply said, "It's really nice." She didn't respond with a lot of enthusiasm, "This is gorgeous! This is beautiful! This is blah, blah, blah."

When I asked if she thought he was disappointed because he'd hoped she would have been more impressed, she said, "Well, if he was, he should have told me that instead of being accusatory all the time." So that's when their relationship started to derail—and they became sort of locked in this new dance. To help shift their pattern of communicating, I thought it might be useful for Terry to learn how to cool someone off when emotions are running high.

Here's the short version of what I recommended. I invited Terry to consider that her son's feelings were hurt because she hadn't been enthusiastic enough; then he displaced these feelings and acted out in another way. Most of us do that at one time or another.

Next, I asked her to imagine her son in that moment again, when he was first showing her the new house and she said, "It's really nice," and to notice what emotion he seemed to be feeling. She said it was sadness, sadness that she wasn't impressed.

Here was a fork in the road. I said, "So if you noticed he was sad, then you could have said, 'I get a feeling that you're sad, sad that I didn't make the right compliment. Is that true?'" She explained that she didn't recognize this in the moment; that, in fact, it wasn't until a year later that she put all the pieces together. Even so, we were talking now about how she *could* handle him. We discussed that it's not about how she felt or feels at this point in time; it's about addressing the other person's feelings so *they* feel like you want to understand and connect with them.

Asking Questions That Show You Care How They Feel

The thing to do when somebody is emotional is to attach an emotion. I've tried this and it works like magic. You might say, "I've got the feeling that you're angry. Is that true? Or upset. Is that true?" If they say, "No, I'm not," then I say, "I'm sorry. If it's not that, what are you feeling?" and I get back whatever the person chooses to tell me.

The next thing I want to do is to understand how big this is for them. So I usually say something like "I see. How upset are you?" or "I see, and you're upset because . . ." At this point, it's important to give them all the time they need to vent, because you're asking these questions so the person can express their feelings, not so you can gather information.

Again, this goes back to the sense that many of us feel undervalidated. Since I started studying this, I'm amazed at how often I find this to be true. I'm astonished. It not only works with my consulting clients, but it apparently also works in serious situations because I read this in a hostage negotiation handbook. It was amazing that the most successful negotiators are the ones who instead of reading the mind of another person, they just go far enough to try to guess at what the other person's emotion is and then they feed that back. The goal here is to allow the other person to know that *you* know what *they* are feeling.

So the question is "I'm trying to get a sense of what you're feeling and I think you're feeling sad. Is that on target? If it's not that, what are you feeling?"

Terry and I played out several scenarios of how things might unfold if she asked her son this question. And how she might need to explore his response to make sure she really understood it. To do this, we role-played: "So how pissed are you, or how sad are you?" And then, after giving her son all the time needed to form a response, we role-played "And the reason you're so pissed is because . . . ?"

At this point in our little psychodrama, Terry realized she didn't know how he would respond to this open-ended question. He might say, "I'm pissed because you blew me off" . . . or "because you were inconsiderate" . . . or "because you never liked my wife" . . . or "because you never approve of anything I do." Terry came to understand that it didn't matter what her son actually says. That specific thing is not that important. *What's important is the exchange itself.*

None of this is problem solving! All of this is simply allowing people to say what's true for them. Let's quickly review the approach that Terry and I worked through. Up to this point, we've asked four things. (1) We've asked the other person to attach an emotion. (2) We've asked what the emotion was. (3) We've asked how emotional they are. And (4) we've asked the reason why they're so emotional.

We've allowed them to say whatever they want to say, and we have *not* argued at all.

Exploring Next Steps

The fifth question is "What needs to happen for that feeling to be better?" The important part here is that you're allowing the person to go inside themselves and find out what needs to change.

When we discussed the possibility of Terry asking her son this, we explored how she might hear "Well, I need you to apologize," or "I need you to leave immediately," or "I want you to like my wife," or whatever it happens to be.

When most people have a complaint, you'll notice that they want someone else or circumstance to change. It's often something external. So just accept that and never argue.

Once you know what the upset person wants, you can ask two more questions. First, "What part can *I* play in making that happen?" After you hear what they want you to do, then you say, "And what part can *you* play in making that happen?"

Here's what's true. When we can play a part in creating the change someone wants, they can probably play a part, too. Once the other person feels heard and felt, we've moved into a constructive dialogue.

Terry agreed to try this approach and she later told me that, even though it was uncomfortable for her, it did jump-start communication with her son. They had a real dialogue and her son knew that she really did care how he felt, which was the first step to healing things between them.

No Spin: Just Positive Intent and Authentic Inquiry

As you imagine doing this with people in your life, this approach may seem pretty radical. People talk about winning people over with razzle-dazzle, dress for success, and persuasive positioning. I've come to understand that what really works in communication is relaxing with the other person, being nice to them, and keeping the focus on them.

Here's why this works. Most people are really doing the best they can. Again, that's not Pollyanna thinking, that's just reality. And if you want to be efficient and effective in navigating bumps in communication and relationships, you have to be authentic. You have to give other people the credit for their humanity.

You'll find that the magical part of deciding to get along with somebody else is when you change yourself—all of a sudden you get along better with them *and* with other people, too. That's the marvelous part of this. It's easy. We don't have to do anything to anybody else. We make a little alteration in the way we think and the way we manage our feelings and it's like magic. Abracadabra, we easily get along better with people.

It was surprising, and a little bit embarrassing, when a dear friend told me how much I had changed during the course of my NLP training. To be honest, I thought I was a pretty nice guy beforehand. I mean I had friends, I was successful in ways that were important to me at the time, but I was told by a number of people who knew me earlier that since I began studying NLP, I became more approachable and easier to be around.

I wasn't really sure what approachable meant, since I'm not outside myself. But when I step into third position and just observe myself, I see this big guy with a deep voice, who talks fast, moves fast, and takes initiative to make a lot happen. That could be kind of off-putting. I can see that. If I were a person who's gentler, more thoughtful, more deliberate, somebody like me could seem pretty damn abrasive.

I never realized that. I thought I was just being an action-oriented guy, making a difference, getting things done. I thought I was being a brave soldier, so it was really astonishing for me to realize that for some people that act was a little hard to take. That's why I say the good news here is that the biggest part of getting along well with others is an inside job.

If you're loaded with stereotypes and if you think you know too much about what other people are really like, you're likely to get into trouble. You're *not* going to actually hear the person, and they're going to know it. If you're too preoccupied with meeting your own needs, with getting feedback from someone that says *you* are a great person, if you need to be interesting more than you want to be interested in others, then you're going to put people off.

Here's what you should be asking yourself: "How can I interact with another person? What can I learn from them?"

The impact this shift could have reminds me of the nineteenth-century story about Johnny Appleseed. It's an American myth about a guy who wandered across the country casting apple seeds onto the ground and leaving beautiful apple trees wherever he wandered.

It's kind of a sweet thing to think about. Wouldn't it be nice if, like Johnny Appleseed, we could scatter curiosity . . . optimism . . . self-approval . . . hope . . . and acceptance wherever we passed? By actually recognizing people, really interacting with them, being interested in them, and complimenting them, you can. It's amazing how much you can sincerely change the way people feel about themselves.

You can begin to play with this right away, and see for yourself how magical it is. You have everything you need to practice. First, you have your own brain to fine-tune, and you can do that whenever you decide to sit down and go inside and see what's going on. And you have other people. You can experiment with them endlessly. You've been doing it all your life anyway. Now you can do it a little more deliberately.

The Bird's-Eye View: A High-Level Summary

The three steps we've been talking about are, of course, sequential. First, we need to help the other person feel safe by managing our own state and behaviors. Once that need is satisfied, we can ask questions to demonstrate our curiosity and communicate that we think they're interesting. And once they feel good about the interaction *and* themselves, they need to *feel* felt—that you "get" how they're feeling. This way, they can be free to express their feelings.

And remember, if you end up in emotional territory: name the emotion, confirm your impression, and sympathize with it. Whenever you try something on from the other person's point of view, you can relate to it better. There are places in here where you might say something like "You know, I'd be upset, too." Then you gauge the extent of the emotion and give a lot of time for them to respond so they get everything out. Saying, "The reason you're so upset is because . . ." gives them more time to vent.

After they've completely expressed themselves, then you invite them to tell you what they need to move forward. You could say, "Tell me, what needs to happen for that feeling to subside, for you to feel better?"

Let me share a story from the other day; this interaction illustrates the approaches we've been talking about. Here's what happened.

I went to the grocery store and another person was parked pretty close to me. I opened my door and it clicked against their vehicle and I thought, "Oh, I hope I didn't hit the paint," and then I saw that my door was hitting their hubcap so I didn't worry about it. I turned around to do something and I hit it again.

It was a large truck next to me, so I got out, walked toward the back of the car, and this young woman came out of her truck and she was pissed. She said, "Sir, you hit my car twice with your door!"

Instead of saying, "I did not. I hit your hubcap! Relax, take a chill," I just said, "I didn't know you were sitting in the car, but I understand what that must have sounded like to you, and that would really make me angry, too. I'm really sorry I did that, but if you come around here I'll show you that there was no damage at all because my door was hitting your hubcap."

She came around and saw it and said, "Well, you hit it twice," and I said, "I know. I'm really sorry. I turned in my car to do something and I just bumped the door again. I can understand how that would sound to you sitting in your truck. That would seem pretty thoughtless."

As soon as I said, "That would seem pretty thoughtless," because that's how I would have felt if somebody had banged my car twice, she felt completely validated. She said, "Oh, okay then," and that was it. It wasn't like we exchanged phone numbers and invited each other to lunch or anything, but it cooled her off.

The message here is to allow the other person to really understand that you get how that feels, and if somebody had done that to you, you'd have the same feelings they do. It's simple, but critical because that validates their feelings. And even though it's simple, many of us habitually react in a more defensive way, but real understanding builds bridges, rather than creates separate turfs.

Remember, the action sequence is a little like the emergency instructions on a plane. Make sure you've got your own oxygen mask on before you try to help the person next to you with theirs. So you've got to consider what *you* are thinking. Your experiences, beliefs, values, and boundaries are driving you all the time. You use these to help you function, and to achieve your goals. But your map of the world and your needs are only *part* of the picture, right?

We live in a world of other humans, and if you want to be really successful with other people, go meet them in the world *they* live in.

This approach shouldn't create a conflict of values, unless the relationship requires that you betray yourself in some way. In that case, you need to make a judgment call. But most relationships aren't that threatening, are they? They don't require that you betray yourself. They just require that we be more flexible in what we can accept from others.

So I find myself thinking, "Well, okay, if I'm going to get along with so-and-so, I don't have to be a hypocrite and pretend to be interested in NASCAR racing or mixed martial arts or something I'm not; but I can be interested in *their* interest in it. I *can* be interested in understanding that this individual has a passion."

The important thing to me is not the being able to accept someone else's *values;* it's being able to accept *the other person,* period. Now, if they value cruelty or bigotry or something that violates my deeply held values, then we're probably not going to be buddies, but it doesn't mean I can't be courteous or even compassionate when I'm with them.

Try to keep in mind that someone's offensive values or behaviors often stem from unhappiness, or some pain from their early life. When I presuppose that every behavior comes from a positive intention, I can say to myself, "That person's anger or meanness is an attempt to recover from something." It doesn't mean I'm compelled to condone how they behave, or that I want to be around them a lot. I can just accept them.

And, because I have flexibility and personal resources, I often think about how I could give them an alternative way to be relieved. I don't usually act on that unless somebody hires me as a coach or consultant. And occasionally I get an opportunity to interrupt something negative that's going on, and perhaps keep it from escalating. Sometimes, in passing, you can just sort of squirt a little oil into an interaction and maybe lubricate it a little bit with an offhand comment, but it's preceded by respect and understanding. Like Johnny Appleseed, you can have an impact as you move through the world. Learning more about others will help you to create an even more positive ripple effect.

In the next chapter, you'll learn how to go beyond "mind reading" other people so you can get a better sense of their world *and* how to connect with them.

Key Ideas

- We all process experience in a similar way, yet because our experiences are different, we create different inner worlds, different "maps" of how the world works.

- As we drop our automatic filters and preconceived notions about others, we can become a clear receiver, which allows us to really experience their reality.

- Being the way each of us is is a *choice*. We can always choose to rewire ourselves—strengthening a quality we already have—or borrowing ("Modeling") one from someone who has a quality we admire. And, if we don't like a change we made, we can change it again to make it better.

- Getting feedback from other people about what they'd like us to keep doing, stop doing, and start doing offers us helpful insights that may enable us to improve our interactions and relationships.

- The different parts of the brain have different jobs. The instinctive "fight-or-flight" part is triggered first (along with lots of chemistry)—before the part that thinks things over.

- Because many people don't feel "seen" and "validated," these feelings can affect their interactions.

- Shifting between the three perceptual positions, as appropriate, can increase one's effectiveness. It's best practice to operate from first position so we know what we see and feel. Then we can briefly visit second position to try on something from someone else's point of view, or go to third position to get more complete and objective information.

- Because the brain generalizes, our initial impressions are gathered in a process called GGNEE. We immediately notice someone's gender, generation (age), nationality (ethnicity), educational (socioeconomic) level, and then we imagine what emotions they're having.

- People who are masterful at connecting with others manage their inner state *and* focus on the other person so they don't bring any personal uneasiness into their interaction.

- Making someone else feel safe, interesting, and "felt" are critical steps to being good company.

- Making someone feel safe, interesting, and "felt" can be accomplished by asking questions about what someone does or likes to do, why that's important to them, and potentially confirming any emotions that came up for them.

- Paying attention to how the other person is responding to our efforts to engage enables us to "zoom out" (visit third position) and access if we're out of sync and make adjustments, especially when we have intense feelings.

- To get in rapport, people subtly mirror the person they're interacting with, sometimes matching their body language, rate of speech, or breathing (among other things), while being careful not to mimic the other person.

- Honoring personal space requirements and making meaningful (but not invasive) eye contact can help us make someone feel safe, yet "seen."

- Being focused on the other person and being versatile in how we communicate gives us more options about how to respond, especially in difficult situations.

- Cooling someone off can actually be easy. Taking the following five steps can defuse the emotional charge in a situation and make it possible to restore harmony.

1. Confirm an emotion. "I've got this feeling that you're X (angry or upset or sad). Is that true?"
2. Gauge how big this is for them, and allow them to vent, to get it all out. "How upset are you?" or "The reason you're so upset is because . . ."
3. Determine what they need to move forward, allowing them to go inside and find out what they want. "What needs to happen for that feeling to be better?"
4. Identify what they'd like you to do. "What part can I play in making that happen?"
5. Explore what steps *they* need to take to feel better. "What part can you play in making that happen?"

 To enhance the skills you learned in this chapter, check out the recommended Bonus Activities at our special "Essential Guide" website: http://eg.nlpco.com/5-1 or use the QR code with your phone.

Discoveries, Questions, Ideas, and Stuff You Want to Work On

Discoveries, Questions, Ideas, and Stuff You Want to Work On

CHAPTER SIX: MORE THAN "MIND READING" OTHER PEOPLE

What's going on inside them for that to be true?

> The single biggest problem in communication
> is the illusion that it has taken place.
> —George Bernard Shaw

Communication challenges happen all the time, don't they? Sometimes we're careless about our choice of words. Occasionally someone is overly sensitive to something we said, *how* we said it, *when* we said it, or that we didn't say something they think we *should* have said—or done. It's easy to miss subtle clues that, had we been paying closer attention, would have alerted us to how another person was thinking or feeling.

In NLP, we say that communication is redundant because people are simultaneously communicating in all three systems—visual, auditory, kinesthetic. That's good news and bad, isn't it? When someone is congruent, we get one message through all three channels. When they're not, we get all kinds of mixed signals.

In this chapter, you'll explore how to "mind read" other people by noticing their nonverbal behaviors and the language they use that reveals their inner worlds. You'll discover additional ways to get in sync with someone and build rapport once your observations have given you insight into how they're thinking or feeling. In the next chapter, you'll learn secrets of deepening rapport and making your point.

A $500,000 Example:
Communication in All Three Channels

When I ran a manufacturing firm in Silicon Valley, I had a potential client that was a biotech company located in Florida. I'd been on the phone a couple times with the president of that company—and we didn't get anywhere. I didn't like him. Frankly, I thought he was just trying to hustle me.

He began the conversation by asking for discounts instead of asking about the equipment. He was rushed and didn't have the time to listen to what I had to say. I felt he didn't care about the science of our equipment. I thought he was a jerk.

Even though the company was a perfect prospect for us, my marketing team had never been able to get an appointment in this company. That's why they kept trying to draft me to approach the client again. Because of how I felt about this guy, I said, "I don't think this is going to happen; let the sales representatives call on this account. When the powers that be finally find out they need the best equipment in the world, maybe they'll contact us."

About a year and a half later, I was in Boston at a biotech conference with my marketing VP, Susan. This event had a lot of workshop breakouts—each one addressing different aspects of our industry.

After one of these breakouts, we were walking down to the lobby, where many of the participants gathered between sessions, Susan kind of nudged me and said, "Hey, that's that guy from Florida." When I saw him, I thought, "Oh damn, I've got to say something to him. I can't back away. I'm the CEO. I can't just pretend I don't see him."

As I was walking over to introduce myself, I noticed the guy was built like a football player. He was wearing an open-necked striped shirt with a sport coat. It was evening and after dark in Boston, but his sunglasses were up on his forehead. He had a gold chain around his throat, a good suntan, good slacks, good shoes, and he was sprawled out in his chair. It was clear to me this guy was obviously really comfortable where he's at.

He was a dominant, physical guy, but as I said, I'm six foot three and sizable myself, so I leaned down and put out my hand—I really kind of stuck it in his face. I interrupted the conversation he was having so he had to look up at me. When he did, I had this big smile on my face and said, "Hi, I'm Tom Hoobyar. We spoke on the phone a couple of years ago. I'm the head of ASEPCO."

He looked at me and took my hand and shook it. As he shook it, we had a good handshake—and all the while I was smiling. I had absolutely no sense of embarrassment or detachment from it. Then he said, "You know, my science people have been telling me that I ought to talk to you," and I said, "Yeah, that's what my marketing people said."

He said, "Have a seat and we'll talk," and I said, "Okay, if you buy me a beer." He laughed and said, "Okay, and you buy the next one," and I said, "I will."

In very few words, what I had done was to match him. Once I saw that he was such a physical guy—the kind of guy who likes to slap you on the back—I was able to match his body language and his kind of abruptness. I couldn't tell any of that on the phone, but in person, I could tell that's the kind of guy he was.

He saw me—and it helped that I was the right size, his size. That was a match. The way I grabbed his hand, the way I stuck it in his face and introduced myself with no embarrassment, and then in maybe two sentences—that was also a matching. It turned out he was from New York, so I also matched his speech, which was more accelerated, a little more clipped: "You've got to buy me a beer first."

I didn't just sit down in the chair opposite him—I plopped down. When I did, my marketing VP, who was a very classy lady and was still standing, rolled her eyes because she knew I was doing a bit of an act. Then I just told her, "Here, pull up a chair." So she pulled up a seat and I introduced her in case she could fill in any details that I lacked—or needed to run with the ball after this meeting.

He and I talked about Florida and about California and how his weather was more humid, and we ended up talking about gardens. I had a little garden in my backyard, he had a garden in his backyard, and we talked about how refreshing it was for each of us to get into the garden and get our hands dirty after a day's stress of running a company.

Before we were done talking, we were leaning toward each other. Not just because it was a crowded hotel bar, but because we were in rapport. Near the end of the conversation, we'd arranged for my engineering people to talk to his engineering people and really get the details of what they needed so they could work something out.

As we parted, I said, "I've had my fill of beer. I've really got to go eat some dinner," and he said, "I've already eaten, but I'm really glad you stopped by." He said, "I thought you were some kind of geek. I just didn't know that we'd get along so well."

I said, "Yeah, it was my fault. I didn't handle that phone conversation well at all, but I'm really glad that we had a couple of drinks together and got to talk."

We walked away, and because of that encounter our companies did about a half-million dollars of business together. So what's the lesson there? It's that you can gain a lot of insight and traction in relationships when you pay attention to more than just what a person is *saying*. We want to consider their nonverbal behaviors and the deeper structure of their language.

In this example, my soon-to-be client gave me all kinds of clues to how he was feeling in the moment. People around us are doing this all the time. When we're able to notice posture, body position, use of personal space, facial expressions, eye contact, and so forth, we get a tremendous amount of information—and this is *before* we consider what they said and how they said it!

Keep in mind that nonverbal communication carries a lot of weight. Researcher Albert Mehrabian of the University of California, Los Angeles, discovered that 55 percent of the *emotional* content of communication is based on what someone sees. Thirty-eight percent is based on what they hear in terms of how something was said. And only 7 percent of the emotional content is based on the actual words. That means that over half the impact that we have on each other when we're communicating is visual.

Powerful Telegraphing:
What *Your* Nonverbals Communicate

Ralph Waldo Emerson said, "What you do speaks so loud, I cannot hear what you say." Because this is true, we want to remember to pay attention to our own nonverbal behavior *first*.

Much of our nonverbal behavior is driven by the limbic system—which is the *primitive* brain. Because these behaviors are completely automatic and unconscious, they're a pretty accurate reflection of a person's inner state. This is good news for you because you've already been learning how to notice and manage your own inner state. You recognize that when you're *not* anxious, distracted, or incongruent in some way, your body language sends a message that you're safe and approachable.

Our nonverbal cues are a bit like magnets. They can repel people. "Wow, that guy is angry—or he thinks he's pretty important—I think I'll steer clear of him." They can also attract people. Nonverbals can signal that you are open to someone—that you like them—and they have a feeling that you like them if they have a feeling that you *are* like them. This goes a long way toward helping us make a connection with someone.

Traffic Signals:
How Other People's Nonverbals Provide Direction

Nonverbal behavior is so interesting and compelling that many books have been written about it and you can find some excellent information about it on the Internet if you want to delve into the details and nuances of this subject.

We're going to focus more on what nonverbals you might notice than on what *meaning* may be behind those behaviors. Here I'd like to give you a quick overview of what you may want to notice so you can *build* on your observations to more effectively create rapport.

A NOT-SO-OPEN BOOK: NONVERBAL COMMUNICATIONS TO CONSIDER

Nonverbal communications may stem from a current inner state or from habit. Here's a quick summary of nonverbals you might look for.

Personal Space

As you know from Chapter 5, an individual's personal space requirements vary from person to person. Someone's tolerance of another's proximity is influenced by culture, size, gender, and often age. In America, most of us are comfortable with at least three feet of separation—but not more than five. If you use this as a general rule, you'll be in good shape.

Personal space also includes how much of their allotted space someone uses. For example, when they're seated, do they fully stretch out
their legs in front of them? Do they also put both hands behind their
neck with their elbows pointing out? Use of personal space can also
be shaped by culture. When I was working in Japan, for example, I
decided to make my gestures smaller and take up less space when I
was moving around and even sitting (which wasn't so easy since I'm
six foot three).

Body Position

Even though body position is about how you are in relationship to
someone else, it's not just about distance. Are you face-to-face with
someone? At an angle? Is one of you sitting and one of you standing?
Is there a big disparity in height? Body position factors may influence
your ability to easily match someone.

Posture

In this context, posture is about more than whether someone is
standing up straight. It's more about whether their posture is open
or closed—and mostly if their heart and chest area is open and uncovered.

Gestures

Gestures are most often made with the hands and have culturally accepted meanings. A thumbs-up gesture says, "Great job" or "I agree."
Knocking on wood means, "Let's hope." A wave means, "Hi, there"
or "See ya later." A shoulder shrug says, "It doesn't matter either way."
Wagging one's finger at someone means "Stop that" or "Shame on
you." We even have a gesture to say, "Call me." Similarly, if someone

is nodding their head up and down, it usually means agreement. If they are shaking it side to side, it usually means disagreement or disbelief.

Touch

Gently touching a person's hand is very different from roughly poking them in the chest. Supportive touch induces the release of oxytocin in the recipient's brain. The effect of touch is so powerful that it's a frequent subject of research. As I mentioned earlier, studies show that waitresses who touch their customers get higher tips. Petition gatherers who touch people they talk to get more signatures. Teachers who pat a student on the back find that these pupils are more likely to participate in class.

Touching among groups and teams is powerful, too. Two psychologists from the University of California, Berkeley, recently analyzed ninety televised hours of professional basketball, exploring the power of touch. After looking at every team and every player in the league, they identified fifteen different kinds of touching—including highfives and flying shoulder bumps—and determined that the teams that touch the most win the most!

Eye Movement

It feels completely different when someone is batting their eyes than when they're glaring at you, doesn't it? It's also different if they're staring off into space or staring *at* you! Whether it's appropriate to look directly at someone—and for how long—is often shaped by culture. In Chapter 5, we talked about "the gaze," how making eye contact and holding that gaze a little longer (but not too long) helps someone feel seen. If you have a teenager, you're probably quite familiar with eye rolling, followed shortly by "Whatever!"

In NLP, we also think about *how and where* the eyes are moving and what this tells us about the way someone is accessing information. For example, when the brain is recalling something that's already happened, most people's eyes look up and to the left (which is the observer's right). In contrast, someone imagining an experience like an upcoming vacation would most likely look up and to the right (the observer's left). Ah, but I digress.

Facial Expressions

Happiness, sadness, fear, disgust, and surprise are easily recognized emotions because facial expressions are very universal. A genuine smile shows on the whole face, doesn't it? Not only do the lips curve up, but the person's eyes get brighter, too. A person who's startled will most likely raise their eyebrows, their eyes will widen, and their mouth will open. If they're confused, their brows may furrow and their lips tighten.

Physiological Response

Blushing, blanching, the flaring of nostrils, the eyes tearing up, and the trembling of someone's chin are all examples of physiological responses. Changes in breathing are, too. I often notice when someone has begun to hold their breath; because if I'm in rapport with them, I find I'm unconsciously holding my breath, too!

Locomotion and Pace

Locomotion refers to the style of physical moment. Shuffling or tottering along is very different from rushing or moving quickly. Pace also describes the *way* someone moves. Is it jerky or graceful? Easy or deliberate? Gradual or sudden?

"Paralanguage"

As you may recall, Mehrabian's research said that 38 percent of a message's emotional content comes from *how* it was said—or, more accurate, how it was *perceived* to have been said. This auditory component of nonverbal communication is called paralanguage. Separate from the words themselves, these are audible cues that may telegraph information about someone's inner state and feelings. Volume, inflection, speed, intensity, tone, rhythm, pitch—a change in any of these aspects can significantly alter the way the message is delivered, and received. Sarcasm is an excellent example of tone that has an impact; it may be funny or it may be hurtful.

According to communication experts, other examples of paralanguage include laughing, pausing or hesitating, talking too much, interrupting, or talking over someone. And we all know that silence can speak volumes—because it can feel companionable or tense.

Again, we want to focus on what we can objectively *observe* about nonverbal behavior, not assign meanings that may only apply to a generality rather than a specific person or context. As you can see, there is a real range and richness to nonverbal communication. Our quick overview will heighten your awareness of signals you already knew about—and hopefully make you even more curious about what you see and hear.

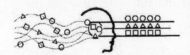 **Discovery Activity:
Recalling Nonverbals of a
Positive Experience**

Right now, you might be focusing on other people's nonverbal behaviors—but that's only half the picture, isn't it? There are always at least two variables in a communication equation—the other person and you.

With this in mind, it helps to be aware of the nonverbal cues you often use. They can provide you with insight into how you're feeling—and into the impact these are having on your communication. Let's take stock for a moment. Make a mental movie of the last enjoyable interaction you had—and watch it objectively from the outside, from third position. As you watch yourself, notice what you looked and sounded like.

Were you standing or sitting close to the other person? How comfortable did that feel?

Were you facing them, standing behind them, or sitting side by side at a bit of an angle? Were these body positions determined by the environment—or did you influence how you were physically in relationship to one another?

Was your posture open or closed—so that your heart was exposed? If not, what were you doing to cover up your heart? How open were the positions of your feet/legs and arms/hands? What specifically do you notice?

Because this is a memory of an enjoyable interaction, there may have been ways that you and your companion were mirroring each other's body language. What synchronicities do you see now?

Did you use touch to connect with the other person? What did you do—and how did that feel?

What gestures and facial expressions did you use? How did these reflect whatever you were feeling?

Think about your eye contact with this person. How would you describe it? Can you recall the color of their eyes?

And what about your paralanguage? Was your dialogue fairly synchronistic in terms of tone, volume, and speed? If not, how were you out of sync with your companion?

Now that you've revisited that experience, take a moment to capture what you learned. Make note of what worked well in this interaction—and if you notice something that could have been even better, make a note of that, too.

Review this list of discoveries and consider if these nonverbal behaviors are typical for you when you're with this specific person. Are these cues typical whenever you're enjoying yourself?

Stand outside yourself and reflect on these nonverbal cues that may have contributed to your companion feeling safe, interesting, and "felt."

As a closing step to this activity, you might refer to the lists you made in Chapter 5 about what makes you a good companion. Look for similarities between that list—and this mental movie. Give yourself some positive acknowledgment for behaviors you'd like to do more often—or even more effectively.

Of course, not all interactions are pleasant and when they're not, the nonverbals are likely to be very different. To explore these contrasts, complete the next exercise.

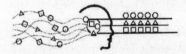 **Discovery Activity:
Identifying Nonverbals from
an Uncomfortable Situation**

Think about a recent interaction where you felt uncomfortable. Don't pick something big or traumatic—just choose an experience where you didn't feel like your best self. Perhaps there was a situation at work or with your family that didn't feel good. What was that exchange?

Make a mental movie of that interaction—and watch it from third position. As you watch yourself, notice what you looked and sounded like.

Were you standing or sitting close to the other person? How comfortable did that feel?

Were you facing them, standing behind them, or sitting side by side at a bit of an angle? Were these body positions determined by the environment—or did you influence how you were physically in relationship to one another?

Was your posture open or closed—so that your heart was exposed? If not, what were you doing to cover up your heart? How open were the positions of your feet/legs and arms/hands? What specifically do you notice?

Because this interaction was a little uncomfortable, there may have been ways that your body language mismatched your companion's. What differences do you see now?

Did you use touch to connect with the other person? What did you do—and how did that feel?

What gestures and facial expressions did you use? How did these reflect how you were feeling?

Think about your eye contact with this person. How would you describe it? Can you recall the color of their eyes? Did you notice yourself looking away or down?

And what about your paralanguage? Did it match your companion's in terms of tone, volume, and speed? If not, how were you out of sync with your companion?

Now that you've revisited that experience, take a moment to capture what you learned. Make note of what worked well in this interaction—and what could have been better.

Review this list of discoveries and consider if these nonverbal behaviors are typical for you when you're with this specific person. Are these cues typical whenever you're feeling uncomfortable?

If you could stand outside yourself, how do you think your nonverbal cues supported or inhibited your ability to make your companion feel safe, interesting, and "felt"?

As a closing step to this reflection, refer to the lists you made in Chapter 5 about what makes a good companion. You might even consider the behaviors that trusted friends asked you to stop doing—or start doing. Look for opportunities to improve how you're interacting with others. Pick one behavior you'd like to change and practice doing a preferred behavior the next few times you find yourself feeling uncomfortable.

In Another's Shoes: The View from Their World

Because *you* already know what you were thinking and feeling in these two recollections, you don't have to imagine what's involved—you *know*. Now suppose for a moment, that when interacting with someone else, you noticed some of the nonverbal behaviors that you exhibited in the *uncomfortable* situation you just revisited. If so, you might suspect that that person feels like you felt. Would that conclusion be on target? *Maybe*. If you have a strong second position, you may really be in tune with the other person and be able to understand them with a useful degree of accuracy.

Here's what I'd recommend you do when you notice what feels like uncomfortable nonverbal behavior. First, check in with yourself. Are *you* feeling comfortable? Second, step into third position and objectively observe what signals you've been sending.

If, after these reflections, you determine that the discomfort isn't yours, avoid matching a behavior that feels intense. For example, mirroring someone's scowling expression or an aggressive stance might match them, but it might also contribute to escalating the negative feelings. ("Oh yeah, well take *that*!") However, it might be beneficial to lean away a little if the other person is leaning away or to match their breathing.

Although matching often happens naturally, it's a little bit of an art, too. So let's explore intentional matching a little further.

Just Like That? How Matching Nonverbals Creates Rapport

People have a language of their physical movement. As I said, postures and gestures are habitual with most people, and it's like a dance. So interacting with them is like dancing with them.

Now, I'm not talking about a conversation with a waiter or a toll-taker at a tollbooth where you don't have time. In those situations, your nonverbals are limited to eye contact ("the gaze"), facial expressions, and paralanguage. But if you're really interacting with someone—having a conversation with them, interviewing them, making a sales pitch, or participating in a business meeting—you can begin synchronizing with them. This is an irresistible subliminal message to them that you like them and you *are* like them.

So here's what you do. Set your intent to notice the nonverbal behaviors we just reviewed. Notice someone's gestures. Notice their posture. Notice their overall body movement—their head tilts and their nods, their facial expressions, and their breathing—and gradually begin to match those. You want to be careful not to mimic them—so don't imitate them so obviously that they catch you doing it. You'll be amazed at how easy it is to just match their posture. Their legs are crossed? Then cross yours. Their hands are on the arms of their chair? So are yours. One hand is on a knee, the other hand is on the table? So are yours.

I do this when I'm coaching people and it just deepens our rapport. It's never viewed as disrespectful or artificial at all—and here's why it's not. This is a language we all know. You probably won't remember learning it because it won't be in the foreground of your memory. But this kind of unconscious conversation is happening all around us—all the time.

Restaurants are a great place to see this in action. When people are getting along well they're leaning toward each other, they're staring into each other's eyes, and their mouths are slightly open and smiling. They're nodding, their heads are tilted, and they may even be reaching toward each other. Their feet may be in contact under the table if they're a romantic couple. They'll be facing each other open, heart to open heart, and they will be matching each other's gestures. Their body postures will be similar.

You can even observe this natural, unconscious communication in groups. You can look at people sitting in an audience and see subtle behaviors that telegraph someone's attitude or inner state. As you look across the rows—and I've seen this in training classes—you'll see a bunch of legs all crossed in the same direction. Then you'll see somebody with their legs crossed the other way or legs apart. We have told ourselves that this difference is probably just a matter of comfort, habit, or space limitations. But here's something to consider: those things may not true. Most nonverbal behavior is run by the primitive brain, which says, "I like this person. I want to be like this person because I want to communicate," so we synchronize. The person who is mismatching the group is probably out of sync—or may be distracted and not really present.

Here's what I'm suggesting—just get ahead of the curve. Simply match someone's body or paralanguage (rate, rhythm, volume of speech, etc.) so it signals your brain and the other person's brain that you want to be in rapport. It doesn't really matter which came first—whether you become fascinated and then you match their body language, or whether you match their body language and then become fascinated. For many people, this is a relief—they find they can more easily put someone at ease nonverbally than coming up with just the right thing to say.

When you can influence your environment, it may also be helpful to consider how the body position dynamics will play out. A friend of mine, who was planning to sing at a party, brought not only his guitar and amplifier, but also a tall stool. When I asked him why he bothered to bring his own seating rather than just use the folding chair they'd set out for him, he said that he felt more comfortable being eye to eye with people when they came up to talk with him or make requests. As I watched him that night, I could see that he was absolutely right—that being seated on a stool made him easier to approach and talk with.

Similarly, if you're talking with a client, it can sometimes be helpful to be seated at a forty-five-degree angle to one another—rather than having to present to them across the barrier of a desk. This affords you the opportunity to be on the same side and yet be in a physical position where you can easily see them and notice their nonverbal behaviors. This side-by-side position is especially helpful when you are discussing a problem. Put the problem opposite the two of you—so it's out there—something you're addressing together.

Nonverbal behavior is all around us, isn't it? It works with all of us, all the time. Now, when you notice a behavior and decide to match it, you're just doing something with intention that you've been doing unconsciously for years.

The More the Merrier? How Matching Works with Groups

Some of my clients, who frequently work with teams or groups, have asked me about how to effectively use these nonverbal communication tips when they're interacting with more than one person. As you might imagine, I watch each of them carefully to notice their unconscious communication. What is each person's posture and body position? What are their gestures and facial expressions? How do these differ when they're interacting with me—as compared to when they're interacting with one another? It's a fascinating exploration.

But as you know, observing is just the beginning. How do you make a connection with each person? The trick is to spread your attention among the participants. Although you can't mirror each person's body language simultaneously, you can use an open body position, extended eye contact, a smile, their name—and, of course, you can still engage each person by asking open-ended questions.

Just the Opposite: How Breaking Rapport Can Be Useful

Staying open and curious serves you well in most interactions. However, there are exceptions. One client asked me whether there might be situations where someone would *intentionally* be closed or send a signal of discomfort.

Think about it for a moment. When would you want to break rapport? Imagine, for example, that someone is making an inappropriate advance—or perhaps somebody's had a bit too much to drink and they're going on and on—and you want to break off a conversation.

The way you break off the conversation is to break rapport. The first thing you do is break the synchrony of your body language and start positioning yourself to leave. In other words, you mismatch their gestures, you mismatch their posture, and you turn yourself away from them as if you wanted to leave. That will break rapport.

In a civil, social conversation like a cocktail party or with somebody who's fairly sophisticated, switching from extended eye contact to distracted eye contact will send a signal. They will immediately start looking away from you because they will understand that they're being dismissed. This is also something that other people may do with *you* when you talk too much or focus on something that's not of interest to them.

Most people recognize when someone is not receptive—simply by a person's willingness to make eye contact. But with someone who's a little more aggressive, you can use your body language to communicate: "This is an unwelcome conversation and I'm ending it right now." Although you're usually focused on building rapport, you can use your matching skills to *mismatch* someone in order to establish a clear boundary.

For the most part, however, you want to focus on creating safety and interest. As you become more comfortable within yourself and with the different communication skills you're learning, you will make others feel at ease, you will gain insight into what's going on in their minds, and you will find them opening up to you.

With this in mind, I invite you to become a keen observer and listener. When you're focusing your nonverbal communications lens on people you know, disconnect yourself from whatever your habitual way of thinking about them is—and just objectively observe them.

Set your intention to look and listen for nonverbal cues with everyone—with family members, friends, coworkers, even people in restaurants, airports, and stores. You'll find it's easier to do this when they're communicating with others. Be curious as you notice how they're behaving with other people when they're not focused on managing the impression they're creating.

Galaxies Away:
Why It's Important to Step into Another's World

Political commentator and author Walter Lippmann said, "We are all captives of the picture in our head: our belief that the world we have experienced is the world that really exists." Yet *most* people don't realize that their world is not the only one, that, in fact, it's shared by few or *only* by them. So they focus on *how* people are like them, and people who *are* like them, and when someone is different than they are, they often experience that difference as something that's "wrong."

In Chapter 4, you discovered some new things about how you create your world. How you use pictures, sounds, and feelings to make sense of things. And how your brain's efficiency strategy helped you form beliefs and develop meta-programs and preferred communication channels. You learned that each of these ways of being is revealed in your language. While all this rich and complex processing is going on inside you, it's also going on inside *other* people.

Now you can build on this understanding of yourself to improve the way you interact with others. You can take a look inside yourself and check, "Do I really know what they mean? Does that feel okay to me? Is that something that I believe, too?"

The Grand Canyon:
How Missing Details Create Gaps in Understanding

Even though we use the same language, we often don't know what someone else *really* means. Despite this potential disconnect, people seem to be conversing all the time.

Without asking questions to get the details that put us on the same page, we don't *really* know where someone else is coming from and how they reached the conclusion that they did. Yet we rarely go into much detail with others. Asking who, what, when, where, why, and how may seem unnecessary or even a bit intrusive. So instead, what we do is kind of hallucinate.

Here's how that works. When people tell you something is hot or something is really good or it's beautiful or it's tasty, the only way for you to accept that statement at face value is to fill in the information gaps in your mind by providing *your* understanding of those words.

This happens because language is designed to abbreviate, to summarize, to give us the bare bones. The trouble is we don't all have the same bare bones. We don't have the same reference experiences, so we frequently don't really know what people mean. Even if you're in the same family, the same company, or same group of friends who frequently have shared experiences, you may still not know what someone *really* means.

When somebody says, "I had a terrible time at that party," all you know is they didn't like the previous experience they had. There are lots of missing pieces to this puzzle, aren't there?

You don't know what kind of party it was. Was it *this* person's birthday party? Were there two people or thirty-five? You don't know what they mean by having a terrible time. Were they wearing uncomfortable shoes that made their feet hurt all day? Did they see an old flame, who was with someone else? Did somebody make a remark that they allowed to poison their whole day? You really have no idea.

Now, in this person's mind *they* know exactly what they're saying, right? In an effort to understand and enjoy rapport, you get sucked into making assumptions and that leads you down the wrong path. In our sincere desire to understand, we unconsciously fill in the missing pieces. A great intention, but not always a great result.

When these gaps occur, as they frequently do, it's important to understand that the other person isn't deliberately giving you only a part of what they're thinking. They're just being brief because *they* know perfectly well what they're saying. *They* know exactly what they mean.

When you fill in the gaps from *your* personal reality, you're really just making guesses or assumptions. In contrast, you can more accurately imagine what's going on inside someone else when you step into the *other* person's reality. Although some people call this "mind reading," it's really just a brief visit to second position.

If you're going to be successful in understanding what a person means, you need to leave your point of reference and step into theirs. Asking myself, "For that statement to be true, what must be going on inside that person—what's it like in *their* world?" reminds me that this person's world is being reflected in their language—and that they are inviting me to step into their world.

Zooming In and Out: Tips to Understanding Someone Else's World

---

Remember, what someone is saying is complete enough for them; it just doesn't have enough information for you. If you can stay curious and emotionally loose while you're trying on what might be true, it helps.

Some people ask clarifying questions in a way that feels like an interrogation or in a way that makes other people feel silly because they should have been more specific. However, when you ask them from a sincere place of wanting to be better company, you'll find that asking questions will help you know people better. You'll begin to understand how they think and to really enjoy the unique and miraculous divinity in each human being. We're all so different.

If you really dig in, you'll notice these differences. Because there are plenty of these, it's quite an adventure! Here are a few tips to keep in mind when you're gathering information to understand someone else's world.

Zoom In: Focus on Them

The way to "try on" someone else's world is to concentrate on their behavior, *not* your reactions. When you stay focused on their behavior instead of your feelings, you can avoid hasty reactions. This in turn frees you to have more choice in how you ultimately respond. Among other benefits, you can avoid a lot of drama this way.

Rather than focus on how *you're* feeling, keep your attention outside yourself, focused on the other person. Although your feelings provide information that may be important to notice, they are about *your* reality. As you focus on the other person and begin to understand their reality, they will then feel safer, more interesting, and understood—simply because of the quality of your attention. *And* they will tell you more, because you are making it a pleasant experience to do so.

Sounds simple, right? While it is simple, it's not always easy. Interestingly, a long pause in a conversation or an extended silence may truly test your ability to step outside yourself and stay focused on the other person. If this feels painfully awkward to you, you might notice that you fill the silence with your own inner chatter. Some of us tend to berate ourselves for that or something we did, saying to ourselves, "Oh, that was a dumb thing to say. Oh, why did I say that? I'm always doing things like that." After all this chatter, we're off in our own little world and we've left the conversation completely!

With people you know and trust, you've probably found that silence is comfortable, or at least tolerable. You don't assume it means something. Instead, you just allow the silence, right? You know they might be thinking about what they want to say, thinking about something else entirely, or not really thinking about much of anything! When it happens during conversation, particularly if it's the other person's turn to say something, just smile at them. If the silence has more intention than a pause, you can always explore it if you want to.

Zoom Out: Visit Second and Third Positions to Get Perspective

Once in a while when you're asking questions and exploring someone's world, they may be thinking, "Wow, the way this person is approaching me is really different." They may like it and feel felt, or they may feel a little vulnerable because the way you interact is unfamiliar and more personal. If they're really uncomfortable, they may send you subtle signals to back off. When you get this feedback, just notice it. Then step back a little and use your nonverbal communication skills to reestablish safety and rapport.

Similarly, if you hear a remark that puts you off or sparks a bad feeling about yourself, zoom out and disassociate from the remark. Your feelings result from your interpretation, right? So it's always important to keep in mind that a comment may not have been intended the way you heard it. Avoid engaging in a reaction that's going to shut down your curiosity and openness, because it will limit your ability to hear and gather information.

When some people hear a remark that seems critical of them, they get angry. With me, if somebody says, "You shouldn't have done that," I simply say, "Oh, I shouldn't have done what?" (Of course, tone is all important here.) Rather than sounding defensive, I try to show that I'm genuinely curious and interested about this person's concern.

In response to my request for more information, they might say, "You shouldn't have talked so angrily to that person."

"Hmm . . . what did I say that made you feel I was angry?" Notice how this question is simply gathering information about their model of the world. I'm not arguing with them. I'm not denying anything. I'm just gathering information.

They might say, "Well, you said this and this and this in that tone of voice." Once I understand how they reached their conclusion about my behavior, I can either try to correct the impression I meant to give, or I can ask myself, "You know, if I were that person, how might my behavior have seemed?" Going into second position like this allows me to try on whatever was described to me. When I do this, I'm using my own body as an instrument to gauge how that behavior might have looked, sounded, or felt.

Then I might think, "You're right. If I had heard that in that tone of voice from a guy like me, that would have made me feel pretty yucky; so I'm going to apologize to them. Thanks for bringing that to my attention." This allows me to have a very sane reaction, right? It's not a big deal, and it doesn't need to become a problem between me and the person who's sharing their interpretation of something I did, or didn't, do.

Here's another example. Sometimes because I'm so passionate about NLP, I really get on a roll and it's hard to shut me up. If, in response to my oversharing, somebody said, "You're pretty stuck on this stuff, aren't you? You think you know everything," I'd probably go into third position (objective observer) and say, "What specifically do I do that makes you think I think I know everything?" In asking this, I'm going to get some behavioral feedback that may or may not be useful. What I hear may teach me something about me, or it may teach me something about the other person. Either way, *my* mind-set is that I'm going to enjoy getting that information.

Then, with genuine interest, not defensiveness, I'll say, "Hmm, I don't think I know everything about NLP. What makes you think I know everything about NLP? Did I say something like that?"

My openness and curiosity in these kinds of conversations are echoed in my nonverbal communication. My posture and facial expressions are saying, "I'm open and safe." My tone is sincere and curious. If these visual and auditory cues were incongruent, it would make the other person uncomfortable.

Slow Down: Watch for Yellow Lights of Incongruence

In a perfect universe, people would be congruent and it would be easier to get a sense of their distinct inner realities. But we're human, so we're not always consistent. I'm certainly not! As a refresher, someone's ambivalence may result from something simple, like having to choose between going to a great concert or going parasailing. Or it may indicate an internal conflict or some violation of their values.

When people are incongruent, we read that like it's a flashing yellow light. Each of us has internal radar that sorts for "Something's wrong with this picture—slow down, be careful." People notice our incongruity, and you want to notice theirs. Because people are always communicating in three channels—visual, auditory, and kinesthetic—you get a lot of information to evaluate. And when what someone is saying doesn't match your experience of them, it's a good time to give them some space or ask them questions.

Imagine, for example, that you see someone you know at a party and they seem a little off. They're saying, "Oh, it's really good to see you," but they're looking past you or they're leaning away from you. In this situation, how would you feel? You might conclude that they didn't really want to see you, they'd rather be talking with someone else, or that something's wrong with you.

Because you kind of know this person and sense that something's off, you might say, "Is everything okay?" and they say, "Sure, I'm fine." If they say this in an irritated voice, that's incongruity again, right?

Sometimes honest sympathy will ventilate the issue. Just asking, "Is anything troubling you? Is there anything I can do?" can be helpful.

You might hear "No, it's not a big deal. My boyfriend said he'd be here on time and he's not here yet and I know he forgot that today's my birthday and I'm just pissed at him." Or "No, no, it's nothing. I have something on my mind. My wife's having surgery and I'm waiting for a call." So you may find out that what people were too polite to tell you was troubling them, or you may not. If I get two or three denials in the face of my earnest concern, then I respect their privacy and I leave it alone.

When someone's tone of voice, posture, facial expression, or body language, and your sense of their energy, don't match their words, it's often a reflection of some kind of inner conflict.

Here's a simple example. Last week I was watching an actress being interviewed on a talk show. I was fascinated to notice that her body was incongruent, top to bottom. Her feet were under the chair. Her knees were away from the person she was talking to. Her hands were folded very comfortably in front of her. Her shoulders and head were turned to the host. Because she was listening and seemed relaxed, she seemed very comfortable in her conversation.

Although her hands and her face appeared relaxed, her lower body looked frozen, like she didn't really want to be there. She was very incongruent. As I watched her, I stepped into second position and actually put my body in this incongruent position. Boy, was that uncomfortable! When I stepped back into first position, I imagined that she was probably very committed to making a point or selling whatever movie she was there to promote. But part of her, the deeper inner part of her, really wished she didn't have to be there.

When I see this kind of incongruity in someone I'm interacting with, the only thing I know for certain is that this is a person who needs a better level of comfort. Usually I'm up for helping them get that. And if they are, too, I do. If not, I don't take it personally.

Noticing incongruity is critical to establishing or maintaining rapport, and to gathering good information. Whenever you notice incongruence or some evidence of conflict, slow down and be cautious. You may be stepping into a busy intersection—simply because that person has some kind of conflict going on at that time, which may have nothing at all to do with you.

Think of this advice as framework for the adventure of exploring someone's world.

Detective Mode:
How Questions Fill in Gaps and Facilitate Understanding

When people talk about an experience, their verbal description will be incomplete. Let's zero in on language itself for a moment. As you know, it's really just shorthand; it's efficient, but it leaves gaps. In Chapter 4, you learned how you naturally delete information. Now you'll notice, really notice, how often other people do it, too.

In NLP, the Meta Model is a way of recovering missing information when you're being asked to fill in the blanks. Here are some examples that illustrate gaps and what you might say to get more information so you can understand their experience.

If somebody tells you, "I had a terrible time at that party," go inside yourself and see what you get. Can you make a representation of that? If it's even kind of fuzzy, you immediately know you need more information, like who, what, where, when, how, why. In your picture of the party, many of those details were missing, right?

Clue: Unspecified Nouns and Verbs

Because so many pieces of the puzzle were missing, you could ask lots of different questions. You could start by asking, "Which party?" (surprise: it may not be the one you both just attended) and get some more details about the party itself. Or, in contrast to gathering these facts, you could say, "When you say you had a terrible time at the party, what made it a bad time? What happened that made it a negative experience?"

Sometimes, despite well-intentioned body language and tone, when you ask someone such a direct question, it can sound like you're challenging them. To soften your questions, you can frame them with "Can you tell me?" or "I'm curious," or "I'd like to know."

In addition to missing people, places, and things, some people's descriptions are missing actions or processes. Imagine, for a moment, that your boss told you, "This is completely wrong." There are lots of possible reactions you might have, right? You could be frustrated, defensive, angry, indifferent, or anything in between. Those reactions would come from being in your world and filling in the blanks.

But if you tried to make a picture of what went wrong by stepping out of your reality and into your supervisor's, all you know is that something isn't the way he wanted it. Simply saying, "Well, okay, what was supposed to be done?" will fill in the *what* and the *how*.

If he said, "Well, the pages are supposed to be stapled along the top, and these are all stapled on the left edge," now you have useful information, right? And based on this, you can decide or discuss next steps.

This kind of communication happens all the time, doesn't it? It's kind of amazing that misunderstandings aren't even more commonplace than they are. If you adjust your attention to pick up this information, you'll be astonished at how much missing information there is in the things people tell you, and how easily you can fill in the gaps.

Clue: You Can't Put It in a Wheelbarrow

Here's another example of how meanings are hidden. These are action or process words that are turned into things, like *frustration, production, knowledge,* and *freedom.* Those descriptions really ought to be verbs or adjectives such as *frustrating, produce, knowing,* and *be free.* So, in NLP, when somebody uses these kinds of words, we call them "Nominalizations."

A nominalization is an abstraction that is undefined. Now, what's hiding in this bit of jargon is a powerful concept. It's something theoretical pretending to be something with a real existence. An easy way to recognize a nominalization is to ask, "Can I put it in a wheelbarrow?" It's like truth, beauty, and the American way. None of us really knows *exactly* what those things mean because they're pretty abstract.

If somebody says, "This is another day of frustration," you'd have to say, "Oh, who's frustrated?" When the person says, "*I'm* frustrated!" then you can say, "What was it that made you feel frustrated?" "I worked all day to get the proposal out this afternoon, then the delivery guy didn't pick it up in time to get to the prospect by the deadline."

Ah, now you have a better understanding of that person's frustration, right? The lesson here is don't understand too quickly. It's really important that you slow way down, and then you'll get an accurate sense of what's going on in the other person's head. If you try something on, either by making a picture of it, or sensing how it feels, you'll know if you have enough information.

I have a friend who often tells me a story and ends it with "See what I mean?" And then we'll laugh because we do this dance all the time. We've been friends a long time, so she's used to me saying, "No, I don't really know what you mean, but I want to. Let me tell you what I think I heard you say and I'll ask a few questions so you can help me fill in the gaps, okay?"

Clue: *Always/Never, All/None, Everyone/No One*

Another way that people leave out details is by using what we call "Universals." For instance, when you hear somebody use words like *all, none, everyone, never,* or *always,* you know that's really exaggeration, right? Other than gravity, there are VERY few things that are *always* so.

Here are some examples. "You never help me" or "His family always hates me; nothing I do ever pleases them." Or "I'm never going to learn to use this computer program."

When most people use these words, they're usually describing behaviors. *These universals show the limits of that person's world, the limits they're experiencing at a specific time or about a specific subject or person.*

In these situations, you can really do someone a favor by injecting a little good-humored perspective with questions like "Really? *All* the time?" or "Really? You've never ever done *anything* right, ever?" When I ask these questions, it's usually with kind of a half smile. What I get in return is kind of "Well, yeah, sometimes I get things right, yeah, maybe when I was fifteen." Now they're laughing, you're joking, and the two of you can get back to reality because those universals are "never" realistic.

Clue: Have To, Should, Must, Need

Another information gap that's less obvious is when people can say, "I *have* to do this. I've *got to* be there. I *should* call them. I really *must* meet the deadline." When they're using those kinds of words, these seem reasonable and you might be tempted to just accept them at face value. Yet if you did, you wouldn't really have a complete picture. To get one, you could say, "Hmm, I'm curious, what would happen if you didn't do it?"

Well, most likely *something* would happen if they didn't get it done . . . maybe they'd get a fine . . . maybe they'd get a lower grade on a paper . . . maybe they would miss a birthday. But the world wouldn't end. And maybe nothing would happen, no one would notice, and *that* would be a different kind of something to deal with.

Here's the thing. In the human mind, when you say words like *have to, must,* or *can't,* what your *brain* does is stop at that word and think, "Okay, I can't, because if I do the universe is going to end. I'm going to die. It's all going to be terrible." Whenever you hear somebody using these words, called words of "Impossibility" or words that are "Required," the best thing to do is to invite the person to examine their limitation. Asking, "What prevents you from doing it?" or "What would it be like if you *could* do it?" encourages the brain to consider other possibilities.

Clue: Absence of Criteria or Evidence

Another glimpse you might get into a person's world is when they say, "Oh, it's bad," or you hear them say, "It's all good." What's all good? In NLP, we call this the "Lost Performer." Who is the judge of whether something is good or bad? How do you know it's good? "That's the best kind." "That's a fact." Really—according to whom? In each of these examples, there are big information gaps.

If a woman says, "My husband certainly loves me," you can say, "Oh, that's wonderful. How do you know he loves you? How does he show his love?" and then she'll tell you what, in her inner world, means he loves her. "It's because he said so this morning, because he bought me a ring, or because he always takes out the garbage."

Clue: Effect with No Known Cause

The last illustration of a person's limitation is called "Cause-Effect." Imagine that somebody says, "He made me angry." You'd want to know how that happened, right? So you'd ask. In response, they might say, "Well, it was his tone of voice." Now you'd probably ask what his tone was like, and they might say, "He was just abrupt and pissy with me."

By asking questions, you can start unpacking people's conclusion-making and find out whether that's really an accurate conclusion. You can discover if that's something they believe, and if it is, that's useful. And if it's not, it allows the other person to give you more information.

Different Journeys:
How Beliefs Distinguish Our Inner Worlds

Sometimes when people make unconscious statements, they present it as fact. A well-respected colleague of mine once said in one of our monthly meetings, "Time will get away from us and the business will collapse if we don't do this." His dire prediction provided a peek into his inner world. Even though his statement wasn't on target, he let us all know how concerned he was about what would happen if we didn't take action quickly. This was just his belief.

As you know from Chapter 4, when you start listening carefully to your own language you can get a good look at *your* beliefs and you may get a picture of *your* inner world. You may hear yourself say things like "You know, every time I get a project it's such a mess when I get it that I can't possibly finish it on time."

Even in our internal dialogue, these are statements given as fact, but they're *not* fact. When you hear a belief, go inside yourself and think for a moment, "Is that true? *Every* time I'm given a project, even if it's kind of a mess, is it true that I can't finish it on time? What if just a few sections need extensive editing? I could finish that on time." Or, with the belief about the business collapsing, it's important to ask, "Is that really true? Will the business really come to a grinding halt?" Probably not.

On a lighter note, you may hear one of a teenager's beliefs when they exclaim, "Well, I can't wear those shoes with *this*!" You can ask, "Oh really? Why not?" And you might hear something fascinating, like "Well, because they're totally the wrong color blue." With further exploration, you may come to understand that the blues have to match *exactly*. Some of the beliefs you'll hear will strike you as being pretty funny, including some of your own.

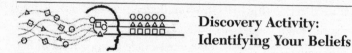

Discovery Activity: Identifying Your Beliefs

Before we consider how to uncover *other* people's beliefs, let's see what happens when you reveal a few of your own. Complete the following sentences by filling in the first thing that comes to your mind.

I am _____.

People are _____.

Life is _____.

Now, read each completed sentence and try it on. Have you ever heard yourself express this point of view before? Does this feel true to you? Would you be likely to disagree with someone if they completed the sentence differently?

How long have you had this thought?

When you're done, just put this activity aside for a moment. We'll come back to it.

Roots of Beliefs: The Importance of Experience and Belonging

In Chapter 4, you learned that *most* of your beliefs were formed when you were young. This happens in two ways. Some beliefs are sort of cause and effect. They're formed from personal experience, like "If I cry, someone will come and feed me or change my diapers." As an adult, this belief might be expressed as "If I let someone know what I need, they'll respond," but the emotional reaction that's linked to this belief may be more like a child's. That's because the belief that's still creating the motivation is one a small child came up with in an effort to make sense of the world. Isn't that fascinating?

In contrast, other beliefs come from unverified information—like the family or local wisdom; they're simply learned and integrated. It's a tribal kind of thought. By sharing similar beliefs and views of the world, we feel not only some sense of order and control, but also a sense of belonging. Initially, these beliefs of belonging relate to our families because our very survival rests with being cared for and accepted. Later, this kind of tribal thinking may extend to include the school we go to, the community we live in, the company we work for, a spiritual congregation we practice with, or even social and political groups we affiliate with. Most of these groups have shared beliefs that drive their motivations and behaviors.

Beliefs that are acquired like hand-me-downs can be tricky because beliefs filter the information we let in. Here's an example. One day my neighbor's eight-year-old daughter said, "I'd never marry a rich man." This really caught my attention, so I said, "That's interesting; how come you wouldn't want to marry a rich man?" She looked at me like I was incredibly stupid or from another planet and said (like it was the most reasonable thing in the world), "Because rich people aren't happy."

When she answered my question about her belief, she revealed another belief. While it's possible that she actually *knew* some rich people and based her conclusion on her experience, it seemed unlikely to me. These were beliefs she'd heard in her tribe and accepted without question. Even though I was a little alarmed about her conclusion, I didn't argue with her. I simply gave her some statistics about how the lack of money is a source of conflict in many marriages and explained that marrying someone who had money might eliminate those problems. This line of reasoning didn't seem to shake her conviction.

In contrast, a former girlfriend's mother had always told her daughter when she was little, "It's just as easy to fall in love with a rich man as a poor man." Of these two beliefs, which one seems the most limiting, and which one seems the most empowering?

It seems quite possible that my neighbor's daughter might, in fact, decide not to hang around with those unhappy rich people, unwittingly limiting her possibilities for friendship and marriage. Again, in contrast, my girlfriend's mom simply opened the door to possibility, so she could consider all men as potential candidates.

In a nutshell, all of us form beliefs, most often from our earliest days. Without some adult experience that calls a belief into question, we can carry these thoughts as truths through our whole lives. Even though many beliefs are unconscious, it helps to notice them and bring them into the light for further examination. Then the most important question we can ask is "How is this belief working within us? Is it empowering us or limiting us?"

These beliefs are evident in how someone completes the sentences you just did in the last activity: I am . . . People are . . . Life is . . .

I love exploring beliefs, and often when I'm talking with a new friend, I like to say, "Just for giggles, I'd like to play a game. Complete this sentence for me. Life is like a _____." I'm always intrigued by what they come up with. For example, I've heard,

"Life is like a game."

"Life is like a contest."

"Life is a battle."

"Life is an adventure."

"Life is a circus."

"Life is a journey."

People come up with all sorts of metaphors that give you an indication of their beliefs about life. A battle and a circus, are they talking about the same thing? Absolutely. And in addition to having diverse beliefs about life, people have beliefs about themselves and about *other* people.

The parts of the world that really impact us are what we say to ourselves about our lives, how we characterize them, and how other people treat us. How other people treat us, of course, is a little more complicated because that's mixed in with how we treat them and what their beliefs are. In many cases, we draw conclusions from what other people do (or don't do) that aren't really justified by what they did in that one specific situation.

Here's the bottom line. People's attention, even in conversation, is frequently *internally* focused, although it may *seem* like they're listening to you. This experience is so common it is frequently expressed as a joke along the lines of "Listening is *not* thinking of what *you* are going to say next."

In general, people are mostly concerned with themselves. They're much more focused on their own thoughts, feelings, choices, and behaviors than anyone else's. That's not necessarily bad or selfish; it's just the way most people work. It's one of our basic survival characteristics.

Said another way, once you recognize and accept that, most of the time, someone else's attention is on their own experience, you will find it a lot easier to understand people and why they do what they do.

As you know, understanding how your beliefs motivate and shape your experience can help you recognize how powerful they are in your life—and how powerful *other* people's beliefs are in their own lives.

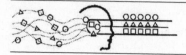

Discovery Activity:
Exploring a Personal Belief

Let's revisit the activity you did a moment ago. Choose *one* of the beliefs you discovered when you completed the following sentences.

I am _____.

People are _____.

Life is _____.

When you consider this belief now, is this something that people in your family believed?

Based on who you are today, is this something you still think is true, or something you simply accepted and once believed?

Although many beliefs originally embodied a positive intention, like keeping us safe, or helping us belong, they still impact our behavior.

So, is the belief you identified empowering, or limiting?

If it's limiting, is this something you'd like to change?

One of the beliefs I'm fortunate to have is that I'm lucky. I'm pretty sure I got this from my parents. They were people who looked for and focused on the positive things in life. I remember that even when times were hard, they encouraged my brother and I to count our blessings and be grateful. So, feeling that I'm lucky is a belief I want to keep and continue to feel empowered by.

But if I had a limiting belief that "people are always out to get you," that's something I might want to change. If I'd had this belief for a long time, I would also have lots of evidence that it's true, simply because that's what I'd been looking for. A way to loosen up this belief would be to identify counter-examples, examples that show how this belief isn't *always* accurate.

Perhaps I could think of someone who was often nice to me, or I could remember a friend, teacher, or coworker, who once stood up for me when someone else was being unkind or unfair. Maybe there was a time when a complete stranger let me go ahead of them at the grocery store checkout when I was in a hurry. Even a small example can begin to loosen up a limiting belief.

If I couldn't identify any counter-examples in my own experience, I could look for these with others. If you decide to do this, don't pick the person who seems to have everything going their way. Instead, pick someone you know pretty well who's had some tough breaks, then step into second position with them and notice anything that flies in the face of "People are always out to get you." Perhaps this individual got a raise or a promotion. Perhaps someone gave them free tickets to an event. Perhaps a person who owed them money paid it back. What in this person's experience could provide you with a kernel of evidence and hope that "people are always out to get you" is not true?

Your beliefs are powerful, and so are other people's. You might be wondering what to do when you encounter another person's belief that's different from yours. Imagine, for a moment, that someone across from you is stating something as fact that you *know* not to be fact. What do you do about that? Do you jump right into a debate? Let's hold this question for the next chapter, when you'll learn several ways to explore what the other person thinks and create an opening to consider a different point of view.

For now, I recommend that you notice the belief and continue to learn about your companion. Do them the favor of being curious about them, and continue to gather information about them. Usually, people find this kind of conversation to be a very pleasant experience.

They find you fascinating because you're fascinated with them, so this is a win/win situation.

Wants and Needs: How Exploring Beliefs Uncovers Motivations and Meta-Outcomes

---

Because unconscious beliefs shape our decisions and behavior, when people tell you about something they want or need, you'll often discover that the stated goal is not their *real* motivation. There's something called the goal-behind-the-goal, or "Meta-Outcomes." In learning about the Well-Formed Outcome in Chapter 2, you explored the meta-outcomes related to a goal you chose.

So how do you learn about *someone else's* meta-outcomes in a conversational way? Imagine, for example, that a neighbor tells you, "I've got to go down and get my car washed this afternoon." In response, you could say, "Oh, that's a good thing. I do that once in a while, too. How often do you get it done?"

"Oh, I get it done every week."

"What's important to you about that?"

"What? Are you serious? It's important to take care of my things," or "Well, in this neighborhood everybody's car is shiny, and I don't want to be the bum on the block," or "If I don't do it, my wife takes it to this place that costs fifty-two dollars, so I take care of it." You'll get some kind of reason. The more you peel the layers of the onion, the more you'll learn about someone's beliefs, meta-outcomes, and real motivations.

Two of my favorite questions to uncover unconscious motivations and beliefs are "What would happen if *that* occurred?" *and* "What's important about that?" These provide me with interesting information about and insight into others. It doesn't put people on guard. Because it just gets them thinking, these are great questions that elicit honest feedback from people.

Also, when I'm trying to learn about someone's reasons, goals, and dreams and the goal-behind-the-goal (meta-outcomes), the big question is "If that happened, what would *that* do for you?" This question is like magic, so I usually ask it again, building on what they just told me, "And if *that* happened, what would that do for you that's even more important?" Here's an example of what these questions might reveal.

Imagine that someone told you, "I've got to finish my courses and get this degree."

"Okay, and if you get the degree, what will that do for you?"

"Well, then I can enter my chosen field of microbiology."

"That's great. And if you enter your chosen field, what's even more important about that?"

"Well, then I'll be doing work I like and I'll be getting paid well."

"Great. So doing work you like and getting paid well, what does that do for you?"

"Well, then I can buy a house, get married, and have kids. Are you crazy? What do you mean what does it do for me?"

Then you can laugh it off and say, "Right, and is that the most important thing in life to you? Having a house and having kids?"

"Yes! Having a happy family and a sense of belonging is really important."

When you're *genuinely* trying to learn about somebody, they don't get resistant or resentful. Instead people really appreciate your sincere interest. Do you know how little this happens in industrialized society? Just think about it. Unless somebody is making cocktail party chatter, people rarely ask each other questions beyond "What do you do?" or "Where are you from?" Almost no one ever asks questions that sincerely dig down, do they? Your authentic interest and inquiries will be a refreshing change.

Beyond Belief:
How Language Reveals Other Personal Preferences

Belief statements are *one* reflection of individual preferences. A person's language will also reveal their preferred representational system, their key meta-programs, and how they operate in relationship to time. Knowing how to notice these preferences will prepare you for modifying your own preferences in order to maximize how you communicate (which you'll learn about in Chapter 7).

Preferred Channels: Representational System Preferences

How would you know about someone's representational system preferences? Imagine you were talking with someone and they mentioned their vacation plans, saying, "We're going on vacation in July. We've got reservations and we're saving our money. We're going back down to the Caribbean!"

You might say, "Oh, you've been there before. When you think about going back there, what are you most excited about?" and the person will tell you any number of things. Whenever they slow down, you can pick one thing to build on and say, "And what's important to you about *that*?" or "What do you like best about that?" or "What's the best time you ever had on vacation?" With any of these questions, you'll be able to gather more information.

If your companion processes primarily in visual terms, they might say, "The colors of the Caribbean are so bright . . . the costumes people wear are so vibrant . . . and the water is this sparkling emerald green." Their description provided you with snapshots, right?

If their processing is primarily auditory, someone will talk in terms of sound. You may hear, "I love waking up to the sound of the surf . . . I sleep great when I can hear the rustle of the trees in the wind . . ." or "the local music is an amazing sound; their instruments are made from steel drums, old bottles, coconuts, and driftwood!" Hear the difference in these sound bites?

Or you'll get a kinesthetic description. "You know, I just feel wonderful when I'm down there. I love diving into the warm water and riding the waves . . . squishing the sand between my toes makes me feel like a kid again . . . I'm so relaxed my stomach has settled down . . ." or "I love the food! The spices are kind of hot, but the beer is ice cold." Notice how these feelings and sensations shape the experience of the listener.

Again, everyone uses all three channels, but you'll find that people favor one over another. They'll lean toward feeling and emotional words or tune into sound words, or they'll focus on vision words. This is information most people don't ordinarily get. Noticing these personal preferences will give you additional insight into how the unique human you are with actually works—and how best to communicate with someone through their preference.

Preferred Patterns of Processing: Meta-Programs

In Section 1, you learned that about additional filters that we habitually act on, called meta-programs, which are patterns of processing information that we've adopted and automated to help us make decisions and motivate ourselves.

To refresh your memory, the following chart highlights some of the key meta-programs. In Chapter 4, when you were initially introduced to these filters, which ones seemed to best describe you?

Meta-Program	Answers the Question
Options/Procedures	Is it more important for you to do something the "right way" than it is to have alternative ways of doing it?
Toward/Away-From	Are you more motivated by moving toward something that has a potentially positive outcome, or away from a potentially negative consequence?
Proactive/Reactive	Are you more likely to take the initiative to act, or wait for someone else to do it—or for something else to happen?
Internal/External	When you evaluate something, are you more likely to use an internal personal standard, or to ask for someone else's feedback?
General/Specific	Do you most often deal in the "big picture"—or in the details?
Match/Mismatch	When making comparisons, do you notice how things are alike, or where there are differences/discrepancies?

As you think about meta-programs, remember that these behaviors are expressed more as a continuum than as extremes. But when you consider the two extremes, there's likely to be *one* in the pair that you can barely understand or have trouble tolerating. If so, the *opposite* one is your preference. Meta-programs are so much a part of us that when you try them on, you may discover you have strong feelings about the "rightness" of one versus the other.

Because meta-programs are unconscious and personal, they can be a source of conflict between coworkers, significant others, teammates, and even strangers. Because meta-programs are now on your radar, a part of you will be looking for them and wondering how they're influencing your interactions.

If you're "externally oriented" and like to get feedback from other people before moving forward, you might be really irritated to come back from vacation and find that your coworker put information about a new product on the company website *before* "testing" it with a sample group. This frustration might be really severe if *another* of your meta-programs was "reactive."

And if your orientation is "away-from" *as well as* "specific," you might feel challenged by a spouse who comes home waving two tickets to Paris and saying, "I got a great deal! We leave day after tomorrow, so get packing!"

A New Aspect of Meta-Programs: "Content" and "Domain"

Another important meta-program is called "Content." The "Content" meta-program recognizes the importance we assign to these five basic elements, called "Domains," of life: People, Information, Things, Activity, and Location. It's a revealing aspect of our nature. Are we "people-people" or do we collect antiques? Do we remember based on where we were, or what we did, or whom we were with, or what we had or what we learned?

With a little attention and practice, you'll notice how someone's possessions or conversation will reveal how they prioritize these five elements.

All of us relate to these domains and unconsciously rank them one through five. For instance, my personal "sort" is probably People, Information, Place, Activity, and then Things. Possessions and things like that are pretty low on my list of awareness. Relationships (People) are the first things that occur to me, and next for me is information.

These content "sorts" are context-based. For example, my wife, Vikki, sorts content this way—People, Activity, Place, Information, and Things. We're aligned in a lot of ways, but, at home, she's much more proactive than I am in terms of creating our environment. She watches HGTV and I'll watch the Discovery Channel. She's looking at Place and Things and how they may be arranged (Activity), and I'm looking at history and science and stuff like that, because I'm an information junkie. We have these overlaps *and* we have these interesting differences.

As you become more aware of your meta-programs and see them in others, you'll notice how commonalities can be a source of comfort and connection. And how differences can be a source of curiosity or conflict. There's no right or wrong about this. It's all just preference. Fortunately, things are just not neatly black-and-white—you're this and I'm that—and never the twain shall meet.

A Case in Point: Meta-Program Content

Here's how a forty-one-year-old client of mine who was an engineer used his knowledge of meta-programs to increase his versatility and comfort. He was married to a woman whose top three priorities were Things, Activity, and Place. She loved to go to flea markets.

Because his initial "sort" was Information, Activity, and Relationship, the very thought of going to a flea market and all the stuff there made him a little crazy. Once he realized this, he started researching what the vendors were selling by asking them where the items came from and their history. Just by focusing on information, he was able to amuse himself and make it a more enjoyable experience.

Consider a person whose top three priorities are Information, Place, and Activity. That person's not likely to be warm and fuzzy. That person probably lives in his or her head. Their home, the place they actually live, is going to be very important to them, so you don't want to mess with it. You might not even be welcome there. Quite frequently, they're really attached to what they do, and relationships aren't very high on their list. I know some superb teachers who are like this. While we like and respect each other, it's not like they often call me saying, "Let's go hang out." I don't take it personally—it's just how they operate. It's just personal preference.

The Common Thread: How People Relate to Time

The element of time touches many aspects of our lives, so the different ways people relate to it always reveals something about their unique world.

Time Orientation: Through Time and in Time

A person who's *through* time is someone who can see the past, present, and future simultaneously. This perspective is likely to make someone a good observer and excellent planner. In contrast, a person who is *in* time is very associated, very in the moment. This person has the capability to really enjoy life in the moment. However, they may not excel at planning or keeping commitments. To them, a commitment is something that happened in the past and planning is something that happens in the future. When someone is *in* time, it makes sense that these behaviors would present a challenge.

When you understand *your* orientation to time and recognize that someone else's is different, it's easier to stay away from making judgments about it and accept that this is just how they operate.

Cultural Time Orientation: Monochronic and Polychronic

Cultural differences in time orientation often create friction. I just moved from Silicon Valley in California, where it's very diverse. People from all over the world live and work there; so cultural differences about time make communicating challenging.

Psychologist and author Allen Bluedorn, conducting research about time, found that in communication, especially nonverbal communication, there are really two major divisions for time: monochronic and polychronic.

Monochronic time is linear. That's Germany, Canada, Switzerland, Scandinavia, most of Europe, and the United States. We're very linear. We like schedules. We show up at the agreed-upon time for an appointment because that's what's important to us. We say time is money and that you can't ever get it back, so culturally that's what we're about. It makes sense that in the 1300s the first clocks were built in Europe.

Polychronic time is a system where several things can be done at once; it's a more fluid approach. Polychronic time is common in southern Europe, Latino cultures, Native American cultures, Arabic cultures, Mexico, and India. Relationships are much more important in these cultures, and there's much less attention to accounting for every moment.

If you were at a friend's house in a polychronic time culture and there was something going on there that was going to make you late for an appointment, you'd just go ahead and be late, because the relationship is what really matters. Since that less formal perception of time is accepted, being late wouldn't be the same kind of issue or an insult that it would be in a monochronic time culture.

These are broad generalities, of course. Yet among the people you know, you'll probably notice that their different approaches to time are based on the culture they're in or the one they're from. When we lived in California, a lot of the housekeepers were Hispanic and some of our friends would say, "The housekeepers are late again. They're just lazy." That judgment stems from a linear orientation to time, right? These housekeepers weren't lazy; they were probably taking care of their children or looking in on a friend. They were just operating from a different set of values.

As I began exploring time and wanting to write about it, I realized how profoundly it affects people's approaches and beliefs about so many things. And I began to wonder if additional research about time had been done recently.

Time Orientation: Now and Then

Phil Zimbardo, a prolific professor at Stanford University, has written a lot about psychology and lately he's been talking about how time operates differently in people's lives. (There's a wonderful animated presentation of his key concepts on TED and YouTube.)

Some of what he describes will not surprise you, because these patterns are things you've probably noticed in your own life and in your interactions with others.

He says people are past-oriented, present-oriented, or future-oriented. Interesting, huh? If they're future-oriented, they're obviously more focused on the future than on the present or the past. They're good planners. They're very goal-oriented. They tend to have higher grade point averages, be health conscious, and save their money. They can delay gratification, so they have pretty good ego control and self-esteem. However, because they are sometimes too far in the future, they may have trouble locating themselves in the present. As a result, they may be less able to enjoy present activities and may be a little less affectionate to people immediately around them.

People who are past-oriented are actually looking back at the past; they're relating everything that's happening to what's already happened. These people operate primarily from negative past perspectives or positive past perspectives. They base their outlook and decisions on these experiences.

If, for example, a past-oriented person has had sad, painful, or traumatic experiences they haven't gotten over, they're going to be pessimistic. They tend to expect less out of the future and are hesitant to take risks. In contrast, people who have happy pasts are going to be quite optimistic, enthusiastic, and ambitious; they expect to repeat or create a good experience that they feel happy about.

People who are present-oriented can pretty much be divided into two categories: hedonistic or fatalistic. If they're fatalistic, they think that fate's in charge of their life, so they live more passive lives, believing they have little or no personal power. If they're hedonistic, they like to enjoy life. They're impulsive, they're spontaneous, and they're risk takers. They tend to lose themselves in the excitement of the moment and have passionate relationships. One conclusion: you simply don't want someone who is present-oriented in a planning capacity.

There are many more subtle distinctions. But always ask yourself, "Where is this person in relationship to time? Are they thinking about and living in the past, in the present, or in the future?" Someone's orientation to time impacts what we learn about them, what we choose to say to them, and what might be possible in a relationship with them.

A New Approach: How to Apply Your Understanding of Nonverbal Behavior, Beliefs, and Personal Preferences to Interactions with Others

---

Setting your intention on understanding someone else's world can help you establish rapport, enhance your communication, and deepen your connection. You can also begin to enjoy discovering all the ways people are different instead of being puzzled or even annoyed by the differences.

Of course, trying to notice and explore all these different pieces of someone's world can be a little overwhelming, especially when you're meeting someone new. Here's something easy you can do to practice and hone your skills.

Discovery Activity: Exploring Someone's Inner World

Just for fun, complete the following questions to see what you already know about someone you're close to. Right now, think of someone you know pretty well.

Person:_____

How are they in relationship to time?

When they describe something (especially an experience that has emotions associated with it), what does their language tell you about the representational system they're processing in? Are they more visual, auditory, or kinesthetic?

What meta-programs do you notice in their behavior? Is their orientation more:

- Options or Procedures?

- Toward or Away-From?

- Proactive or Reactive?

- Internal or External?

- General or Specific?

- Match or Mismatch?

How would they rank the meta-program content domains—people, place, information, activities, and things?

How do you imagine they'd complete these sentences?

I am _____.

People are _____.

Life is _____.

What beliefs do you notice that they mention fairly frequently?

Do these beliefs seem to be empowering or limiting?

Of course, these answers are just a starting point. As you interact with the person you've identified, try to see them with fresh eyes. Be curious and ask questions about missing information that you normally would have just filled in. As you get more information, consider which of your initial observations were on target, and which ones were not. (To get an outside perspective, invite this person to take the quick assessment you did in Chapter 4 to get a brief profile of their meta-programs.)

During your next several interactions with this person, notice how the communication or feelings may be different from before—simply because you are stepping outside yourself, and focusing on really understanding *them*.

This practice experience will help you use these same observation and questioning skills with others you know or are just meeting. Noticing what's missing in someone's communication, recovering lost information, discovering what someone really wants, recognizing their preferred representational system for processing, identifying how someone is in relationship to time, and distinguishing their meta-programs will help you understand and appreciate *their* world. No one's way is wrong—it's just different. These differences reflect the richness of human experience.

Using the information and skills you learned in this chapter can change your life. And because this way of communicating alters the way you touch the lives of others, you can help make the world a better place. In the next chapter, you'll learn how to put these discoveries to work so you can be even more effective and persuasive.

Key Ideas

- Nonverbal behaviors like personal space, body position and posture, gestures, facial expressions, etc., provide important information about another person's inner world.

- Naturally (or intentionally) matching someone else's nonverbal behaviors in a subtle way can create a sense of safety and rapport.

- "Trying on" a person's behaviors to see how they feel is a kind of "mind reading" that enables someone else to step into the other person's world.

- Because language is linguistic shorthand about someone's experience, it has gaps in information. The NLP Meta Model provides a process to gather missing details.

- "Zooming in" helps us focus on another person and understand their world. "Zooming out," when interactions feel a little tense, enables us to give someone room to exhale and affords us the opportunity to go to third position to objectively assess what's going on.

- Noticing incongruities between what someone is saying and how they're saying it (how their body looks or what their tone sounds like) is like approaching a yellow light; it pays to slow down and evaluate the situation before rushing on.

- For better or worse, beliefs filter our experience. Most beliefs are formed when we're young and they still drive our behavior years later.

- Beliefs can be detected in people's language.

- When we uncover beliefs, we have a chance to discover how they influence us.

- Exploring a person's goal-behind-the-goal (the meta-outcome) enables to us to have greater insight into what's most important to them.

- Paying close attention to someone's language is one way to identify:

  > that person's preferred sensory channel
  > the meta-programs that influence them
  > how they are in relationship to time.

 To enhance the skills you learned in this chapter, check out the recommended Bonus Activities at our special "Essential Guide" website: http://eg.nlpco .com/6-1 or use the QR code with your phone.

Discoveries, Questions, Ideas, and Stuff You Want to Work On

_____

_____

_____

_____

_____

_____

_____

_____

_____

_____

_____

_____

_____

_____

_____

_____

_____

_____

_____

_____

_____

_____

Discoveries, Questions, Ideas, and Stuff You Want to Work On

Chapter Seven: Making Your Point Easily

How can I help people understand what I mean?

Thaw with her gentle persuasion is more powerful than Thor
with his hammer. The one melts, the other breaks into pieces.
—Henry David Thoreau

Much of the previous content has been dedicated to understanding how to thaw things out in ourselves and in others. By learning how we process our experience we thaw out our well-developed, well-intended foundation of patterns. Making these automated and sometimes rigid patterns more fluid readies our internal environment for change and enables us to bring our most comfortable, congruent selves to any interaction. And by being genuinely curious about how *others* process, we bring a welcome warmth, refreshing honesty, and increased understanding to relationships.

This chapter is about connecting the dots—building on what you've learned about yourself and others—to help you further enhance communication and connections.

Chronicle: High Points of the Journey So Far

We've covered a lot of ground together so let's quickly open our mental files so we can easily connect previous concepts with new ones. Because you're already familiar with the content, the following refreshers appear as suggestions.

- Work from the inside out. First, notice what's happening with you. Use your NLP tools, especially sub-modalities, to change your emotional reactions and improve your personal experience.

- When you're comfortable and congruent, consider what's happening with others around you. Set your intent to focus on being interested, not interesting.

- To signal that you are safe, use your body language and slightly extended eye contact to show that you're open and interested.

- To understand what someone really means and how it is in *their* world, use the Meta Model to fill in gaps left by linguistic shorthand.

- Pay particular attention to other people's nonverbal communications and subtly mirror one or two of these behaviors by matching their posture, gestures, rate of speech, or tone of voice.

- Notice people's language, because it will reveal their preferred meta-programs and representational channel, their relationship to time, and their beliefs—all of which give you insight into their worlds.

- When you hear a belief from someone, explore the related meta-outcomes and consider how that belief may be empowering or limiting that person.

Because you've been practicing these behaviors, you've learned even more about yourself—and others. This chapter will help you take your skills to the next level and support you in making connections with others and being *understood*.

It may surprise you to learn that getting people to "buy in"—to move them from resisting—to listening and considering what you say actually doesn't depend so much on what *you* tell them. It's more about what you get *them* to tell you—and what goes on in *their* brains during that process.

A book called *Just Listen* beautifully illustrates this phenomena. The author, Mark Goulston, is a psychiatrist who teaches hostage negotiation to many different government agencies. He's used to dealing with people under tremendous stress. He says that the most important part of communicating with somebody else is the quality of your listening skills—*not* what you say.

So, the way you and your message are received isn't really influenced so much by your haircut, what you wear, or the firmness of your handshake. It's based on how the other person feels when they're with you. It's based on how safe, interesting, and felt they feel—and how *you* helped them feel that way. Sound familiar?

Physical Connection:
How Touch Enhances Connections and Impact

Touch is one way you can influence a person's experience of being with you *and* their recollection of that connection. Because we talked about the power of touch in earlier chapters, you may recall that waitresses, petition signature collectors, and basketball teams that use appropriate touch enjoy improved results. Touch will, without question, enhance *your* ability to warm up even casual connections.

For example, research has shown that babies don't thrive if they're not touched and cuddled when they're infants; their brains will not develop well and they won't gain the weight that they need to. In fact, the Touch Research Institute at the University of Miami School of Medicine has carried out more than one hundred studies and found evidence of the significant effects of touch—including faster growth of premature babies, reduced pain, decreased autoimmune disease symptoms, lowered glucose levels in children with diabetes, and improved immune systems in people with cancer. All these benefits— just from a nurse's touch!

Cincinnati Children's Hospital is one of a number of leading health centers in the United States that now use healing touch therapy. Their director said, "Research has demonstrated that patients who receive healing touch experience *accelerated* wound healing, relaxation, pain relief, and general comfort."

In addition to these details about research and touch, I'd like to share a personal example of how touch left an impression on me. You may recall that in my first meeting with my wife, she repeatedly touched my arm at the café and said, "Tom, it was just the funniest thing." All these years later, I can still feel that spot on my arm.

When I was thinking about that gift, I realized that my father was like my wife in the way he used touch. He was an immigrant from Assyria, who moved to the States to enjoy greater safety and religious freedom. He was a big strong farm boy, who went to UCLA and played football; later he became a preacher, and ultimately, because he was a truly talented tenor, he became a professional singer.

I grew up in the Los Angeles area right after World War II and noticed that my dad was always throwing his arm around people and hugging them. At that time, men here didn't really do that. I remember noticing that his friends and associates seemed kind of uncomfortable when my dad would embrace them, so I asked my mom about it and she explained, "American men aren't used to being as demonstrative as your father is."

But here's the thing. Everybody loved my dad, everybody. They just lit up when he came in. Because he gave people his full attention, he had an ability to make each one feel very special. In addition to being brilliant and talented, he was the kindest man I ever met. He brought heart to everything he did—and one of the ways he showed his heart was to touch people. People around him felt the way I feel when I'm around my wife.

So, what's this have to do with you and why should you care?

Here's my experience. I love my dad and I adore my wife, but I don't think that they're really more magical than the rest of us. Well, maybe a little bit because they had this *instinct* for touching people and making kinesthetic contact. But it's touch itself that's really magical.

Since I've adopted my wife's habit of touching others, I've substantially warmed up my relationships in my family and among casual acquaintances. I will pat somebody on the shoulder or touch their arm when I'm saying something—particularly when greeting them, complimenting them, or saying good-bye. It appears to be more than acceptable; it seems to deepen our connection.

This new habit of touching has also made *me* feel more at home with other people. I feel more relaxed because I've had contact with them. I feel like we're more in the groove with each other. I end up joking with people more than I used to, even when I'm waiting in line with complete strangers. Because of touch, I end up making more human-level contacts, instead of connections that are limited to my role in a particular situation.

So, if you haven't experimented with touch already, make a commitment to do it in your next two or three interactions. You can do it quietly, a little bit at a time, so nobody needs to notice anything, until you're comfortable reaching out to others even more. Try to increase the number of times that you touch the people around you. It can be as demonstrative and frequent as the ways my wife or my dad used touch, or it can be just a quick friendly pat, but give it a try.

As you know, NLP calls these touches anchors. Anchors, when you do it this way, just as it happened with my wife and me, are kind of little reminders that you were there. Our skin is chock full of nerves, so touching and being touched definitely brings us closer to each other. Again, these kinds of anchors are completely subliminal and completely unconscious, so using the power of touch will just leave people with the impression that you're warmer or more relaxed or more outgoing. Not bad, right?

Oxygen Mask First: How Managing *Your* Inner State Keeps the Focus on Others

It's impossible to overstate the importance of paying attention to and managing *your* inner state. It's like putting your own oxygen mask on first, right?

I confess, doing this didn't come easily to me. As I told you, I'm a big guy, I move kind of fast, and I've got a deep voice, so these qualities were an asset when I was in the military. And I had developed a habit of being a bit blustery and domineering. Then, while studying NLP, I became aware of the way I came across to people and I wanted to change that.

So one of the things that I did during the NLP workshops was to learn how I could enter a room and not be noticed. I wanted not to be distracting in any way—so I wanted to enter the room without people noticing my arrival.

I practiced on a class of fifty NLP students that I was coaching. Any time I'd been out of the room, I'd pause—and before I entered the classroom, I would consciously check on and attend to *my* inner state. I'd put my virtual oxygen mask on. I would purposely calm myself down, center myself—then open the door and slip in. I graded myself by how many heads turned. And when I was able to do this so that the only person who looked up was the one nearest the door, I figured I'd gotten this part mastered. I could slip in like an expert high diver who enters the water with only the slightest ripple.

For you, managing your inner state might mean bringing your energy up, rather than quieting it down. If, for example, you tend to be a tentative or shy person, you might want to amp up your energy. The way to do that, of course, is to think about the other person. Imagine them feeling a lot like you do. After all, few of us get enough attention. Each of us is out there pretty much on our own, playing and fulfilling our different roles.

Nobody really expects that we're going to pay attention to *them*. So before you meet somebody, imagine in your mind, "I'm going to meet somebody wonderful. I don't know anything about them and this is going to be a game. I'm going to enjoy learning as much as possible about them without it feeling like they've just been in the third-degree hot seat."

Your goal and your intention in meeting somebody are really what drive the experience. After all, if you know what you want from the meeting and how you want that process to feel, you have a clear and worthwhile focus. In this case, getting to know the other person is your goal. This really frees you from worrying if you have something in your teeth, if your fly is zipped, or if you're making a good first impression. Believe me, if you're genuinely interested in the other person and it shows, you *will* have their attention. They will enjoy being around you.

So once you're under control, take care to avoid a common pitfall of persuading. When people try to persuade other people—when they get into selling, urging, encouraging, and arguing—all of those behaviors make the other person feel pushed. What's lacking from most social interactions where a person feels pressured is the opportunity to exhale, to just relax and ease into being with people.

Think of the people whom you enjoy being around. Are they pushy? Needy? Narcissistic? Or are they calm, relaxed, centered in themselves, and genuinely interested in you? Just think about that. Your intent is to help the other person feel safe, relaxed, and at home with you. So, instead of accelerating the energy, you want to step back a little to give them some psychological air, and if you feel like you're picking up too much speed, "zoom out" and briefly visit third position to assess how the interaction is going.

Your ability to use a person's name in conversation, to use extended eye contact and touch, and to match their nonverbals and their language are charmers. Once the other person feels safe and felt, you can show more interest in them in terms of asking them questions about what they do, what they like, what would it be like if they could do, have, or be something different, and what *that* will do for them; then listen and just let the other person run with it. As they do, they'll give you more information about themselves—and you can ask more follow-up questions.

People who are busy with *their* stories and their talk about "me, me, me" are the ones who give the impression of being insecure. They often turn others off because they don't seem to be interested in anyone but themselves. People who try to be interesting (and I was guilty of this in the past) are probably insecure. People who are self-assured are interested. That's the big difference. To be genuinely interested in someone else allows you to feel self-assured. It gives you information *and* it creates the impression that you are self-assured, open, and safe.

So, when you're talking with people, in addition to the questions you learned in Chapter 5, you want to ask questions that get at how they feel or think about something, as well as what they've done in the past or might like to have happen in the future. As they answer, they begin to feel known by you. And as they become known by you, they'll be more comfortable and will share even more of themselves with you. Cool, right?

Rules of the Road:
Quick Tips to Navigate Uncharted Territory

Before we explore challenging and sometimes difficult situations, where persuading may feel more like negotiating, here are a few simple rules to keep in mind.

1. Don't interrupt. When somebody starts talking, let them go. Be mindful to keep the flow going and manage any desire to think "out loud."

2. Don't ever contradict. If they say something that you feel you ethically have to take issue with, a better way of doing this is to agree with their viewpoint—say, "That's an interesting viewpoint. I understand that, and I wonder if *this* would also be possible, or if this has any interest or validity for you." (Since I've been able to adopt the attitude that whatever anyone says is interesting and fits in with their world, I find I no longer feel compelled to contradict or correct them.)

   A long time ago, I read about something Thomas Jefferson said he learned from Benjamin Franklin: "Never take issue with another man. If you prove him wrong, you've made an enemy for life, and if he proves you wrong he'll think you a fool." Thomas Jefferson said that Ben Franklin was the best-loved man in the colonies because he was the least argumentative. Interesting, isn't it? And it's kind of a little nod to the principles of NLP.

3. Avoid using the words *but, why,* and phrases starting with *you.* Replacing the word *but* with *and* usually encourages discussion.

Here's the reason: when you use the word *but* in a sentence, its job is to negate everything that went before that. You can say, "I understand where you're coming from, but I feel differently." As soon as you say the word *but*, it means everything that went before that is a lie; it negates a whole part of your statement. People know this and still many people use it—letting it negatively impact their rapport *and* their message.

Because *why* is also a word that often makes people feel challenged or even attacked, it can undermine the feelings of safety and comfort that you've worked so hard to create. Think about it. "Why do you do that? Why did you wear that? Why do you think that?" *Why* doesn't support feelings of rapport. If you must use it, if there's no other way to ask about something specific, then soften it by saying, "I wonder why that's so. What do you think?" Much better words to use are *who, what, when, where,* and *how.*

Imagine that someone (even you?) has an issue that sounds like this: "Why does this keep happening to me?" or "Why do I always get the short end of the stick?" To answer this question, the unconscious mind has to agree that the person always gets the short end of the stick; so it will produce a reason, even if it's not true. "Why" means there's no dispute, so the mind will make up a reason, which further cements the feeling or belief.

Although I discovered that "why" questions were good to ask when I was doing product development—"Why does this thing keep blowing up?"—I discovered that it's definitely not useful in building relationships. So I trained myself to substitute "How come?" for "Why?" and I recommend that you play with this or find an alternative that works for you.

Starting a sentence with the word *you* is less black-and-white in its effect. You can use *you* in conversation easily. "You have a great tan. I'll bet you had a great time on vacation." The problem is when you *start* with the word *you*, it can sound accusatory. "You always

do this. You did that." Unless it's a compliment, there are very
few sentences beginning with the word *you* that are going to put
people at ease.

4. Get the other person's name and repeat it so you can remember it;
then use it during your conversation.

5. Parrot the other person. All you need to do when they say something is repeat the last two or three words as a question. For instance, if somebody says, "I'm really tired today," all you have to
say is "Tired?" and that will invite them to go on and explain more
about what made them so tired. Were they out late? Did they run
a marathon? Are they having trouble sleeping? Parroting invites
them to give you more of a glimpse into their world.

You might imagine that simply repeating someone's words will
make the other person feel mimicked. Yet, if you do repeat their
words back to them, *without* any interpretation, they'll really feel
heard. You can also do this in a conversational way. If, for example,
I said to someone, "How's your day going?" and they said, "Oh,
don't ask," then I would say, "Okay, now I've got to ask. How's your
day been? What made you say that?"

6. Dig deeper. If you're pretty comfortable with the person, you can
even just say, "Because?" or "And that was because?" and see what
they tell you. These are nice ways of saying "why?" and it leads
them to give you more of a story. What you want is to avoid questions that have a yes-or-no answer.

7. Open the door to possibility. If somebody says, "Oh, I couldn't do
that," say "Oh, I know it's too hard, it's almost unthinkable, but I'm
wondering, what would it be like if you *could*?" The underlying
sense of that phrase is "I agree with you. I'm not disagreeing with
you. I agree with you that you can't, but I'm curious. I wonder what
would it be like if you could."

Here's an interesting thing about the way humans work. Whenever we hear a question, we're inclined to answer; we almost can't help doing this. Even if we don't respond out loud, we answer the question in our heads.

For example, if I were to say, "I wonder what your father would look like if he had green hair. Imagine that your father was there in a picture out in front of you; if he was standing maybe ten feet away from you with green hair, would it be light green or dark green? I don't know; what would it look like? Would his eyebrows match his hair?" Now your brain is making images—because that's the way brains work.

So questions are really powerful tools for guiding experience. You just want to make sure that when you're guiding someone's inner experience you're guiding them in a direction that will be pleasant for them to experience, so they'll like being around you.

Suppose someone lets me know how their day went, saying, "My boss was really short-tempered today. I think something is going on. He gave me an assignment and wouldn't give me any direction on how to do it." I'd say, "Oh, so you got an assignment and you didn't get the information on how to do it," and they'd say, "Yeah," and *then they'll go on*! The point is, they will feel that you really understand them. Because they feel heard, they're likely to tell you more.

8. At some point during this exchange, I could also say, "If I were you in that situation, that would make me feel pretty frustrated—or I might feel unappreciated." Using "feeling" words helps someone feel felt. As soon as you do that you've crossed over, and at some point in the conversation—and this happens time and time again—the other person leans forward and starts to talk. When that happens, that's the exhale. This is the point where you can talk.

9. Check for agreement. If you have something to propose, do so—and then check for agreement. For example, you might say, "How do you feel about this solution?" If the other person is hesitant or unwilling to reach an agreement, ask them, "What changes would you like to see that would make the agreement more acceptable, more fair?"

These nine recommendations will help you navigate the unpredictable waters of communication. When you're listening to another person, remember that it's always useful to ask yourself, "What has to be going on in that person's world for this to be true for them?" This question not only gives you a shot of empathy for the other person, it also gives you an insight into how they may be feeling.

The Local Language: How to Communicate According to *Someone Else's* Preferences

---

As you know, our language shows how we construct our thoughts, our inner reality—whether that's mostly through pictures, words and stories, feelings, or even scents or tastes. In Chapter 6, you learned that the predicates people use, their meta-programs, the way they reference time, and the beliefs they state as fact, reveal what's true for them. These details provide clues for how to deepen rapport and be persuasive.

There's an old saying, "When in Rome, do as the Romans do." Each of us has preferred modes of speech that reveal our preferred sensory arena. Once you know how someone is processing their experience, you can adapt your language to be more like theirs, right? That gives you a lot of power to connect with them, to have them feel that you are on their side, that you understand them. A funny thing is that when you step this far into someone else's world, you really do become more simpatico. You genuinely have a deeper understanding of their world—and consequently a greater appreciation for them as a person.

Let's explore an example of discovering and using someone's preferred channel of experience as revealed in the predicates they use.

ADAPTING TO PREFERRED REPRESENTATIONAL CHANNELS

Imagine that someone uses a lot of visual language. "It was clear as day to me." "It was the blackest sky" or "It looked completely wrong." How could you show them that you're on the same page?

If you're a highly visual person, too, this might be easy. But what if you were kinesthetic; would that feel like more of a stretch? (Remember, as kinesthetic processor you might *naturally* say, "I'm following you" or "That makes sense to me.") By shifting from your natural preference into *theirs*, you could say, "I see what you mean . . . I can imagine that . . ." or "That's crystal clear to me." And if you wanted to further explore what they were talking about, you might say, "I'm trying to get a clear picture of what you're looking for. Please tell me more about what you'd like to see happen. Can you shed some light on that?"

A salesperson selling a car to this visual person might say, "This car looks like it meets all the criteria on your list. Can't you just see yourself driving it? Imagine how great it would be to use this car for your summer vacations. I'd love to see a photo of your family in it when you go the Grand Canyon next month." If he wasn't getting a favorable response after showing them the car's features, the salesman could say, "It appears to me like you're hesitant, that this one's not *exactly* what you're looking for. I can keep an eye out for a car like this in that deep blue color you like . . ."

Speaking someone's language makes it easier for them to get the message you're sending simply because they have less to translate into their *preferred* channel of processing.

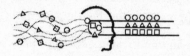

**Discovery Activity:
Using Predicates of
Preferred Channels**

So, how can you learn to speak someone else's language? Practice. Because making the adjustment may not come naturally to you, think of it as a game. Play with the language rather than be concerned whether it's right or wrong. Just for fun, read items 1a, 2a, and 3a. Then complete items 1b, 2b, and 3b to produce a short list of conversational phrases that you often hear. For example, after reading the sample visual word, you might write "I see what you mean" or "Feel free to look around" in the space provided in 1b. You can refer to (and add to) these whenever you're writing or when you want to adapt your language to someone else's preferred channel.

1A: LOOK AT THESE SAMPLE VISUAL WORDS

Descriptors: *clear/cloudy, light/dark, colorful/drab, big/little*
Verbs: *imagine, envision, see, watch*
Nouns: *vision, snapshot, picture, image*

1B: LIST COMMON CONVERSATIONAL VISUAL PHRASES YOU CAN IMAGINE

_____

_____

_____

_____

2A: LISTEN TO THESE SAMPLE AUDITORY WORDS

Descriptors: *loud/quiet, harmonious, dissonant, clear/flat*
Verbs: *whisper/shout, hear/listen, sing, echo*
Nouns: *sound/note, noise, tenor/tone, pitch*

2B: LIST COMMON CONVERSATIONAL AUDITORY PHRASES YOU CAN RECALL

_____

_____

_____

_____

3A: TRY ON THESE SAMPLE KINESTHETIC WORDS

Descriptors: *scary/inviting, chaotic/calm, sad/funny, good/bad*
Verbs: *sense/feel, reach/grab, kiss/slap, fly/fall*
Nouns: *impact, turnaround, crash, exploration*

3B: LIST COMMON CONVERSATIONAL KINESTHETIC PHRASES YOU FEEL ARE ON TARGET

_____

_____

_____

_____

For additional demonstrations and/or examples, go to http://eg.nlpco .com/7-1.

Adapting to Meta-Program Preferences

Adjusting your communication style can go a long way to creating harmony at work or at home. If someone's meta-program preferences are different from yours, try on theirs—and demonstrate your increasing flexibility by communicating in theirs. Let's take an example.

Imagine that your natural preference is *specific* and *away-from* and that your boss, who wants an update on a project you're working on, is a *toward* and *general*-oriented guy. You've noticed in the past that when you explain what you've been doing and spell out all the details, he kind of glazes over midway through your update. You'd like to avoid getting that reaction—and to feel more comfortable providing him with the information he wants. So, what can you do?

You could step into his shoes by asking yourself, "What's important to him about this project *and* what concerns might he have about it?" In trying to answer this question, you might reflect back to what he told you when you got the project and what his vision for it was—or even recall questions he's asked you during other project updates. Once you've identified some of your supervisor's criteria related to this project, you could make a brief outline that enables you to gift-wrap your succinct update in terms of *his* criteria. Give him the high points and be prepared to provide relevant details if asked.

Continuing with the scenario, imagine that you need your supervisor's support to light a fire under another department manager who looks like he won't deliver his group's part of the project at the agreed-upon time—which will really put you and your team up against a wall. If your boss is *toward* and you're *away-from*, you'd want to phrase your request accordingly, right?

You might *want* to say, "It's really a burden for my team when Bill's department drags their feet and makes it hard to meet the deadline. Can you do something?" But it would be more effective to say, "I know that this project is key to the new product launch. It's so exciting that we'll be the first in our industry to introduce this innovative tool. Can you help Bill's group stay focused on the target—so the whole project team can meet its deadline? I want to make sure we enjoy the longest window of opportunity we can." That's pretty different, right? Which one do you think would get the boss to encourage Bill's group to step things up?

These kinds of adjustments aren't just helpful at work—you'll find them helpful in all your relationships. Imagine that you and your significant other want to purchase a house. In this scenario, you're *proactive* and *toward*. You've found a house you like and are ready to move forward. Because your mate is more *away-from* and *external* you might *want* to say, "Let's get going on this right away; this house is really perfect for us. I can see us living there."

After stepping into your significant other's world, you *might* say instead, "Buying a house is a big decision for us. It seems like there are a lot of things we really like about this place and I don't think either of us wants to lose it to someone else. I'm wondering what kind of support will help us be more certain about our decision. Didn't your sister just buy a great house? Maybe she has some ideas, or what about Lee from your book group who used to be a Realtor?" This second approach reflects the significant other's world and is more likely to get a favorable response than "Let's do this"—isn't it?

Adapting to Time Differences

If someone you love or work with has a very different relationship to time, this can create some serious conflict. Part of this discord comes from the meaning we attach to these differences. Imagine, for example, that you are someone who's *through* time and your best friend is *in* time. Because of this difference, you often find yourself at a restaurant waiting twenty minutes before he shows up.

You might interpret their being late any number of ways. "He's so inconsiderate. He doesn't really want to spend time with me. I'm never as important as his work." Any of these things *might* be true but it's just as likely that because he's *in* time, he gets caught up in the present moment. He actually is unaware of what time it is, or how much time he needs to allot to the process of stopping what he's doing and getting on the road to meet you on time. He's only thinking about right now.

This difference might turn out to be a deal breaker for you; if it's not, what are some ways you could adapt your behavior and influence his? How could you try on what it's like to be more in the present moment? What would make you more comfortable during the times you are waiting for him to join you? Could you bring a book or play a game on your phone? If you're home, could you take that time to talk with a friend on the phone? How could you *enjoy* the waiting, so you're not telling yourself a story about why he's late or feeding the negative emotions that sometimes come up while waiting?

Perhaps you clearly identify occasions where it's critical that he's on time—such as meeting your parents for dinner or leaving for the airport two and a half hours before the flight. Maybe your partner would be open to setting a reminder alarm on his phone fifteen minutes before he needs to leave to meet you. Identifying nonnegotiables and useful tools can help you meet in the middle, because asking an *in-*

time person to be on time all the time could require more prompting than either of you would like.

Talking About Different Beliefs

Communicating about beliefs is fascinating, simply because someone else's can be so different from your own. Asking yourself, "What has to be going on in that person's world for this to be true for them?" is especially helpful when it comes to differences of opinion—or differences in beliefs.

As you now know, beliefs are mostly out of a person's awareness and are stated as fact. Because these ideas shape the person's view of the world, they are often dearly held—and can become a source of conflict.

Recently, I had a difference of opinion with a family member, and they were being pretty aggressive with their viewpoint, so I said, "And it *could* be something else. I'm just curious to know if you ever considered these possibilities." What I said might have, but didn't, make things better.

As things got hotter and hotter, I finally said, "You know, I bet you feel like I'm attacking you, and I'm getting the feeling you're attacking me. I don't want to attack you and I bet you don't want to attack me. I think we're reacting, not from our hearts now, but from our fears. Could we restart this conversation and get on the same side and just share what we feel and what we think?"

And he responded with "Oh yeah, sure, you're right. This is getting to be too much of a pain in the neck." He was really relieved when I suggested this, and it paid off for both of us. (In Chapter 8, you'll learn more ways to manage conflict.)

As a reminder, the first two rules of the road are critical when there's friction: don't interrupt, and don't contradict. I confess that, in the past, when I felt criticized, I'd contradict or get defensive. I felt compelled to stand up for myself—or to immediately give the other person solutions for their problem. I learned the hard way that having all the answers may earn someone a gold star in grade school, but in adult conversation, it's not appreciated.

What *is* appreciated most often is to let the other person vent. Until they've *completely* vented, they don't want you to talk. Once they seem to wind down, say, "Tell me more." That's the magic phrase.

In my personal *and* professional life, when I say either "Can you say more about that?" or "Tell me more," the person I'm talking with is usually responsive. Phrasing my requests this way brings me a lot more information, allows the person to settle down inside themselves, and sometimes reveals what it is they're thinking or what it is they're wrestling with. To really understand what's going on with the other person, *continue* to invite the other person to tell you more until they feel completely heard.

A New View:
How the Process of Reframing Expands Possibilities

When you're talking with someone who is experiencing some kind of difficulty, you can hear it in their language and use a beautiful strategy called "Reframing." Simply put, reframing is looking at a statement someone has made—then finding a more positive way to say it.

For example, if someone says, "I just can't get out of my own way today," you could say, "Oh, you can't get out of your own way today? What would it be like if you could?" Then their attention diverts to *if they could,* because questions are a very effective way of directing someone's thinking (including yours).

Have they tripped themselves up physically? Are they dropping papers all over the floor? Is their mind hard to focus? Have they said things they wish they hadn't? There are so many missing details. As you may recall from Chapter 6's discussion of the Meta Model, this is a place where you want to get more information.

Imagine that you do get some additional information and the person says, "Well, I just feel kind of down today. I don't feel like anything I do is going to work out well."

Then I might say something like, "Wow. When I have a feeling like that, I'm just wondering if there's something in there I should listen to." Now I've reframed it from just a down, defeated feeling to "Oh, maybe there's an interesting hint or an intuition in there. I should search for it," rather than to just say, "There, there—just ignore that. Just try to forget about it."

It's important to really listen and consider what somebody says. If they said, "I'm so sick of driving this beat-up old car," I might say, "I know—and I think you were really smart to keep driving that car instead of putting money into a new one while you're going to school."

There are ways of shifting what the person says—by changing the context or meaning they've made—so there's a new possibility that makes sense. Either way, what you want to do is just offer a different perspective on what they said—because we need to loosen things up a little.

I recommend being modest in your ambitions with these shifts. Expecting people to turn on a dime isn't really reasonable or practical. If you can just loosen things up a little when someone has a stiff set of beliefs—or if the beliefs are in their way or are an obstacle between the two of you—you're offering them more choices.

Sometimes just asking a question creates a desired change. Perhaps you can help people to loosen up a bad mood by inviting them to consider how they'd feel if they were in a better mood—by asking them what might need to take place for them to be in a better mood—or by inquiring what sort of shift in their thinking would result in a better mood.

Okay, so what has all of this got to do with persuading people?

When you make people feel better by genuinely getting in harmony with them and attending to their feelings—so it's about them and not you—guess what happens? They feel more comfortable with you, which makes them more receptive to you and what you have to say. According to Robert Cialdini, the author of *Influence: The Psychology of Persuasion,* these individuals will want to return the favor at some point simply because humans have an instinct for reciprocity.

So imagine that someone said, "I can't 'X.'" To reframe their statement for them, you could say, "Oh, so you *want* to 'X.'"

This may seem contrary, but here's why it's so effective. If they said, "I can't 'X,'" they must want to "X" or they wouldn't be complaining about not being able to, right? By saying, "Oh, so you want to 'X,'" you've agreed with them that they want to: you demonstrated understanding them. At the very same time, you've also moved their brain's focus from something that was impossible to something they want.

Let me share an example of a simple reframe that my friend Tom Dotz did with an acquaintance at his favorite restaurant. While he was waiting for his friend, the hostess came over to say hello. When he asked her how things were going for her, she let out a big sigh and said, "Well, I just turned twenty-nine and I really don't know what I want to do with my life."

Because she sounded a bit depressed, Tom was hoping to help her shift to a more positive feeling, so he asked her, "Well, if you did know what you *really* wanted, what would that be?"

Without missing a beat, she said, "I'd go to the Parsons School of Design and get my art degree." This desire seemed so clear to Tom that he was puzzled and asked, "Well, what stops you?"

She said, "It would take five years and I've be thirty-four."

At that point, her expression was bordering on despair so Tom said, "So let me get this straight. You really want to go to art school, but you're twenty-nine now, and you'd be thirty-four when you finished, right?"

"Yes" was the quick reply.

Then he said, "So what's really true is that in five years you'll be thirty-four. Your choice is simply that you'll either be thirty-four with your art degree, or you'll be thirty-four without it."

A look of astonishment came over her face just as Tom's friend arrived at the table. At this point, his conversation with the hostess was interrupted and she excused herself. Tom told me that he never thought much about this brief exchange until a few months later, when he went back to the restaurant. As soon as the hostess saw Tom, her face lit up and she rushed over to him. Before he could even say hello, she smiled and said, "You changed my life!"

Because this looked like good news to Tom, he asked, "How so?" At this point she described the brief conversation they'd had and proudly said, "Thanks to you, I applied to Parsons. I've been accepted, and I start school this fall! I've only got three more weeks here and I'll be moving back east." Then she gave Tom a big hug and led him and his friend to their table.

It was just a quick chat, right? How could it have such a powerful impact as to change a person's life? Here's how: when you make this tiny shift in someone's attention, it engages a whole different part of that person's brain. They move from being stuck to actually considering other possibilities. And to help them along, as you notice them *beginning* (within five or ten seconds) to consider possibilities, you could say, "I know you can't but I'm curious, what would it be like if you *could*?" Then "That sounds great. What would be necessary? Would it take more planning or more time, or do you need more connections or money? What do you think? What would it take?"

As you know from earlier chapters, questions like "What would you like instead?" or "What's important to you about that?" also open people's minds—and open the door to other possibilities.

As someone starts thinking, more and more of the brain is engaged—their blood chemistry changes *and* their mood changes. Even if you just stopped after the first reframe and *didn't* continue to explore possibilities, you will have left somebody in a more positive, hopeful, optimistic state of mind—when before they were negative, turned off, and limiting themselves.

Here's why even a small reframe can make a big difference: When somebody's angry or frustrated, they cannot be curious. People can't have those two emotions at the same time—and curiosity is the natural course of creativity—not anger and frustration. You have a lot more neurons available when you're curious about something.

Super-Glue Removal:
How to Loosen and "Unstick" Beliefs

Even though curiosity is a powerful tool for "unsticking" yourself or someone else, a firmly held belief can be even more powerful. Some beliefs have a really strong grip. So if I were going to help someone with a difficulty, the first thing I'd do is unpack the belief itself. How is the belief expressed? In other words, what is the reality that this person sees or hears or feels?

Is it a voice in their head, or an image, or a feeling—perhaps one they "just can't shake"? For instance, when it's an image, I've found that when they can really look at the image associated with the belief, it's turned out to be a bogus mental movie that just loops around and around, playing over and over. It has an impact simply because it's *stuck* in the unconscious. Since it's usually unconscious, the client is usually only aware of the feelings the mental movie "loop" causes. And then those negative feelings tend to get associated with whatever happens to be going on in his present experience.

Their World: Understanding Someone's Belief

Let's explore an example of how this unpacking process might unfold. A person can say, "I have low self-confidence," but I don't know what that means to them. I can't duplicate their experience in my brain based on that statement. Could you? Probably not. Then I might say, "Okay, I get that you have low self-confidence. Can you tell me a little more about how you experience that?" My ambition at this point is to get enough information, and *specific* enough information, so I can re-create that experience and that feeling myself.

Then I try on what they tell me, and see what that's like. For example, it might be an inner dialogue that sounds like this: "Okay, so if I hear the voice of my college teacher, my mom, or whoever it was, telling me I'll never amount to anything, and I hear it coming from behind and above my head, and I hear it just as I'm about to step out onstage, yeah, that would probably bug the hell out of me. That would definitely limit me."

So now I can say to that person, "Okay, I can understand that. I can re-create that experience for myself, using my body and my own senses as an instrument. Now I can understand and appreciate how you must feel."

The key is to realize that people give us very high-level condensed reports on their inner process because they don't know what their inner process is. But when we help them slow the process down, they can give some key details and we can ask enough questions to understand how they create this internal experience for themselves. Then we do two things.

First, we try to replicate that process in ourselves. We try it on and continue to gather information until we can re-create their experience. Second, we look for the positive intention behind this experience, because nobody has an inner enemy. People have a lot of habits that in the present are completely unwelcome and inappropriate, yet when you find the part that is maintaining that pattern, you'll find a positive intention.

Two Cases in Point: Exploring, Finding, and Shifting a Belief

I had a thirty-four-year-old client who didn't want to talk in public. Because he was a teacher, he *had* to. Fortunately, he managed to find himself a niche where he could do almost all of his work in writing and when he was in class, he basically read from his notes. He didn't really give a presentation at all.

In talking with him, I found out that he'd once, as a little kid, given a presentation at his church. Afterward, although he thought he'd done well, he discovered that his mother was very embarrassed for him. Now, I don't know how he really did (probably nobody knows), but he initially thought he did well. People applauded after his presentation, but his mother was embarrassed because he mispronounced or forgot something—and she made a point of bringing this to his attention.

Even though his mother's intention was probably to help him do better on his next presentation, the shock of her embarrassment went into his experience—and part of his brain said, "Boy, I'm never going to do this again." So for decades he carried this inhibition about talking out loud in front of a group.

As he and I worked together, we found that piece of inner dialogue and came to understand that its positive intention was to keep him from disappointing his mother. His mother had been present at all of his graduations, had been applauding him when he got his doctorate degree, and was now living in a house that he'd purchased for her from his earnings as a college professor.

Although his adult mind knew that she was proud of him, this other part had still been operating. Once he could understand that this childhood belief was just linked to trying to protect him as a little boy—a protection he no longer needed—it went away and so did the inhibition. From that point on, he was able to make an effective presentation, not just read his notes and avoid the audience.

In contrast, I worked with a thirty-eight-year-old attorney who had stage fright about having to talk in front of a board of directors. It turns out what inhibited him was not a voice, but an image. In our discussions, we explored the last time he made an important group presentation. The way he had this filed in his mind was as a picture of him in the well of one of those Victorian-era operating rooms. He was at the bottom, and the seats in the amphitheater around him were raised—so the audience was looking down on him from twenty feet above.

He was down at the bottom and he was about three feet tall. And when he looked up at the seats around him, there weren't people in these seats. They were all like Easter Island figures—these imposing stone statues of odd-shaped heads—and the eyes were all blank.

When I reproduced that image, I could tell him with sincerity and compassion that seeing this in my mind's eye made me feel very unsettled, too. When we examined this unconscious image, we were able to identify the initial positive intention and update his self-image *and* the way he thinks and feels about speaking to the board of directors or anyone with authority.

When we're trying to help ourselves (or someone else) process differently, it's a trap to think that there's a cut-and-dried fix for every condition. There's not.

However, because so many of these conditions can be traced back to similar causes, you only need a small set of tools to help make these shifts. We're all just flavoring our memories and our conversations and our conclusions from past experience. We're generalizing them so that we can operate on them in the future using those principles that we define for ourselves. "That's the way the world is, or that's how the world's always going to treat me."

In an attempt to automate that behavior—like we automate tying our shoes—we make assumptions that can sometimes be limiting to us. So it's always wise to say, "Tell me more," rather than focus on a technique or solution. You'll discover that your voracious curiosity for understanding how another human being works is such a gift.

Understanding is always about someone's *process*. Because it's easy to be seduced by words and content, we might sincerely relate to someone's experience and be excited to move directly to a solution. Replicating another person's process in sensory terms is always the key to really getting their reality.

Because you now understand how your own mind works, you'll remember as they tell you about their process that it, too, can be broken down into feelings, sounds, pictures, tastes, and smells. So when a person gives a really general complaint, like "Well, you know, I don't get this job, I can't do it," you recognize that this is way too limited; you can't do anything with it.

After all, when people generalize about their limits, they've taken themselves out of human experience. What you want to do is take a person to the last time they actually felt the feelings they're describing to you, so they can feel it again. At this point, they can tell you what's going on. They can't tell you at the outset, so you have to guide them back there.

"When was a time this happened for you?"

"Oh, it happened to me last week."

"Oh? Tell me about it." Then you watch and listen. You hear the words, you hear how they're chosen, and you hear the assumptions in their language. You do this because you're trying to become them—to understand how they create this feeling themselves.

My experience of unpacking beliefs and exploring difficulties is that the first, second, and third steps usually involve getting a complaint that's expressed in high-level terms like "I'm detached. I'm uninvolved." You'll get these abstract conclusions that you must pare down into specific pictures, sounds, and feelings that you can reproduce in your own mind and body. Once you can do that, you have the information you need to help yourself—or someone else—make a positive shift.

It's Kind of Like That:
How Metaphors and Stories Support Shifts

Metaphor is another powerful and fun way to help people shift or change their attitudes and attention. It's no accident that we've been telling each other stories since the days that tribes sat around campfires. They'd stare into the flames and tell each other what happened on the hunt, what happened with the baby back at home while you were out on the hunt, and what so-and-so said or did.

If you think about it, there are thousands and thousands of stories in your life—family stories, work stories, community stories, world stories. Let's take a simple story like Jack and the Beanstalk. Jack's mom tells him to go sell the cow because they need money, they need to get firewood, and he gets talked into trading the cow for three magic beans.

So she spanks him with a wooden spoon and puts him to bed without supper, and she's brokenhearted because she lost the cow and this idiot boy came back with beans. She throws them out the window—and the next morning there's a huge beanstalk.

Jack, who's not going to be real welcome at the breakfast table anyway, gets curious so he climbs the beanstalk. He climbs it and climbs it, and gets up above the clouds, and he's in this magical realm where everything is much larger than it is down where he lives. The chairs are bigger and everything's bigger—and, of course, this is a place that's lived in by a giant.

The harp, who is the giant's captive, tells him where the giant keeps his gold and then helps Jack escape. So, as they go back down the beanstalk, they're being chased by the giant, who's roaring that he's going to kill them, and then Jack chops down the beanstalk and the giant falls and is destroyed.

When hearing this, did you at any time think you were the giant? Probably not. You took on the identity of Jack. You went and got conned out of your mom's cow for the beans. You came back home and you went to bed without supper, and the next morning you climbed the beanstalk.

Here's why that happens. The human brain usually identifies with the hero. Each of us is the star of our own lives, right? We all know that. This is more than just a platitude. This is an operating psychological reality: We each live in the center of a world that's created in our own minds. We're pulled out of that world sometimes—if we're at the movies, watching TV, immersed in a book, or sometimes if we're with someone else—but generally, we're in the center of a world of our own making.

So why is this important now? The way we bridge the gap from one soul, from one mind to another, from one heart to another, is with our senses and with the skills that we've talked about so far. We reach out and touch one another. We look into each other's eyes. We get into rapport. We share our experiences with each other.

One of the nicest and most neutral ways to exchange information is to tell a story. Most stories are interesting, right? However, if the story is told by a narcissist, then the story is all about "me, me, me"—and that's probably not going to be very interesting.

It can be a story that happened to you and yet it's not all about you, you, you. It's just about something that happened. If you're simply a normal mortal in the story, you can be astonished, surprised, embarrassed, afraid, frustrated, and the other person will go right along with that because they'll feel the same way.

Stories can entertain, inform, educate, and unite people. You can use stories to help someone make a shift. As you know, when we try to *persuade* someone, they often experience us as pushy—then they push back. You, in turn, might want to try harder. This pushing can become a vicious cycle where nobody can win. What you need to do is step back a little and maybe even zoom out to third position to objectively check things out. But at some point, should you want to *make* a point, you can simply tell a story.

Once Upon a Time: A Case in Point

With my grown daughter, I used to try to strongly suggest that she do certain things. After all, I'm a generation older. I know how a lot of this stuff turns out, but that doesn't get me anything because (surprise, surprise) she wants to lead her own life. She's not interested in letting me lead her life, or letting me get a second shot at leading my own, and she's right.

So what I've learned to do is listen and then—kind of as an afterthought—say, "Look, I don't know if this will work for you, but this worked for me once. It's something you might think about, or not. It's up to you," and I just leave it at that.

Sometimes a story about *someone else's* challenge and success is even more effective than a story about your own experience. If I had a relevant example, I could say, "You know, I had a client who had a similar challenge in her work. She's not you, and your situation is different, but this is what happened . . ."

Then I'd tell her the story of this woman who was being hit on by her boss, or someone who'd gotten credit for work *she'd* done stolen from her, or a guy whose customer had unreasonable expectations. I'd tell her some story that related to the work situation that we were discussing.

Here's the beautiful part about a story. My daughter could be saying in her mind or she could be saying out loud to me, "Dad, I don't need any help with this. I've got it. Thanks. I can deal with it. I'm a grown woman," all of which is true because she's a superb woman. But even if she's quietly protesting, she's going to hear the story anyway out of politeness. And as she hears the story, she's going to identify with that other client that I was talking about, and she's going to experience what that other client experienced. She's going to experience a success. So in her mind, no matter what her attitude, she will have tried that solution on.

A Book and Its Cover: How Appearance and Environment Are Clues to Other Worlds

I won't say that people are like an open book, because while some folks are easy to understand, others remain a mystery. Often, though, the cover of the book will attract you and reflect something about the quality of the read itself, and the same is true with people.

Here's another example of how metaphor works in our lives. Let's say that you're out to dinner with friends and you're joined by somebody you don't know, a friend of a friend. The person is introduced to you as somebody that you might want to get better acquainted with, maybe because you could help each other professionally, or because you want to learn a skill they have, or because you have common interests and connections, or for some other reason he or she is somebody that you'd be interested in knowing better.

Because each of us lives in metaphor, one of the first things you want to do is just to look at them. Our whole lives are a metaphor for what we believe and how we live. We each tell ourselves a story about our lives, and we dress according to that inner story. Our choice of clothes, hairstyle, jewelry, shoes—*everything* reflects that story. Although we may sometimes feel like these choices are forced on us, they aren't. In a life where there are millions and millions and millions of free choices, people are often astonished at how consistently those choices will reinforce their personal metaphors.

A Case in Point: Personal Appearance

I'll give you an example. I like personal comfort. I've had many jobs where I was on my feet all day. I've been in a lot of service occupations and I've been in management for about forty-five years now, usually moving around. So I used to wear moccasins a lot. I'm casual, obviously. I don't wear starched white shirts and neckties. Now I wear Merrells, which are walking shoes that I can slip in and out of easily. I wear Levi's, khakis, or cargo pants, and I like wearing shirts that have two pockets on the front. They're handy for me. I'm a guy who's had lots of different occupations that frequently involved tools so I like to carry a lot of stuff with me.

So what does that make me? That makes me kind of an explorer, a person who likes to go on adventures like safaris. I've got a little knife in my pocket with a little flashlight attached, I have a cool pen that does different things, I have a tiny screwdriver that works on machines and my glasses. You get the picture, right? I try to be ready for just about everything, like a Boy Scout. So you could say a lot of things about me just from the way I'm dressed and the way I present myself—and these observations would help you know how to approach me to make me feel comfortable and interesting, right?

One of the ways to get to know another person is to ask about something they have in their office or home, or about something they're wearing, "That's a really interesting necklace you're wearing. I'm fascinated by it. How did you come to choose that?" and then they'll tell you. It was given as a gift or they acquired it at a certain place, but what you're really interested in is getting them to tell you what *they* value about that possession. What they tell you is important about it will let you know a lot about their values and who they are.

A Case in Point: A Personal Possession

As an example, I had a business associate, who was a fifty-something very buttoned-down attorney. He was a very well placed, very skilled corporate attorney who was very well-off, and for decades we were friends.

Over the years that he provided some legal assistance in my various businesses, I noticed that he always used the same pen. It was sort of a fancy silver pen with some kind of crosshatching on it. I'd never seen one quite like it before so I asked him about it once.

A big grin lit up his face and he went on to tell how this pen—not this particular pen, but one very much like it—had been given to him by his wife when he passed the bar exam, and how he had had it for years and years and years. It was manufactured by Cross and he loved it. But one day he lost it and he didn't want his wife to know, so he contacted Cross and tried to get another one. And because they didn't make it anymore and he couldn't track down another one, he found someone to make him a custom pen that looked exactly the same!

This story gave me a whole new impression of his love for his wife, his appreciation of her support, and his consideration for her. It also let me know that little things were really important to this man. Again, an innocent question opened up a whole world of someone else's reality to me.

As you can see, playing with stories is fun. When you plan to tell a story, be sure the protagonist is interesting. It's probably you or someone you know. And by interesting I don't mean somebody out of a novel, I mean somebody just like you and me. Tell a story about someone who feels real and about something that happened that would be interesting to you. Ideally, this story will contain one or two key ideas you want to share with your listener.

That information could be "I knew somebody who was in the same jam that you're in, and they came out okay," or "I know somebody who was in the same jam you're in, and everything went a little wacky for a while and they survived it anyway. It's survivable," or "I know somebody who had the same opportunity as you did and passed it up, and here's what that cost them," or "I know someone who had the same issue that you have, and here's how they solved it."

In examining my own experience and hearing about other people's lives, I find that we're okay until we become really *convinced* of something, and then as soon as we do that, we shut off all the other possibilities. That's when we get into trouble. There are lots of ways that you can use a metaphor or a story to soften your conversations with people and to loosen their grip on a conviction that's limiting them. Just telling a story is a lot less confronting than directly contradicting someone; it leaves them freer to come to their own choices without having to feel they've "given in."

Toxic Relationships:
How Difficult People Tax Your Personal Resources

You might be thinking, "Cool, I can easily do this kind of exploration and match the way someone processes, or use reframing or metaphor to help a lot of people." Yes, you can—and yet you'll find that making this energy investment will not pay off with everyone. So let's talk a little bit about toxic people.

In my view of the world, a toxic person is someone who's basically kind of a pain in the neck. It may be a bully, or a critic who makes himself feel good by putting you down, or putting other people down. It may be a whiner, who isn't really interested in *any* solution. They'd rather just complain, because that's enough for them. They may be a psychopath of one sort or another. They may be a taker, having no real interest in you, other than what they can get from you. They could be a narcissist. Or they could be someone who is basically just frozen in first position, almost exclusively self-centered.

Remember the first, second, and third perceptual positions? As we've discussed, first position is "I know who I am. I'm me and you're you and we're different and I know what I feel." That's a very authentic position; however, it can be infantile if that's the *only* position a person has.

Second position is "Now I'm feeling *for* you. Now I'm thinking that if I were you, and what happened to you happened to me, I'd feel pretty much like you do." That's the position where you get great empathy and compassion for someone else.

The third position is a fact-finding position where you can evaluate. This position is sort of disassociated because you're not emotional about what you're evaluating. You can be well meaning, you can be kind, but you're not really sucked into the emotions of the moment.

Many toxic people have no second position. They cannot empathize. They cannot feel what it's like to be somebody else. They're not even interested in anybody else; that ability got pruned away when they were little kids. As we discussed earlier, it's necessary for sanity and health to be able to flicker between all three positions appropriately, and that simply isn't possible for most toxic people.

So what can you do about the toxic people who are in your life? If you want your life to be easier and happier, it's wisest and simplest to just remove them from your life wherever and whenever you can.

Frequently, people I'm coaching find themselves in a relationship with a toxic person and, for one reason or another, they can't end it. Maybe the toxic person is a relative, or an employer, or someone whom they feel they *have to* put up with. In that case my advice is "Okay, but don't expect to change that person. The relationship with that person is always going to be a one-way exchange where they ask and you give, so just know that." Just being clear about your choice to tolerate them *knowing* they won't change will help free you from some of the bad effects of having them in your life.

On the other hand, if you're the supervisor of a toxic employee, work with human resources to improve performance, or move them out. As you well know if you have one toxic employee, they affect the whole team and work environment, and not in any good way. They almost always drag the whole team down to their level of behavior and frequently drive off the good ones. It's important to fix the situation quickly even if it costs you something to dislocate and replace the person. If the toxic person is the boss, it's probably worth finding another job, even in a bad economy.

When the toxic person is a family member, this is a challenge that requires good boundaries. That means you have to understand and again accept that there are some people you cannot help or change.

They may not be able to change or they may not perceive a need to change. You can offer information. You can sometimes shift their attention—but that's it. People need to live their own lives—do their own activities, make their own choices.

Communicating your boundaries *can* be done humanely and lovingly—and still get the job done. For example, you can say, "Here's the way the situation is for me. When you do this, it's inconvenient for me, so I don't want you to do that anymore." Or "When you do that, I have this inconvenience, so I can't do that with you anymore." This way, you're not condemning anyone, you're only pointing out what your limitation is—and why you can't do it anymore.

The best boundaries are boundaries that aren't defensive or offensive; they just exist.

There are people whom I've told, "I'm sorry, I just don't have the time for that."

In response, they sometimes said, "Isn't this important to you?"

"Actually, no—it's not. It's important to you and I understand that, but with my responsibilities and where I am in my life, I'm sorry but I can't take the time for that." When this happens, I will usually recommend an alternative—a connection, a book, workshop, or website.

I'm older now and I've stopped beating my head against the brick wall of toxicity. Too many times, my intentions were good, but I was trying to help people live their lives or I was actually trying to live their lives *for* them.

As a result, my investments of personal energy didn't work out well. I suffered, and sometimes the most important folks in my life did, too. When it comes to toxic people, you have to set limits—budget for how many of them will be in your life and how much of your time or other resources you'll spend with them, and do not have any expectation that you'll get anything in return.

Connecting the Dots:
Linking Key Concepts and Skills to Opportunities

This chapter has been about connecting the dots—understanding how to build on things you've noticed about someone's inner world—so you can communicate even better with people you know—and those you will meet.

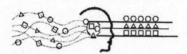 ### Discovery Activity:
Applying Your Discoveries
About Someone Else's World

Here's an activity that will help you apply your knowledge and observations to interactions with someone you already know. In Chapter 6, you selected a person you're close to and answered several questions that invited you to peek into and explore that individual's inner world. You identified the way you think they relate to time, their preferred representational channel and meta-programming patterns, and some beliefs you've heard them express.

Flip back to the notes you made in Chapter 6. For *each* of the answers you gave, list at least two specific things you could do to "try on" their world, or enhance communication with them.

Then, as you interact with this person, use these potential steps, discreetly or overtly, and notice how it changes your experience and the tenor of the interaction.

This activity will help you put what you learned from this chapter into practice. Consistently challenging yourself every day to play with small changes in your language will deepen your understanding and appreciation of its power. In Chapter 8, you'll learn how to build on these skills to more creatively collaborate and resolve conflicts.

Key Ideas

- Moving someone from resisting to listening to considering depends more on what you get *them* to tell you than the other way around.

- Stepping back or "zooming out" gives someone psychological air and space to exhale when they appear to be tense or feeling pushed.

- Asking, "What has to be going on in that person's world for this to be true for them?" is a way to stand in someone else's shoes and get a sense of their internal experience.

- To speak someone else's language, it's helpful to adapt to and mirror *their* preferences, their preferred representational channel and meta-programs, and their orientation to time.

- Beliefs are mostly out of a person's awareness and are stated as fact. Because these ideas shape the person's view of the world, they are often dearly held and can become a source of conflict, or of close agreement and rapport.

- When someone is stuck or seems like they're struggling with a limiting belief, reframing is a simple, subtle, and effective way to suggest a more positive perspective.

- Unpacking a belief to understand how it's expressed (pictures, sounds, etc.) and the associated positive intention increases the possibility of loosening the belief so it can be updated.

- When asked a question, the human mind can't help but create an answer. Asking questions that open up possibilities engages more of the listener's brain—which, in turn, changes their blood chemistry and their mood.

- Metaphors and stories are powerful and fun ways to shift someone's attention and attitude. Sharing anecdotes or tales often works well because the listener instinctively relates to the protagonist and can't help but try on the situation and the solution as they listen.

- Because we all live our lives in metaphor, someone's appearance, their toys, and their environment (in addition to their language) provide a glimpse into their unique map of the world.

- Inner conflicts that have been reduced to a condensed report like "I'm really disconnected" are too generalized and abstract to work with. Finding a specific (ideally recent) experience can provide enough sensory information to "try on" the other person's reality.

- If we establish sufficient rapport, most people will respond well to us. They will accept our efforts to mirror nonverbals, match predicates and meta-program language, as well as loosen and reframe beliefs, which will generally make life more interesting and fun for both of us.

- Our efforts to help someone shift may not always be welcome or appreciated. Sometimes this is because we may have misread the extent of our rapport (and the permission that gives us) or we were inappropriately inserting ourselves.

- Other times our efforts are unaccepted because some people are so self-focused they're kind of toxic. Reducing the amount of contact with such individuals or maintaining clear boundaries can protect our energy and enable us to focus on what's most important in *our* worlds.

To enhance the skills you learned in this chapter, check out the recommended Bonus Activities at our special "Essential Guide" website: http://eg.nlpco .com/7-4 or use the QR code with your phone.

Discoveries, Questions, Ideas, and Stuff You Want to Work On

_____

_____

_____

_____

_____

_____

_____

_____

_____

_____

_____

_____

_____

_____

_____

_____

_____

_____

_____

_____

_____

_____

_____

Discoveries, Questions, Ideas, and Stuff You Want to Work On

_____

_____

_____

_____

_____

_____

_____

_____

_____

_____

_____

_____

_____

_____

_____

_____

_____

_____

_____

_____

_____

CHAPTER EIGHT: CREATIVELY COLLABORATING AND RESOLVING CONFLICTS

How do we get from here to there?

> Creativity is a lot like looking
> at the world through a kaleidoscope.
> You look at a set of elements,
> the same ones everyone else sees,
> but then reassemble those floating bits and
> pieces into an enticing new possibility.
> —Rosabeth Moss Kanter

In NLP, we think that choice is better than no choice. Curiosity and creativity are pathways to more choice—they enable you to play with the different pieces of any situation and discover new possibilities. In this chapter, you'll learn how to build on the knowledge and skills you've learned so far and apply them to opportunities for collaboration, innovation, and conflict resolution.

An Embarrassing Example

To set the framework for the exploration we're about to make, here's a story. This happened during a year I was traveling *a lot*—I was in lots of hotel rooms, lots of restaurants, lots of airports—in lots of different towns. And, because I was *expecting* to see something, I didn't see what was right in front of me.

After a while, when you're moving around that much, you just expect certain things—like the paper towel dispensers in the men's restroom—to work in a particular way. In public restrooms, there are these black plastic contraptions on the wall by the sink, right? Some have little seeing eyes and when you wave your hands in front of them in *just* the right way, they burp out a stingy little towel. Other times, there's a button on the front or on the side—and that's really messy because everyone with wet hands has to press the same button.

Anyway, I was at the sink with wet hands in this men's room. When I waved my hands and nothing happened, I waved them again, closer. Nothing! Then I waved them *under* the place where the towels come out. *Still* nothing. So I waved my hands right *in front* of the thing. Again, nothing! I'm thinking, "Is this damn thing blind?"

Then I saw a little silver round thing on the side. Thinking it was a button, I pushed it. It was a rivet. Next, I pushed on a plate with the trademark and another thing that turned out to be another rivet. Nothing.

Then, being a hotshot engineer and an experienced traveler, I looked at the slot where the towels come out and wondered, "Can I just pull one out even if the machine's busted?" I saw the edge of a towel sticking out so I pulled it and it popped right out.

It worked just like a towel dispenser did in the good old days—turns out, that's exactly what it was. It was an old-fashioned dispenser that *looked like* one of the new ones—no buttons, no seeing eye, just a slot where you reach up and pull out a paper towel.

What really struck me is that the *simplest* thing was the *last* thing that occurred to me, not the first. Because I was on autopilot, I was expecting something and I didn't see what I *might* have been able to see if I had just tried the simplest thing first, or if I'd just been curious.

After this experience, I found myself wondering, "How often am I on autopilot? How often do I *assume* that I know how something, or someone, works? How often do I assume that I know what *I'm* doing or what the *right* way is?" A lot, it turns out. With this awareness, I began looking at my behaviors, as well as how other people were communicating and acting. I set my filters to notice unspecified expectations and challenges, and be curious about what I observed.

I found no shortage of examples! But rather than tell you about all the bumps and bruises I witnessed, I'd like to share a *contrasting* example.

Moving in the Same Direction: Effective Collaboration Using the Well-Formed Outcome Model

An NLP classmate of mine was a senior manager at Hewlett-Packard when we learned how to create Well-Formed Outcomes. At that time, he was leading a $500 million business unit and often fantasized about how much more his team could accomplish if everyone were really on the same page. He said that sometimes he felt that work was like white-water rafting. He explained that because they weren't paddling *together*, the trip had unnecessary lulls, dangerous vertical drops, and difficult points of navigation. And, he said, they were missing a lot of the camaraderie and fun of mastering the big water.

Even though his people were knowledgeable and motivated, he was often surprised by how folks were out of sync when it came to the vision for a project, product, division, or even the whole company. They didn't always see the big picture. And from his vantage point in the organization, he didn't always see or understand the challenges that inhibited progress toward specific goals.

By using the Well-Formed Outcome questions with his direct reports (and theirs), he was able to make the elements of and obstacles to success more visible. In the context of a specific opportunity at Hewlett-Packard, he and his team answered:

- What specifically do we want?

- How will we know when we've achieved that—and when we achieve this, what else will improve?

- Under what circumstances, where, when, and with whom, do we want to have this result?

- What stops us from having our desired outcome already?

- What resources (our existing ones and perhaps additional ones) do we need to help us create what we want?

- How are we going to get there—and what's the first step to begin to achieve this result?

The process of exploring the opportunity together helped him foster honest communication about objectives and issues; clarify key initiatives, philosophy, and company goals; encourage creativity; reward collaboration; and come up with useful solutions.

Because employees were reenergized and results were outstanding, he and his team got noticed. Other managers called to find out what he was doing differently. In a very short time, many HP managers throughout the United States adopted this model. Whenever they started a new initiative or found themselves face-to-face with a challenge, they applied the Well-Formed Outcome questions. Not only did this model provide them with a productive track to run on, it also helped to create a common language of leadership within the company—even internationally!

As you know from Chapter 2, the Well-Formed Outcome model works well when you use it on your own issues—*and* it works well in team or group situations. In fact, it beautifully illustrates Henry Ford's philosophy that "if everyone is moving forward together, then success takes care of itself."

Creativity: How Imagination Expands Possibilities

The Well-Formed Outcome model invites you and others to be creative, doesn't it? It requires you to envision what you want, anticipate issues, communicate with others, and reach a shared solution. *This* kind of creativity multiplies your options.

There's that word—*creativity*. I've noticed that some of my clients associate creativity with unpleasant school experiences. If that's true for you, you might be thinking, "No, wait, *I'm* not creative. I can't draw. I can't perform. I'm not the funniest person in the room." Fortunately, those old yardsticks are gone. As an adult, if you're not an artist by trade, creativity is usually about using imagination, just playing with different elements and possibilities.

A Case in Point: Untapped Creativity

Let's revisit the towel dispenser situation for a minute. Just picture me standing there with my wet hands—waving my hands and waving my hands and waving my hands. But, as you know, that didn't work to turn on this particular machine. There I was talking to myself, "Well, it *must* be a button," which led me to push everything on the machine that looked like it might be a button. But just by pulling on the towel that was sticking out, I got what I wanted. It was the easiest thing in the world, right? But not for me—because I had *assumed* I knew what I was doing. I had assumed I knew the nature of this thing.

Even though this experience was enlightening, it was also kind of embarrassing. After all, I'm a trained engineer. I'm fairly creative. I've got patents on some complex, innovative, and in-demand products. But because I was not in the lab or my writing studio, I wasn't telling myself, "Oh, turn on the creative, Tom." This was different. Because I was in a men's restroom and I wasn't really thinking much at all. In fact, I was barely present—let alone bringing *all* of myself to the task.

FREEING UP INNER RESOURCES

So part of being creative is reminding yourself of all the things that you are, all the resources you have, and all the possibilities that you have. As you know, inner work comes first. When you want to access your creativity, use the same process of calming yourself that you would if you were preparing to enter a room of strangers, participate in a negotiation, or facilitate a conflict resolution between family members or colleagues. Loosening yourself up and dropping your filters will help you get into a more creative state of mind.

The next thing to do when you decide you want or need to be creative is to get yourself unstuck. To do this, start by realizing that whatever issue you're considering, it is *not* part of you. It's not *you;* it's not even about you. It's out there somewhere. So place it out there. By using disassociation to separate yourself from it, you can easily see it at a slight distance. Now you can turn it sideways, upside down, add things to it, pull things apart, and see it in different colors. You can start to play with the issue, whatever it is.

To get your creative juices and confidence flowing, it's also useful to recall other times you were creative, times when you found effective solutions to a challenge. If accessing such memories is difficult, think of situations when you've been part of a creative team and how the powerful synergy of working together helped you find innovative answers.

Expert Advice: The Disney Creativity Strategy

In a moment, I'll share one approach that was identified by NLP leader Robert Dilts. In his book *Strategies of Genius,* he explored the unique creative processes of different geniuses. Using the principles of NLP modeling, he was successful at getting inside their heads and finding out what really goes on with them. What are they saying to themselves? What are they thinking? What are they seeing?

Robert got so good at this, he not only did it with people that he knew or interviewed, but he did it with creative legends in history. In his three-book series, he modeled Einstein, Aristotle, Mozart, Leonardo da Vinci, Jesus, Tesla, and Disney.

As you know, Walt Disney was one of the most creative people to live in the twentieth century. Disney was a gifted film producer, director, screenwriter, animator, voice actor, and entrepreneur. Not only did he create Mickey Mouse, Donald Duck, and Pluto, but he also animated the German fairy tale "Snow White and the Seven Dwarfs" and brought us many other movies. In addition to making films, in the 1950s he got into TV *and* created Disneyland—the first-ever theme park. Because of his genius for entertaining, Disney was even selected as the head of pageantry for the 1960 Winter Olympics.

Today the Walt Disney Company has its own TV channel, musical artists, ice-skating productions, cruise lines—and who knows what they'll create next!

Several years ago, I had the privilege of spending several hours with the Disney Company's number three and four guys. I got to talk with Mike Vance, who designed Disney World in Florida, and then Ken Carr, who designed nearby Epcot Center. They both shared a lot of stories about Walt Disney that perfectly match up with Robert Dilts's take on the man. It's just another way of validating Disney's creativity process—which you'll find amazing. So here it is.

Although Disney's creativity was initially intuitive, over time he developed a process for tapping into his special genius. When he was trying to conceive something new, he would assume three roles that he isolated: the roles of the Dreamer, the Realist, and the Critic. The reason his system works so well is this: he took on these roles *one at a time. He kept the Realist and the Critic in their places until he fulfilled the Dreamer role.*

THE DREAMER

First, he *became* the Dreamer. He said he had a special chair in the room and the Dreamer would appear and sit in that chair—and then the Dreamer would dream. The Dreamer would come up with this crazy ride, let's say Pirates of the Caribbean. While he was dreaming, he'd imagine everything he wanted to be part of that experience.

The ride would go through the bayous. There'd be crawfish. There'd be banjos. There'd be snakes and alligators and dim lights and pirates and "Ho, ho, ho!" and buried treasure and sabers and gold coins and sand—all the things he wanted.

In this role, he would only make notes about everything he could think of that he wanted in that dream, because that's the Dreamer's job. The Dreamer's job is to dream. The Dreamer's job is not to go, "Yeah but . . ." So that was it, just the Dreamer.

THE REALIST

Then the Dreamer would leave the stage and in would come the Realist, who would sit in a *different* chair. The Realist didn't say, "Yeah but . . ." either. The realist would say, "Oh, I see—and I know how you could make that happen. And we could use this over here. No, you probably can't go to the Caribbean and bring that over to Anaheim then stick that in the Pirates of the Caribbean ride, but here are some things we *could* do."

"We could have recorded insect sounds, and we could actually have misters to raise the humidity level. We could have heated air blasted in so if we enclosed the ride, we could actually make it feel just like it was down in the tropics." The Realist is the person who takes the concepts and makes them real.

Now, of course, some limits would apply, right? For example, the Dreamer may dream up antigravity and the Realist can't do antigravity, but maybe the Realist can do a ride where it *feels* like the bottom drops out from under you. So the Realist is the person who realizes the dream.

THE CRITIC

Then the Realist steps aside, and the next person who comes in is the Critic. Again, no "Yeah but . . ." The Critic just says, "Hmm, that's an interesting process. Let's see, do we have liability insurance? Is there any way that that moisture coming out of that humidifier would short the electrical circuits?" The Critic considers ecological factors, things that might be a concern if the Dreamer and Realist got what they envisioned.

So again there is no killer in this process—and there never needs to be. I've been in a lot of market research and product development brainstorming sessions that turned into slingshot fights because folks were just shooting each other down. That's not creativity at all.

Creativity in Disney's strategy is kind of loving, isn't it? It's all *positive*. It's completely focused on getting the biggest dream possible— which means the Dreamer can't be afraid of anything. The Dreamer needs to be fully supported.

Innovation:
How to Use the Disney Strategy with Groups

Even though the "Disney Strategy" was initially conceived and used by an *individual,* it later became an essential part of how the company operates. Not only has this strategy been a critical factor that's enabled the Disney Company to hold its position as an entertainment innovator, but it's also a foundational piece of the award-winning leadership training offered at the Disney Institute. Today, many individuals, teams, and companies use this approach to create new products and services, improve existing ones, and solve problems.

If you'd like to use this strategy with a group to create something new or resolve a problem, here are a few recommendations.

THE SETUP

At Disney, they facilitated this activity using three different rooms: one for the Dreamer step, one for the Realist step, and one for the Critic step. If you don't have adequate facilities to use separate rooms, you could designate three distinct areas in a room—one for each role.

THE ROLES

Because each role in this strategy is critical, most companies choose to have all participants play all three roles—while other organizations sometimes choose to break their participants into three teams and have them assume a *single* role. Although this second method is manageable and takes less time, having *everyone* moving sequentially through the different roles and associated mental states is *much preferred* because it provides a more robust and collaborative experience—and produces even better results.

Having an understanding of the different roles is essential to effectively playing each role and to facilitating this strategy as a team activity. On the following page is an outline excerpted from instructions created by Keith V. Trickey, who developed an in-depth outline for using the Disney Strategy with *groups*. (If you'd like to review his complete step-by-step summary, go to the Bonus Activities link at the end of this chapter.)

Role Guidelines for the Disney Strategy

The Dreamer: The one for whom all things are possible

The Approach: Want to do it
Questions to Consider:
- Why are you doing this? What is the purpose?
- What are the payoffs?
- How will you know you have them?
- Where do you want to be in the future?
- Who do you want to be or be like?
- What range of topics do you want to consider?
- What elements of those topics do you want to explore?

Physiology: Head and eyes looking up, posture symmetrical and
relaxed

The Realist: The one who sorts things out

The Approach: How to do it
Questions to Consider:
- What will I be doing?
- How specifically will the idea be implemented?
- How will I know if the goal has been achieved?
- Who besides me is involved (time constraints)?
- When will each phase be implemented?
- When will the overall goal be completed?
- Where will each phase be carried out?

Physiology: Head and eyes looking straight ahead, posture
symmetrical and centered

The Critic: The one who picks up the pieces that don't fit

The Approach: Chance to enhance
Questions to Consider:
- How do all the elements fit together?
- What elements appear unbalanced?
- What parts do not fit with the overall objective of the project?
- What parts of the project are underdeveloped?
- How possible is this within the time frame?
- Why is each step necessary?

Physiology: Eyes down, head down and tilted, posture angular

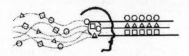

**Discovery Activity:
Applying the Disney Strategy
to One of Your Opportunities**

Let's apply the Disney Strategy to your life. Think of a problem you've been trying to solve—or something new you've been trying to create.

What's the opportunity?

In a moment, you'll have a chance to explore this opportunity from the point of view of the Dreamer, the Realist, and the Critic. You can do this imagining all at once and make your notes after the whole thing—or image it a step at a time and make your notes after each step.

Get comfortable and think of a time when it was easy for you to come up with new ideas—a time when you were able to imagine things you wanted—a time when you were able to dream up lots of possibilities.

Now perhaps in your mind's eye, you see an empty chair and perhaps in a moment, the Dreamer will appear. When it does, invite it to run wild with ideas about the opportunity you've identified.

Notice and remember what the Dreamer wanted . . .

Now think of a time when you were great at planning something—you were able to anticipate and arrange everything—all kinds of details—a time when it was easy to take all the necessary steps to accomplish what you wanted.

Now perhaps in your mind's eye you see a different empty chair and perhaps in a moment, the Realist will appear. When it does, invite it to consider the Dreamer's fantasies and imagine how it would all be possible—what steps you could take to make these things happen.

Notice and remember what the Realist recommended . . .

Now perhaps in your mind's eye you see another empty chair and perhaps in a moment, the Critic will appear. When it does, invite it to consider the Realist's recommendations and identify what concerns you have—and would need to be addressed before you could be fully satisfied with the plans/solution. What additional questions do you have for the Dreamer or the Realist?

Notice and remember what questions or concerns the Critic raised . . .

For additional demonstrations and/or examples, go to http://eg.nlpco .com/8-1.

Creativity can be applied to any situation, right? So you could try this approach when you're imagining . . . a party you want to have . . . a new approach with your boss . . . a specific conversation with your kids . . . how to invite someone on a date . . . whatever! There are countless situations where you can use this three-chair process on your own. Just by assuming the roles of the Dreamer, the Realist, and the Critic, in rotation, you can strengthen your creative muscles and expand your choices.

Up Against the Wall: How the "Conflict Integration Process" Supports Creative Problem Solving

---

Albert Einstein really nailed it when he said, "Problems cannot be solved by the same thinking that created them." Although most of us have heard this wisdom, we still get stuck in our patterns when problems arise and then we feel like we're up against a wall—unable to move. When we're in conflict—with ourselves, someone else, an idea, a process, technology, or even a machine—curiosity and creativity are the keys to finding alternatives that make our experiences of being in the world better.

When you think of conflict and creativity, you may see them as very different things. But a lot of what we've talked about in terms of creativity applies to conflict, too—and here's why. Remember what I told you about that towel dispenser? I was on autopilot and *assumed* I knew how the damn thing worked, but my expectation was wrong and my strategy didn't work. I limited myself.

As I started thinking about conflict, I realized that when I'm interacting with somebody—if I walk in with preconceived notions of who that person is and what they're likely to think, do, or say—I limit my options for connecting and dealing with them.

Loosening Up Positions

When there's a conflict, it's generally because people are locked into their positions. To make communication possible, the first step is always to help folks get unlocked. We can help people release their defensive posture by stepping back, taking a deep breath, and letting go of expectations.

Imagine that someone is wrestling with some sort of a problem. They're stuck. When they're stuck, they're actually feeling *physically* stuck, like they're frozen in place. Our language actually frames it that way, but it's not really *them* that's stuck, is it? It's some kind of issue—something they have to work through—something that's getting larger and larger in their mind's eye and probably taking over.

The trick here is to disassociate them from the issue by literally setting the issue aside and sometimes physically putting the issue "over there" on a flip chart or whiteboard so we can look at it together. That allows us both to be on the same side, facing the issue that's "over there," together.

Now how does that work when you're dealing with people who are at each other's throats? As a senior executive, I've had this happen a number of times, so let me illustrate this process by describing a specific situation—and then highlighting the critical action steps.

A Case in Point: Conflict Resolution

Normally, the office in my Silicon Valley manufacturing company was a pretty happy place, but not on the morning in question. As soon as I arrived, first cup of coffee in hand, the receptionist looked a little nervous and said, "Glenn and Susan are waiting for you in the conference room."

I thought, "Oh, this isn't going to be much fun." These were two of my vice presidents and they were always hassling each other— probably for reasons that stemmed from their different roles. Because Susan was a marketing person, she wanted the company to be the hero for the customer every time—and she was constantly trying to get the prices down and speed up delivery times. As the operations guy, Glenn was always trying to perfect our processes and increase consistency, and as you might imagine, he didn't like exceptions or surprises.

They were waiting for me in the conference room—scowling and sitting across from each other. After taking a deep breath and letting out a big sigh, I sat down where I could easily see both of them. Their heads were down, pretending to be studying their papers.

I reached out and I put my hands down on their respective papers. Then I said, "Stop for a minute. I'm here to help. Let me ask you a question." They both looked up and I said to Susan, "Ladies first. What's up?"

She said, "Well, you want me to make these marketing goals, right? So, we're out there making promises to our customers, and every time I turn around, he stops me."

I said, "Oh. Okay, so I get that you're feeling pretty unhappy about that."

She said, "Yeah, I'm feeling betrayed. I don't know how we can succeed as long as he's in charge."

Now things are getting really hot, so I said, "Okay, Glenn, what's the deal?"

He said, "Well, I'm the operations manager. I'm supposed to be the protector of the company, right? That means overseeing production, that means cost control, and that means reasonable delivery times. But Susan constantly comes in here with orders at the last minute. She goes right past my office, walks right back to the shop foreman, and tells him to stick these in the line and get it done ahead of time— and she doesn't even charge for it. She's going to bankrupt us."

My attitude was "This is going to be fun!"

So I said, "Okay, I've got it. Let me ask you a question, Glenn. If Susan backed off and we handled things exactly the way you want, what would be good about that? What would that do for the company?"

He immediately started listing the benefits. "Well, we'd be on a firm economic basis. We'd be profitable. Our people wouldn't have to work overtime. We wouldn't buy more than we needed because I could stock exactly what was ordered. There wouldn't be these damn rushes."

So I said, "Okay, in spite of what there wouldn't be, what *would* there be?"

He thought for a minute and said, "Well, we'd have increased profits, a better margin on our profits, a lower inventory, more turns on the inventory, and less overtime."

Then I said, "Okay. Susan, if those things were possible, would that be good for us?" and she said, "Of course it would. I'm not arguing that. All of that would be good. The thing is, we won't get the sales that way."

I said, "Okay, now I want to know if we did it entirely your way, did everything that you want—kept every promise that our representatives made and that we encouraged them to make to get orders— what would that do for the company?"

She said, "Well, we'd beat all the competitors. We'd be known as heroes. We'd not only have the best product in the world, we'd also be getting into more places—so we'd have more testimonials. The company would grow faster."

So I said to Glenn, "Is there anything about what Susan said that you disagree with?" and he said, "Well, of course there is. We can't do it that way."

I said, "Okay. I'm not talking about the *way* she wanted to go about it. I'm talking about her goals. Was there anything wrong with her goals?" and he said, "No, we all want that. We've got the best product. We want more users—and we want to be heroes—that's what we all want."

I said, "Okay, so you both agree that we want decent profit margins, that we want less overhead in terms of overtime for the shop guys, that we want as much inventory as we need, but not a lot more, and we want to be heroes to our customers. You've both agreed with that, right?"

They seemed to be sitting there thinking, "How's he going to pull this rabbit out of the hat?" So they're smiling at each other and at me as they share this joke that somehow I just walked into the trap and now it's my problem to solve.

But instead I said, "Okay, here's the deal. I've got some calls I have to make. Let's do this. Let's spend a half day on this. While I make my calls, I'd like you guys to come around here on the same side of the table and put your notepads over here facing that whiteboard."

Once they were settled facing the whiteboard, I said, "Now take turns putting up on the whiteboard three or four ways we might be able to do *all* of this. See what's possible here. Just write as many things as you can and I'll be back in half an hour. Then, over lunch, we'll look them over together. We'll solve this so that we get as much as we can of what each of you wants for the company because I think you're both right. We need to accomplish the objectives you've both identified for the company."

When I left, they were no longer arguing. They were comparing notes to find out what they could do that wasn't mutually exclusive—which got them on the same side of the table behaviorally, not just physically. At first they were on the same side of the table against me, because they thought that I had trapped myself and I was going to have to solve the problem. Yet the truth is that the crux of the issue goes back to Einstein's wisdom—you can't solve a problem at the level of thinking that created it.

How does that translate into our behavior? The level of thinking that created this problem was that Glenn was trying to protect his process, his inventory levels, and his responsibility for shop overtime. Susan was trying to protect her personal goals and her departmental goals of increased sales, better service, and enhanced reputation among our customers. Unfortunately, because each of them was trying to accomplish their objectives at the expense of the other, it wasn't going to happen.

I've seen this hundreds of times. The level at which the people were arguing was not going to have any resolution at all. In companies, there's often conflict between scorekeepers, like accountants and operations people, who have to keep track of things, and the score makers, like the marketing and sales staff.

Because of the kinds of personalities that it takes to succeed in these different areas, these groups often have some unkind stereotypes of each other. Yet the truth is this—no business survives without excellent talent and disciplines in both areas. You have to have growth and aggression, *and* you have to have control. Every organization needs muscle and brains, and you need these inside yourself, too.

A Review Outline of the "Conflict Integration Process"

So here's an interesting thing. This process that I used with Glenn and Susan is a classic "Conflict Integration Process." Let's break it into pieces. I looked at the situation and saw that their horns were locked. They were absolutely head-to-head with no give. There was no real interest in resolution, and no possibility of one, because they were in complete and perfect balance in terms of their conflict.

Then I turned to one of them and said, "And if *that* worked out, if we did it your way, what would that do that would be even better or more important? What would that do that would be good for us, for the business?"

So Susan told me, "Well, if we do that then we're going to get growth and we're going to get a good reputation and we're going to get more sales and enthusiastic testimonials—all good stuff."

Then I turned to Glenn and said, "And if we did it your way, what would that get us?"

He said, "We'd get higher profit margins and lower overtime costs and better inventory controls and a smoother operation. All good stuff."

By "chunking up" to find the goal-behind-the-goal (meta-outcome), I was able to get each of them then to approve of the other person's outcome. Remember how far apart Glenn and Susan were at the beginning of the meeting? His initial goal was to beat Susan into submission and make her stop handing in rush orders. Her original goal was to beat Glenn into submission and make his whole process and procedure more flexible and responsive to her demands. Those initial outcomes were in absolute opposition.

But when I asked Susan for the goal-behind-her-goal, she gave me a very positive outcome for the company—and Glenn could understand that. When I asked Glenn for his goal-behind-the-goal, his meta-outcomes were smoother operations, lower cost, better inventory control—and Susan could appreciate these. What you do, by asking the right questions, is take the goals up to a level where both, or all, people can agree. Typically, this approach produces objectives that anyone with their head on straight would think were a good idea.

However, you can't even begin to explore meta-outcomes until people get unlocked. Because when people are in conflict, they're stuck. They have a foxhole mentality that says, "This is the only way to go. Everything else is idiotic."

So, you might be wondering what happened after Susan and Glenn were left to come up with solutions. When I came back from making my calls, they said, "We need a little more time. We're not ready for you yet"—which, of course, I was thrilled to hear.

Around eleven thirty I came back in and said, "How we doing?" and they said, "We still need a little more time." So I ordered lunch for us all. When the sandwiches arrived, I came back in and ate with them and listened to their process as they had worked it through. What they came up with was a strategy where we could actually make an even more extraordinary promise *and* charge for it.

Because we made offering such service extraordinary, what Glenn did was to hold out a certain part of our process and resources so we could accommodate that. He was happy because there was a strategy for it *and* we were being paid extra for it. Plus, offering this option made us really heroic to our customers because they realized they could get extra service if they were willing to pay for it (which is a reasonable and proven tradition). So they resolved it brilliantly and supported *both* sets of objectives.

This conflict was between two experienced and passionate professionals, who even though they were often at each other's throats, had a deep respect for one another. This exact strategy of exploring and agreeing upon meta-outcomes can work well when several people are involved—or when there's just one.

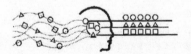   **Discovery Activity: Identifying One of Your Conflicts**

To increase your understanding and mastery of these concepts, let's apply them to your life. So, think of a recent conflict or misunderstanding that you had with someone. It might have been about a situation at work, dinner with a friend, or a family matter.

Take a moment now and go back to that point in time—thinking what you were thinking, noticing what you were noticing. When you have access to those pictures, sounds, and feelings, answer the questions below.

Who were you talking with?

What was the focus of the discussion?

What was your point of view? What did *you* want?

What would having or doing what you want get you that was even more important? (As a reminder, this meta-outcome might be something that's good for you, or for a specific relationship, or for your team or family, or for your company.)

In retrospect, what feelings or point of view inhibited your ability to express the positive aspects of your meta-outcome?

As you think about it now, consider if there have been other occasions when you've had these same limiting feelings or thoughts. If so, identify at least two steps you could take in the future if similar feelings and thoughts come up for you.

For additional demonstrations and/or examples, go to http://eg.nlpco .com/8-4.

Internal Battles: How to Apply the "Conflict Integration Process" to Inner Conflicts

---

Most of the conflicts we have with other people contain some aspect of an inner conflict, don't they? But not all conflicts involve interacting with someone else. So, let's say you have a conflict that's just with yourself—or you know somebody who has one. It often sounds like "On the one hand, I want to do this—but on the other hand, I want to do this."

Here's one I really wrestled with: "On the one hand, I want to spend more time with my family because time passes so quickly and the kids are growing up. On the other hand, I want to excel in my career, which means I need to put in extra hours. So how do I move forward?"

This was my conflict, but for now, as I describe the Conflict Integration Process, imagine it was yours. First, we'll explore this process together using my example and then you'll have an opportunity to apply it to an inner conflict you want to resolve.

Start by focusing on one side—just like I took Susan's issues first. I would start with the hand whose objectives were mentioned first—in my case, that was spending more time with the family. So, imagine you're me. Where is this feeling or part in your body? Where does that feeling come from?

When you quiet down and go inside, you'll have that feeling. Then you allow it to come up, and now what you do is to invite it to travel down into your left hand. The reason for this is that you're going to talk to this feeling or part. In this situation, you don't have a Glenn and Susan at a conference table; you have two conflicting competing parts in your own psyche—and you need to get them separated so that you can communicate with them individually.

First, I focus all my attention on the part that wants to spend time with the family, all that love and all that yearning and all that enjoyment of the kids—very high-value stuff. Focus on that part now—gather the associated feelings and allow these to flow across your collarbone and down your left shoulder and down your arm and through your elbow and through your wrist and into your left hand, as if it were actual stuff, as if it had some substance.

As the substance gathers in your left hand, you can imagine it has some sort of a weight and that the weight actually takes form, a symbol of some sort, perhaps like an avatar, that communicates to you in that moment what that need or drive might be. So you look down at it, whatever it is.

When I did this and looked down at my hand, the symbol I saw was one of the kids' little teddy bears with an ear half-torn. So I've got this little brown teddy bear in the palm of my left hand.

Look down at your left hand and then acknowledge this part. "Thanks very much for coming. I'm glad you're here." This helps make the subconscious process more real.

Now you go back inside and you think about that *other* drive that was also very important—the one that said, "I want to excel in my career and that means I need to put in extra hours to develop the skills so I can really become all that I can become. I want to become better at this so I need to spend extra time either with a senior mentor in the field, studying, or just trying out more things."

So, for you, where's this second "drive" in your body? As you feel it, allow that to move in the opposite direction. You allow that to move up through your right shoulder and down your arm and past your elbow and through your wrist and let it gather into the upturned palm of your right hand.

As it collects, and as it gathers weight, you take a look at that and you see something there. I don't know what it would be for you. What *I* saw was a briefcase, containing a laptop computer, that was folded up and ready to go.

So, now we've got these two separate objects that remind us of these two different motivations—one in each hand. Now we have them metaphorically and symbolically across the conference table from each other, about where I walked into the room with Susan and Glenn.

Now I can turn to the little teddy bear in my left hand and I can say, "If I can spend as much time with my family as you'd like and be with the kids, what would that do for me?" and it says, "Well, you'd develop much stronger bonds in your family. Your kids would grow up to be better kids. They'd be better behaved, more self-assured, and more independent. They'll look to you for advice and guidance instead of people they meet at school. Your wife will be happy. And you'll be satisfied with yourself as a man and a father."

So, after you hear what the symbol in *your* left hand has to say, acknowledge that. "Okay, thank you very much—that all sounds good to me." Then I'm ready to go to the other side—which for me is represented by the briefcase containing the laptop—and I say, "And if I could spend more time at work developing my career, what will that do for me?"

That side says, "You'll have more money. You'll have more recognition. You'll advance further in your career, and eventually you'll have more control over your time so you can take more vacations with your family or do whatever you want to do." Then I say, "Okay, thanks for sharing that—that sounds pretty good, too."

Next, we'll ask the same thing I asked Glenn and Susan. This time, I say to the teddy bear, "Can you understand the benefit to the family of my getting more recognition, more advancement, more money, and more control over my time and my career by investing some time to develop it?" and it says, "Sure."

Then I say to the briefcase, "Can you see the benefit to me as a human being if I have this enrichment of spending time with my kids and being the guy that I should be, and allowing my wife and I to be there for them so we've formed the bonds that will serve us as they grow into the teenage years?"

The briefcase guy says, "Sure. I think about the future all the time."

In the work situation, I left Susan and Glenn alone in that room to allow them to work through the process on their own. Here what we would do is to allow these two objects in our hands to slowly come together. Because they now approve of each other, they understand each other, we just allow them to come together. And as they come together slowly, our hands meet and make a cup that contains these two different representations, in this example the teddy bear and the briefcase. What happens then? They blend, they mix, and they swirl.

As they do and we open our hands, there's a third object there. I don't know what that would be for you, but there's a third object there. When I look down, I see a tent at a campsite. That seems a little weird. So I say, "This is something new. You guys have blended. What did you come up with?"

What the tent at the campsite says is "Invest time now while the kids are asleep—you're still young, you can do with less sleep—and invest some evening hours now, but not when they're awake. You have to run a little harder right now to spend time and be available to your kids so you're not skipping their important events or the couple of hours before bedtime. You're working with them and *then* you're spending time on your own a little later in the evening to get ahead, so that as they get older you'll have this money and advancement and power, and you'll be able to take family vacations with them and be part of their lives."

I think, "That's really beautiful!" Listen to what your new blended part has to say, then bring those cupped hands up and hold them against the center of your chest—and allow that new object to be breathed back into your chest—then allow that to flow through your whole body.

That's an integration. It's not a resolution or a forced compromise. An integration means we move the conflict up one level and we find out what's important about each of those things. We don't want to lose anything. In NLP, we try not to remove or lose anything—we simply shift and add things.

What happens when *you're* stuck inside and you want to resolve it? You need to do the same thing that I did with Glenn and Susan in my office. It's just you—so you need to find a way to separate those two parts of yourself into the two parts that have been competing. Then allow them to look at each other from a slight distance so they can appreciate what each part is trying to accomplish on behalf of you, the you that owns them both and gave energy to them both. In this step, you can easily reach agreement when you focus on the *what*, not the *how*.

Then, as they blend, it's like what happened by the time I came back in the conference room with Glenn and Susan and we had sandwiches together. By then they had blended and they were able to tell me all the brilliant new ideas they had about offering the special accelerated delivery program at a price that would not destroy the company process. Because they were both sincerely endorsing these recommendations, I could tell they had really blended.

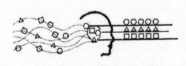 **Discovery Activity: Applying the "Conflict Integration Process" to One of Your Opportunities**

Perhaps as you were reading this, you were reminded of an issue you are or have been wrestling with. Because this is a delicate and deep process, do this in a private space where you won't be interrupted. Ready?

Think of an unresolved issue that's important to you. Really step into the experience of being conflicted, so you can see what you're seeing, hear what you're hearing, and feel what you're feeling.

As the conflict presents itself to you, separate the different parts that have been competing.

Identify where one of the parts or feelings is in your body and invite it to flow through your body so it can come out and present itself in your hand. When it does, thank it for being present. If that part were an image, what would it look like?

Now notice where the *other* part or feeling is in your body and ask it to flow through your body so it can come out and present itself in your *other* hand. When it appears, thank it for being present. If this part were an image, what would it be?

Turn to the part that's in your left hand and invite it to tell you what it wants. When it does, say, "Thank you for telling me that."

Next, look at the part that's in your right hand and invite it to tell you what it wants. When it does, say, "Thank you for telling me that."

Next, ask one of the parts, "What would having what you want do that's *even more* important?"

Then ask the other part the same question.

Now allow the parts to look at each other from a slight distance—so they can each appreciate what the other is trying to accomplish on your behalf. (If you've learned each one's meta-outcome, it should be easy to reach agreement that they both want what the other part is trying to accomplish.) Thank both parts for being willing to see the other's intention.

Then, breathing deeply, slowly bring your hands together so the parts literally come together, too. Allow the parts to mix and blend.

Open your hands and notice the new image that results from this merger. Thank this new part for being there and being willing to operate on your behalf.

Then slowly bring the new image in your hands up to the center of your chest and allow the image to enter your body and become fully integrated.

Take a deep breath and notice how different you feel.

For additional demonstrations and/or examples, go to http://eg.nlpco .com/8-7.

In NLP, we recognize that you don't try to solve the problem at the level of the argument—because you're not going to get anywhere. Classic "Conflict Integration" requires that you bump things up a notch—and maybe a notch after that—until you get to meta-outcomes that are easy to agree on. You can do this within yourself—or you can help another person, who has a conflict they're wrestling with on their own.

The Importance of Meta-Outcomes in "Conflict Integration"

In the past, when companies hired me to help them deal with a conflict, they often wanted me to "mediate it" as if I were some sort of judge. And I'd tell them, "Look, I'm not a judge. I don't know your business. Let's do this. Let's explore each side without arguing for your positions on the issue. I'm sure *those* have already been well expressed—so forget that. Just tell me, if you won, what would winning accomplish." Then, managing the discussion to keep the focus away from complaints and positions, the participants would come up with a list of compelling outcomes.

Sometimes, to reach a meta-outcome that everyone could agree on, I'd need to kick it up a notch and say, "Okay, and if you were able to accomplish *that,* what about that would be of even greater benefit to the company—or what would having that do for the company that's even more important?" Then I'd go over to the other side and say the same thing. Even when there are more than two sides, this strategy works like magic.

How to Increase Communication During "Conflict Integration"

Suppose you find yourself in a situation where people have been at odds for so long that the "fight" has become personal. They seem to hate each other and have damaged each other in different ways. What are you going to do then?

The key is to loosen up the old stuff. One of these things I actually did with Susan at a different time, much earlier in their relationship, because she and Glenn were frequently in conflict. One day when they were really going at it hammer and tongs, I said to her, "I'm just curious, Susan. I'd like you to answer this question. I want you to do some mind reading. If I were to ask Glenn what frustrates him most about working with you, what do you think he'd say?"

She paused and said she didn't want to do it—and I said, "Come on, just throw it out there. I don't think you're in any doubt."

She laughed and then she said, "Well, he'd say that I'm disorganized and I'm demanding—that I'm a prima donna. He'd probably say I want it all my way and I have no discipline and I have no respect for him."

I said, "Okay, if that's true, what would that make him want to do?"

And she kind of smiled, and by this time he's smiling a little bit because he realizes she gets him, and she says, "Well, he'd probably become a bit mulish and maybe a little unreasonable."

To which he said, "Hey, I'm not unreasonable." And now they're at least talking.

Then I turned to him and asked him the same question. "If I were to ask Susan what frustrates her most about working with you, what would she say?" and he started giving me a joking answer, but I held his feet to the fire and said, "Come on, play fair. Do it right. You know the truth. We all know the truth—so get it out there."

So then he played it sincerely and told me what he thought she would say about him, that he's autocratic and dictatorial and rigid, doesn't care much about reality, and just cares about his figures. I said, "What would that make her do?" and he said, "Well, she's a very strong-willed woman and she's really dedicated, so she'd just go around me." Then he laughed and said, "Wow, that's what she does."

At this point, because they each understand that they each appreciate the other person, tension has started to release and things are lightening up. When you're in a conflict situation—if people aren't emotionally ready to deal with the issue, if they're so at war that now they really need to get blood on the carpet—the best thing for you to do is to take a moment and dial things down.

By asking each person or team to tell what the other person's or team's complaint would be about *them,* you get some real loosening up in the dialogue, and *then* you can get back to the issue.

To quickly summarize, the principles of this process are that you separate the people from the issues. Because we are emotional beings, it often feels like a personal threat when we have a difference. It doesn't really matter what the difference is. If it's "Oh, you forgot to dot that *i,*" that's a personal threat. Any criticism can be really risky territory—not only to give, but also to receive—because we're so wired to protect ourselves.

If you want to succeed in this business of communication, *you have to set yourself aside except* as a mirror and receptor. You set your own fears aside because you realize they're as automated as anybody else's. What we're trying to do here is to work at a higher level—with ourselves and with others.

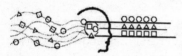 **Discovery Activity:**
Examining Ways You Get
Stuck or Make Things Harder

Because *the only variable we can control in any situation is ourselves,* let's take the opportunity to examine our own behavior. For a moment, go back to the conflict you explored earlier in this chapter in the activity called Identifying One of Your Conflicts.

Now, rewind to the beginning of the conflict and do a little mind reading.

Say to yourself, "If I were to ask them what's most challenging about interacting with me, what would they say?"

What came up?

Say to yourself, "Okay, if that's true—and if I were them, what would that make me want to do?"

Notice what came up—and what you learned from standing in their shoes. How does this new awareness shift your feelings and what's possible?

Different Strategies? What "Conflict Integration" and Negotiation Have in Common

As you can see, differences of opinion and heated feelings are natural. So conflict resolution and negotiation have been hot topics for as long as I can recall. Despite being an avid learner who's been in business for decades, I've probably lost more than I've won in negotiations. Even so, I've always kept trying to learn—asking myself, "What was this? What happened here? Was there any part of the process that made any sense at all? Are the good parts replicable? And what can I do differently next time to avoid the not-so-good parts?"

An Overview: Negotiation

So, let's talk about negotiation strategies because there are a lot of them out there. For many years now, the win-win principle has been the basis of effective negotiation. Shortly after I was introduced to this concept, I had to negotiate a sales deal with SmithKline Beecham. Although they're now affiliated with Glaxo, at the time they were a big player all on their own. I was meeting with their head purchasing officer and he said, "This will be like the Harvard negotiation project," and I thought, "Oh great, win-win." It wasn't win-win. It just meant he'd try to be humane and I should try not to be ornery.

So here's what I know. In any negotiation, you're going to end up somewhere in between what you want and what the other person wants. Whether or not both parties are happy with that end result doesn't really have to do with whether they got everything they came for.

Interesting, isn't it? If it's a business negotiation, there are at least four parties at the table—no matter how many players are physically present. Here are the parties. First, there are the interests of the entities, the two companies. In this case, there was my company and there was the big pharmaceutical company—and there were the purchasing guy and I. His company wanted more for less money; mine wanted more money for less service. We were at complete odds. Where could we meet in between?

Negotiation is *not* "Conflict Integration." A negotiation is a game and you need to appreciate that it's a game. Of course, to win a game, you have to understand the game *and* have skills. Although the desired outcome is different, *many* of the principles of "Conflict Integration"—in addition to NLP skills like anchoring, body language, mirroring of predicates and meta-programs, etc.—are quite useful in negotiation, too.

Negotiation Tips

As you walk into the room, you want to stop and gather yourself. As with any interaction, you want to bring your energy into a relaxed, calm, welcoming state *before* you go into the room because you're probably going to go into a room with a bunch of people. Maybe they're "suits," maybe they're union organizers, maybe they're family members. It doesn't matter who they are, but they're people with an agenda—and you have one, too.

Although you need to be really clear about your bottom line, your agenda and approach must be flexible. Because you have no idea where the negotiation is going to go, you have to accept that you cannot control the outcome. In fact, there may not be an outcome. You may decide that you have to walk away and say, "Thanks, but no deal." You need to own all the possible outcomes so you can be comfortable when those options arise. That way, you're never desperate—which is critical.

In any negotiation, there are four assets at play and on everyone's minds: time, money, energy, and emotion. The more time, the more energy, the more emotion, and the more money that are spent during a negotiation, the more valuable that negotiation becomes, and this makes the outcome *exponentially* more important.

If you understand that these aspects are playing a part in a negotiation game, then you realize that if you're not in a rush or in a hurry—you've already got one of the big variables on your side. If you can take as much time as you want, the other side will feel squeezed by that.

Besides time, there are two other key elements you may be able to optimize. Number one is the amount of information regarding the issue. Who has the most information about it? How can you gather additional information? It's always advantageous if you (or people working for you) have done a lot of homework to accurately and thoroughly understand everything about the issue—the various ways it could be worked out and the associated costs.

The other big element, and this is all perceptual, is *who* has the power. What's that mean? What does power mean? In this case, it means the power to make a decision—so who has the power in this situation? The answer to that may flip back and forth—partly because they may not want you to know who has the power, and partly because different players may be vying for power during the negotiation.

Generally, the person who's in position to win is the individual who has the most time, the most information, and the most power or personal authority on their side of the table. The power to walk away at any time is one of the greatest advantages you can have.

And even though you want to win, you'll do better if you do everything you can to be a charming, friendly, sincere, collaborative, and understanding communicator. You do best if you use all the same skills with people you've just met and with people you love. This approach is more humane and it's easier on you.

By the same token, you should understand that in a negotiation, your beginning position is one of no compromise. Ultimately there will be *some* accommodation. You want to have room to make concessions. So start with your end in mind *and* leave yourself sufficient flexibility. You may be presented with a variety of ways to get where you want to go, and won't have to give up much of what's really important to you.

I don't like playing hardball and I try not to do it. But when negotiations get tough, I've been known to say, "Let's do this: Imagine there's a hand grenade on the table. I'm going to pull the pin—then I'm going to put your hand on it to hold it down and I'm going to put my hand over yours. Now we're going to negotiate until we're both satisfied with the outcome—or until we get tired enough to let go of the hand grenade and it blows us both up."

People have laughed about that, but they got that I was completely committed—that I would spend as much time as was needed to make a deal. I wasn't desperate; I was just willing. The thing is, the more willing you are, the more it shows that *you* have control of time.

Additional Benefits of Using Meta-Outcomes in Negotiation

As you might imagine, meta-outcomes, which are the vital parts of the "Conflict Integration," can also be very useful in negotiation. Although these principles could apply to a negotiation with a teenager about using the family car on a weekend, let's use a business example where there are two or three things on the table.

Maybe we're talking about speed of delivery versus pricing, versus bundling other products if they buy enough quantity. So they'll make a demand and I'm looking at that, and what I'd say before I give anything away, before I say yes to anything at all—in fact, I usually don't say yes to anything until I see the complete deal—what I would do is to say, "And if we did *that,* how would that benefit your company?"

Why am I asking? Because I want to hear them talk some more and I want to see their body language. And if there's more than one person representing their company's interests, I want to watch whether they look at each other or whether somebody is surprised by what the other person says. But even more important than all of that, I want to know what their meta-outcomes are.

Meta-outcomes aren't simple things—discovering them requires that you listen carefully and ask relevant follow-up questions. If, in response to my question about how that would benefit their company, they said, "Well, if we get a lower price, that's important because we have this internal policy that we can't spend more than this without getting some sort of special committee approval, which would slow down the rate at which we can buy your products," I'd have learned something, right? But I still need to know more. So I'd say, "And if you get the fast delivery, what's important to you about that? How does that work?"

And they tell me, "That means we can order it later in our process and still get it into our project," so now I know one of them is just a convenience factor, ordering later. The other one is a bureaucracy factor. If I can get them a slightly lower price and maybe a longer delivery, that will work for me.

Because I've found what their meta-outcomes are, that's something I know and they don't. I've found out *why* they're demanding certain things. And even though it may sometimes feel like they're putting me over a barrel, they're demanding things for a specific reason. Everybody always does. It's a game with a lot of unknown variables at play and at stake. Part of your job is to uncover those elements.

One of the NLP negotiation courses I took was taught by a great guy, an attorney with quite a sense of humor. He went up to the blackboard and he said, "Negotiation is win-win." Then he wrote a quote mark and I thought, "Oh, this will be interesting." Then on the board he wrote "win-win" so it looked like this: "WIN-win."

He said, "Negotiation is a game and the goal is to win the game. It's fine to call the other person a partner in the negotiation because they are your partner in a game, but they're also an adversary in terms of the negotiation." When you can be realistic about this fact, you can still be very humane and fair-minded. And when you can keep this is mind, you'll remember that you're not trying to get everything they've got and that you must never humiliate them, make them feel bad about themselves, or rob them of face.

I got a great piece of advice from a mentor of mine who was the chairman of my company. He always said to me, "Put it the other way around. Walk in *their* moccasins." Because I was always so focused and intense when we worked together, I needed him to remind me to put it the other way around, to look at it from the other person's point of view.

So many of the skills in NLP are about that, aren't they? They're about looking at it from the other person's point of view. Now it doesn't mean you live the other person's life or you do their job. It doesn't mean that you have to agree with their point of view. It just means you develop an understanding of and appreciation for their position. It gives you insight, empathy, and more clicks on your dial in terms of how to satisfy their needs—and yours.

When you're negotiating, it's as important to learn about the other person as it is when you're talking with a friend, loved one, or colleague. We live in a world surrounded by other humans. The more we can learn about them, the less concerned we become about ourselves and the more effective we are.

Powerful Emotions: How to Facilitate Discussions with People Who Are Upset

---

In earlier chapters we touched on how to deal with difficult people and situations; let's explore this a little further now. Every once in a while, I need to deal with people who are angry. Maybe I made them angry or maybe they were angry when they got on the phone or in the room, but it doesn't matter to me. I could accuse them of waking up on the wrong side of the bed or of not getting enough love lately, but that wouldn't be helpful. Regardless of what made the person angry, you have to work with the human being in front of you.

So, when I'm interacting with someone who is in a bad mood or was angry—or angry with me—the first thing I want to know is how they feel. I don't feel attacked when somebody's angry; I just feel they're angry. And I want to know how they feel. How angry are they?

So I might say, "If I had to guess, I'd say you're feeling really angry. It might be because I was late on that phone call two weeks ago," or if I have no clue, I'll say, "It feels like you're really angry. Can you tell me about it?" and let them go. Remember, we want to help people exhale. Until they exhale, until they relieve the pressure, there's no listening or real communication anyway, so you let them exhale.

When they seem to run out of steam, you can say, "Tell me more," or you can ask the question "Is that because of . . ." and let them go. Then you can say, "How upset are you?" and let them tell you that. Next you say, "Is there anything I can do to contribute to changing the situation?"

"Well, no. I just wanted you to listen—that's all. I just had to blow off some steam. Thanks a lot."

Once they've been heard, they're probably ready to let you be heard. Or they'll say, "Yes, you can. You can keep your damn promises. When you say you'll call me at a certain time, call me at that time."

I wish I could say that I've never responded defensively to getting feedback. I've been guilty of blasting back with "Well, you're no better," or "Look, I had this going on. If you're not adult enough to understand that . . ." I've done a lot of that kind of reactive behavior and it's cost me.

So when we're interacting with someone who's emotional or people who are generally kind of difficult, it's important to remember that they're the ones who are uncomfortable. They're involved in something that's hard for them; so don't respond with discomfort of your own. Just get what's happening there and that *these* are the folks who are really in pain, not you or me.

So before you can have a communication with them that's in your own self-interest, you need to do something to help loosen that up. The key here is you can't label them in advance, "Oh, that guy's just another pain in the ass. He wants everything in the world." You can't do that. You can't say, "Oh, they're lazy. If they had taken the time to do X earlier, they wouldn't be in this trouble right now."

Drop all your judgments. Most of us live in glass houses, right? If you can just accept that, it doesn't matter that you're not as imperfect as some other poor slob. For the moment, we want to be in league with this person. Because we want to work *with* them, we want no defensiveness at all on our part. We're just there to be of service and to listen.

In my own mind right now, I can hear a voice saying, "Oh right, you're just going to lie down? You're going to be a doormat? You're going to be a punching bag? They won't have any respect for you." That dialogue comes from an old map of the world. It's simple to understand, but it's not true.

For almost two decades, I've been practicing fairly sophisticated communication with people, and I've learned that sincerely seeking to understand them makes their respect for you go up and your stress level go way down. When you don't have the need to defend yourself or to get even or any of that stuff, you can be much more humane dealing with other people. The most powerful position is the one you don't need to defend.

Now, is it a lot of fun to be yelled at or to be abused or even to hear somebody's emotional baggage? Of course it's not; but so what? If you sign up for the job of communicating with your fellow humans, you have to take them as they come. Sometimes that includes bad breath or bad manners, and sometimes that includes pretty bad feelings. It is whatever it is. You're going to care about them anyway because all these conditions are temporary.

When someone's upset, they're a lot like a patient in the emergency room. Because they're in the grip of some kind of pain or emotion, they're in fight-or-flight mode. They're not thinking; they're *feeling*. So, when you're with them, don't focus on being mad, afraid, or defensive. Instead focus on them. The more resourceful you can be, the more helpful you can be, *and* the more appreciated you will become.

So, if after you've let them completely vent, you're clear that there's nothing you can do about this—if this is just something that they had to get off their chest and they thank you for it—you can move on or you can say, "I'm curious: what's impossible about this that you really would want?"

This does two things for them. First, you're still talking about something "out there." In fact, as I hear my own language, I'd probably say, "What's impossible about that?" because that would put it even further away in their physical mind. Then let them tell you what's impossible about it. Next you could say, "Okay, what would make it possible?" That's a very simple and very powerful question: "What *would* make it possible?"

Asking these kinds of questions—"What would it be like if it did? What would it be like if you could? What would it be like if we worked this out?"—shifts the entire basis of thought from impossibility to desire. I find that sharing Nelson Mandela's wisdom often inspires people to embrace possibility. He said, "It always seems impossible until it's done."

As you know, these kinds of questions create a significant physiological response in the human brain; they actually engage more neurons. Then people truly have more brainpower to work with because when it's impossible, it's impossible. It's like having your foot caught in a trap. All you can do is tug on the trap and feel the pain.

But if you imagine what it's like for something to be possible, now you're not focusing on the impossibility, you're focusing on: "Wow, what would it be like? And what would make that possible? Hmm, I wonder what things need to be rearranged? Maybe there's a little more wiggle room over there than I thought." It just starts to loosen up the mind, so it can move forward and entertain options.

The Unexpected Strategy:
An Approach to Consider When *You're* Upset

What if *you're* the person who's upset? Perhaps there's someone in your life who's been a problem for you, disappointed you a bit, or hasn't stepped up. This person might be a family member, a coworker, a client, or a vendor. For me, I found more of these challenges at work than at home. And when somebody who worked for me dropped the ball, I used to call them into my office and say, "What's your problem?" Not an ideal response, right?

A better thing to do—and this is something I tried only a few times before I retired, but it worked like magic—is to call them in and say, "You know, I've been thinking about you and about the demands I place on you. And I think I owe you an apology."

Because the other person's expecting to get called on the carpet, this really throws them for a loop. They're thinking, "Huh?"

I say, "Yeah, the more I think about this, I imagine that you must feel like I don't take you into consideration, I just impose things on you. I give you unrealistic deadlines—I have no sympathy for your personal issues—and you must feel like you can't get it done and, even if you do, you're not going to be appreciated. I want you to know I'm really sorry for creating a situation like that for you. I apologize and I'm going to do better."

The person's waiting because they're thinking, "This is one of those psychology sandwich things." You know, the kind of sandwich where you give them a compliment, then you give them a criticism, then you give them a compliment.

What I'm recommending is a different kind of approach. This is where you don't give them a compliment, you give them an apology of substance—and then you thank them for their time. In other words, you just did the unexpected and you made them feel heard. You made their feelings feel felt, and you didn't demand anything from them. You left it with that.

When people have this kind of experience with you, it's like a "reset"—and they'll return to being their best self. If they have more they'd like to talk with you about, you've just made it safe and inviting for that, too.

Whether an opportunity is internal to you, with one other person, or with a group, you now have several new, effective ways to facilitate creative collaboration and "Conflict Integration." Although these strategies are useful with most people, I recommend that you consider using these approaches with people who are occasionally difficult, but not with people who are just plain toxic. This will help you maintain your personal integrity and control of your life.

Whenever you're interacting with others, you, and they, have a more positive experience when you are curious and creative. Creativity is about multiplying choices. Most of what we've talked about throughout this book is about increasing your choices.

When you think about your life, the things that pinch and the things that hurt us and the things we regret are usually limitations, occasions and places where we believed our choices were restricted. NLP is all about creating *more* choices so you can have more of what you really want.

Key Ideas

- Having expectations or being on autopilot filters out information—which limits thinking and options.

- The Well-Formed Outcome model (Chapter 2) can be used effectively alone, with a partner, or with a group.

- Creativity is about multiplying choices. People can free up and more easily access their creative talents when they quiet inner dialogue, loosen up, and drop their filters.

- Part of Walt Disney's genius was to employ his inner Dreamer, his Realist, and his Critic separately and in sequence whenever he wanted to create something new. He'd use each of these mental roles in a positive, collaborative way. His strategy can be used alone or with a group.

- People engaged in a conflict often feel stuck, and then their emotions take over, which puts them in a fight-or-flight mode.

- Learning someone's goal-behind-the-goal enables you to understand what's really important and usually makes it easier to find common ground.

- Once people in conflict can agree upon mutual goals or meta-outcomes, then they can work together to achieve those goals in a way that's acceptable to both of them.

- The same kind of sorting process and identification of goals-behind-the-goals can be used to help someone who's experiencing an internal conflict. Once this person's competing parts find common ground, the remaining steps of the "Conflict Integration Process" can be used to resolve the issue.

- If a conflict has been going on for a while, the fight may have become personal—and the "gloves are off." In these situations, it helps to ask each party, "If I were to ask the other person what's most difficult about interacting or working with you, what do you think they'd say?" Next we'd build on their answer by asking, "Okay, if that's true, then what would that make *them* want to do?" Then, of course, we'd ask these same questions of the other party. These inquiries enable them to see and depersonalize behaviors that they've been judging.

- Although negotiation is a game where someone wants to and will win, some aspects of the "Conflict Integration Process" are still useful—such as: centering yourself, using rapport skills to get people talking, zooming out, noticing nonverbal behaviors and language patterns, and learning about the goals-behind-the-goals.

- Effective preparation for any negotiation includes considering *all* possible outcomes– including "no deal"—so feelings of desperation are not driving behaviors and decisions.

- In most business negotiations, there are at least four sets of interests involved—the other person's and yours, as well as their company's and your company's.

- The four assets at play in most negotiations are time, money, energy, and emotion. If someone's not in a hurry to agree on and implement a solution, they may be able to leverage time to *their* advantage.

- In any negotiation, it's critical to have access to all the information related to the issues—and to understand who, on the other side of the table, has the authority to make a decision.

- When dealing with difficult people, it's important to help them feel heard and felt by asking questions, letting them blow off steam, naming the emotion—then moving them from being stuck to considering possibilities.

- If someone is upset with another person, a very unexpected and effective way to approach them is to say, "I've been thinking about the expectations I've had of you—and I think I owe you an apology. The more I think about our situation, I imagine you must feel like I don't take you into consideration . . ." This helps the other person feel felt, doesn't add any new demands, and frees them up to go back to being their best self.

To enhance the skills you learned in this chapter, check out the recommended Bonus Activities at our special "Essential Guide" website: http://eg.nlpco .com/8-13 or use the QR code with your phone.

Discoveries, Questions, Ideas, and Stuff You Want to Work On

_____

_____

_____

_____

_____

_____

_____

_____

_____

_____

_____

_____

_____

_____

_____

_____

_____

_____

_____

_____

_____

_____

_____

Discoveries, Questions, Ideas, and Stuff You Want to Work On

_____

_____

_____

_____

_____

_____

_____

_____

_____

_____

_____

_____

_____

_____

_____

_____

_____

_____

_____

_____

_____

_____

_____

_____

CHAPTER NINE: MAINTAINING YOUR MOMENTUM WITH NLP

What's next?

> Your life will be no better than the plans you make
> and the action you take. You are the architect and builder
> of your own life, fortune, and destiny.
> —Alfred A. Montapert

R ecent research suggests that many of us buy books but never read them. We buy memberships to the health club, but never go. We buy clothes we never wear and power tools we never use. The list, as you might imagine, goes on and on.

Having gotten this far in the book, you're already an exception. You've demonstrated your genuine commitment to improving your life. In using the NLP principles and techniques you've explored, I know that you've experienced some positive personal changes—and I hope that you're motivated *to continue* to enhance your new skills.

Journey Highlights: What You Learned

Before recommending ways you might do that, let's step back for a moment and reflect on a few highlights of the territory we've covered together. You've learned about:

- NLP's key presuppositions

- How you "work" using your body, brain, and mind

- The way you use all five senses to process, sort, and store your experiences

- How to notice incongruity in yourself and in others

- How your mind uses a shorthand to take in, filter, make sense of, and manage incoming data

- The power of intentional and unintentional visual, auditory, and kinesthetic anchors

Building upon these basics, you discovered:

- How subtle shifts in sub-modalities can create big changes in your remembered, present, and future experiences

- The importance of where *you* are in the experience, whether you're associated or disassociated

- New ways to prevent and minimize personal stress

- The ways you motivate yourself and how to get unstuck when you are distracted, procrastinating, or resistant to doing something specific

- Nonverbal behaviors that might provide clues to what is going on with someone else and shapes how they are in the world

- Ways to create good connections with others by easily building rapport, demonstrating interest, and making them feel felt

Building upon these basics, you discovered:

- How people process differently and that by adjusting *your* natural preferences—representational systems, sense of time, meta-programs, etc.—you can more easily and effectively communicate

- The power of beliefs—and how each individual's beliefs shape their experience, decisions, interactions, and identity

- Ways that conflicts occur and how to increase collaboration for more enjoyable relationships and successful outcomes

HANDS-ON EXPERIENCES:
NLP TECHNIQUES AND STRATEGIES YOU WORKED WITH

- Creating an anchor
- Shifting sub-modalities
- Enhancing your self-concept
- Mirroring/Matching
- Reframing
- Using metaphors
- Asking the Well-Formed Outcome questions

- Using the:
  - Auditory Swish Process
  - Eye Movement Integration Process
  - Conflict Integration Process
  - Curiosity Shunt Installation
  - Disney Strategy
  - Godiva Chocolate Process

Next Steps: Options for Additional Development

At this point, it might be tempting to put this book on the shelf and move on to a new resource that will help you continue to enhance your life and get more of what you want. Before you do that, consider this: In exploring NLP, you've *already* established an excellent foundation to make powerful personal changes. Why not build on that?

Rather than seek out the next book or online course, what would it be like if you could expand how you use NLP *even more*?

I've found that the more I learn about NLP, the more I learn about myself—and the more options I have for successfully making the changes in myself and my life. If you've been making notes or keeping a journal about your discoveries and dreams, you may already have a list of changes you'd like to pursue. Pick one. When you've made progress with that, pick another. You get the drift.

The goal is to keep NLP in the foreground of your busy life—to use the principles and processes frequently enough that they become part of how you think and operate. If that sounds like a lot of work, it doesn't have to be. In just five to ten minutes each day, you can strengthen your knowledge and skills. This small investment can pay big dividends.

If you're someone who likes having a track to run on, we've created a 21-Day Guide that can get you started. You can use the preprinted guide at the end of this chapter or go online to access a version you can type into. Of course, it's just a guide—you can do the activities sequentially, or skip around. You can even repeat all the activities— just using a different focus.

I said in the Introduction that *NLP is more important today than ever before*. Because technology keeps us in constant connection, we are continuously stimulated by information and interactions with others that we hardly have time to think. By now, learning NLP has provided you with insight into your personal thinking patterns—and helped you manage and change these if you wish. And you've learned whole new ways of dealing with other people and understanding how *they* are thinking and feeling. Great tools for the road ahead, aren't they?

I'd like to leave you with a final thought that was well expressed by Samuel Johnson. Here it is: "Life affords no higher pleasure than that of surmounting difficulties, passing from one step of success to another, forming new wishes and seeing them gratified."

Now you have new tools to do exactly that. I wish you an exciting and rewarding journey—and I appreciate the opportunity to have shared mine with you.

21-Day Guide:

The Next Steps to Creating the Person You Want to Be

This guide is adapted, with NLP Comprehensive's generous permission, from *NLP: The New Technology of Achievement.*

The best time to complete this portion of the book is *after* you've read all the chapters. This guide builds on the NLP ideas and techniques you've explored throughout the book and applies them in *new* ways. Continuing to play with these ideas and processes will increase your mastery of this breakthrough technology and allow you to integrate them as a way to naturally navigate life.

Even though there are recommended activities for each day, there's no rule that says you can't do more than one a day, as long as you're giving each activity the full attention it deserves. Once you've completed this program, you may want to return to the days that you found most useful or appreciated the most, and repeat them for greater benefit. Or you may want to return to the days that didn't seem to offer you much; repeating these opportunities might produce different results or reveal something about yourself. You can also simply repeat the entire program from the beginning. Do any of these activities as often as you like, until all of your goals are reached or you feel you've learned everything this book has to offer, whichever comes first.

 Although there is workbook space provided on the following pages, you may prefer to use your own notebook or download one of the online versions by going to: http://eg.nlpco.com/21-1 or use the QR code with your phone.

Week 1: Going for Your Goals

Day 1: Finding Your Current Coordinates

In order to achieve anything, you need to know where you want to go, right? It's *also* critical to know where you are right now so you can plot a course from here to the fulfillment of your dreams.

Almost all of us, probably without ever really thinking about it, have divided our lives into what we like and what we don't like. NLP cofounder Richard Bandler remarked that while we're clear about what we like and don't like, we probably haven't noticed that we can subdivide our likes and dislikes into the *things we like or want but don't have*—for example, a new car, a vacation or a promotion—and the *things we don't like or don't want and have*—like too many pounds, a quick temper, or badly behaved pets.

To begin, consider what you really like about your life. These can be significant achievements—like hitting a home run, receiving your first "A," or getting an important promotion, and they can also be the simplest of moments—listening to the sound of waves, watching a child sleep, savoring chocolate ice cream. Make your list as long and full as your time allows.

To simplify this process, you can use the following worksheet or one of the online versions. For now, just complete column 1, indicating the things you *want and have* in your life.

Now to the more expected question: What do you *have* that you *don't want* in your life? Many of us spend much of our lives on this question in one form or another. As you consider this question, feel free to include those extra pounds, troublesome habits, being stuck in traffic, days your boss is a jerk, or whatever it is that "rains on your parade." Complete column 3 of your worksheet, making this list as long and as full as your time allows.

Now to the NLP question: What do you *want* in your life that you *don't have*? This is the time to write down your "wish list." Begin anywhere—with your work, home, love life, finances, or whatever. Include your important dreams and also write down at least a few of the everyday dreams, too—like sunny skies, clean sheets, or fresh-brewed coffee. In column 2, write these ideas and make the list as full as your time allows.

The final column is the less-thought-of category: what you *don't want* in your life and you *don't have.* If you're like most people, you probably haven't spent much time mulling over this possibility, so take a few minutes now. There are obvious things like a dreaded disease, crushing debt, a crippled child, chronic pain, the inability to work, etc. There are also many other things that you've never thought of wanting, and you don't want to try them—hang gliding, a prison sentence, a trip to a toxic waste site, etc. Include several of these on your list, too. Capture these ideas in column 4 on the worksheet.

Finding Your Current Coordinates Worksheet

Follow the instructions on the prior page
to complete each column below.

1 **Want & Have**	2 **Want & Don't Have**	3 **Don't Want & Have**	4 **Don't Want & Don't Have**

Take a look at your four lists. Make sure you have at least
several items in each column and that each item
that you wrote down is real and specific.

Once you've reviewed and refined your completed list,
answer the questions provided on the next page.

Looking at your lists again, notice:

- Which list is the longest and which is shortest
- Which list was the easiest to create and which was the most difficult
- Which list feels most familiar and which one is least familiar

As you look from list to list, are you comparing items of equal importance, or do you find you have "mountains" on one list and "molehills" on another?

Right now, which list currently draws your attention more?

As you look over your answers, how do you feel about them?

Do you like the items on your lists, or do you want to change some of them?

As you go to sleep tonight, let your mind wander over how things are, and how you'd *like* them to be. If anything significant comes up, add it to your list.

Day 2: Discovering Your
Motivation Direction and Priorities

Yesterday you discovered your current coordinates. Today you'll focus on two of the lists you made: what you *Want & Don't Have* and what you *Don't Want & Have*. Which list currently occupies more of your attention? Remember the meta-program that describes a person's motivation direction as *away-from* or *toward* (from Chapters 4 and 6)? The *Want & Don't Have* list is another way of describing a *toward* motivation, while *Don't Want & Have* is another way of describing an *away-from* motivation. Notice which list is more important to you now. Begin with that list first. Review the items and prioritize them. What do you want to change most? What do you want to change next—after that, and so on? Use any ranking system you like.

After you finish prioritizing your first list, do the same with the second list.

Once you have prioritized both lists, consider which change, if you were to get it, would make the *most* difference in your life. It might be one of your top-ranked items, and then again, it might seem at first to be a minor one. For example, how much difference would it make to everything else in your life if you began each day in a good mood? What small but significant change could you make in your day now that would encourage this—the perfect latte, a healthy breakfast, upbeat music, stimulating conversation, comfortable shoes? Review your priorities again to identify items that seem most likely, once they shift, to produce the *biggest* change. Star or highlight these items.

Day 3: Making Your Dreads into Dreams

Look again at your prioritized list for what you *Don't Want & Have*. If this is one of your longer lists, today's activity will be even more important for you. When someone has a well-developed *away-from* motivation direction, they naturally pay a lot more attention to what they *don't* like and *don't* want. While this can be motivating, they ultimately won't experience much satisfaction. As they get further away from what they don't like, they get relief and less stress, but not excitement, satisfaction, or achievement. To experience a sense of fulfillment an *away-from* person needs a reorientation of attention. They can tremendously benefit by redirecting attention from what is *not* wanted to what *is* wanted. This activity, using the items you already listed, will help you explore redirecting your attention from what you don't want to what you do want.

Copy items from your newly prioritized *Don't Want & Have* list onto the next page.

Next, take each item you *Don't Want & Have* and think of a positive phrase that means the same thing to you, but is something you *Don't Have & Want*. For example: If you *Don't Want & Have* a few extra pounds, what you probably *Don't Have & Want* is a slimmer, more muscular body. If you *Don't Want & Have* a dead-end job, then you *Don't Have & Want* work with more opportunities. Create a transformation for every *Don't Want & Have* into a new *Don't Have & Want* that is satisfying to you. Write down each transformation for future reference.

Dreads into Dreams Transformation Worksheet

Don't Want & Have   *Transformed into a new* ⇨   **Don't Have & Want**

e.g., a few extra pounds   ⇨ ⇨ ⇨   a slimmer,
more muscular body

Day 4: Turning Your Dreams
and Desires into Achievable Goals

Review your *original* list of *Don't Have & Want* and yesterday's new list of *Don't Have & Want*. Compare these two lists and merge them according to your current priorities. You may want to arrange them in their new order. Of course, as new items come into your awareness, feel free to add these to your list.

 Now pick *one* of your top-priority goals, and take it all the way through the Well-Formed Outcome model using the worksheet on the next two pages or downloading one of the online versions from http://eg .nlpco.com/2-1 or use the QR code with your phone.

Well-Formed Outcome Worksheet

1. **What specifically do you want?** *Describe your desired outcome or state in a positive, sensory-based way that's an appropriate chunk size and also addresses WHAT ELSE having or achieving your outcome will do for you (Meta-Outcomes).*

   _____

   _____

   _____

   _____

   _____

2. **How will you know when you've achieved what you want?** *Determine if the "evidence" you're focused on is appropriate and timely (soon and regular enough).*

   _____

   _____

   _____

   _____

   _____

3. **Under what circumstances, where, when, and with whom, do you want to have this result?** *Reflect on the context(s) in which you want to have this outcome and evaluate the ecology so you can consider how achieving this result may affect other areas, aspects, or people in your life.*

   _____

   _____

   _____

   _____

   _____

4. **What stops you from having your desired outcome already?**
   Identify and explore any feelings, thoughts, or circumstances that seem to inhibit movement toward your outcome.

   _____

   _____

   _____

   _____

   _____

5. **What resources will you need to help you create what you want?** *Determine what resources you ALREADY have that will help you (knowledge, money, connections, etc.). Consider additional resources you'll need to move forward.*

   _____

   _____

   _____

   _____

   _____

6. **How are you going to get there?** *Identify manageable steps to help achieve your result, consider multiple options to get where you want to go, and determine the FIRST step you'll take.*

   _____

   _____

   _____

   _____

   _____

Day 5: Making Your Goals Irresistible

Most of us are drawn to what we find attractive. It fills our attention and directs our decisions and behavior. Now that you have turned your dreams and desires into *achievable* goals, you can make them so compelling that you will naturally be drawn toward them. Remember to *only* use the following steps with goals you've fully taken through the Well-Formed Outcome questions, because it's possible to make unwise or impossible goals compelling. (Unrequited love and quixotic dreams are two examples.) There are better uses of your energy and this technology.

Take one high-priority goal from your list and begin by imagining the goal in your mind's eye and seeing yourself having *already* achieved it. If the goal isn't already a movie, have it take the form of a movie now. Increase the size and brightness of these images, adding vivid colors and dimension. Notice the way this intensifies how attracted you feel to the goal. Continue to increase the movie's size, brightness, and color as long as the feelings of attraction are intensifying until they plateau; then hold them there. Add rich, exciting, upbeat music to your movie of the goal. Have the music become surround sound so it's coming from all directions. Hear strong, supportive, encouraging voices cheering you on to your future. Fully enjoy this mental movie and the associated feelings.

Having done one example *thoroughly* and experienced the effectiveness, you'll easily be able to take any of your other goals through this same process at any time you desire.

Day 6: Creating Inevitable Success

Creating inevitable success means setting your brain on the path to achieving your goal in such a way that it's working on your goal all day long—whether you are conscious of it or not. When you've vividly imagined that you have already achieved your goal *and* foreseen a possible path to get there, traveling the actual path becomes much easier.

This is the process of "chunking" down a journey into the actual steps you need to take to get there. To accomplish this, you'll need to imagine going into the future to become the "you" who has *already* achieved your goal.

When you momentarily become the future "you" who has already achieved your goal, you can visit what is now your past and review the actions and decisions that inevitably led to this achievement. As you review the steps you took, you'll notice different resources that helped you along the way.

Then, keeping this path in mind, return to the present to plan for your future and take the necessary actions in the present.

Having *thoroughly* completed this process and experienced how effective it is, you'll easily be able to identify the steps and resources you need to achieve an important goal.

Day 7: Appreciating the Rest of Your Life

Stephen Covey's book *The 7 Habits of Highly Effective People* identifies the importance of personal renewal—physical, mental, social/emotional, and spiritual renewal. Yet, with the ever-increasing reach of technology, the demands of life seem to expand well beyond the available hours in a day. As we juggle and struggle to keep up, many of us move rest and renewal to the bottom of the list. This decision can come at a price—to our well-being and to our relationships.

Today's activity is as important as each of the rest of the days in this guide. It builds a foundation for heightened awareness, appreciation, and positive action. Looking back to Day 1, you'll see a list titled *Have & Want*. These are things that you want in your life that you already have. In the rush to keep up, grow, and achieve, it's often easy to forget the good things in your life and how far you've come.

Take time today to review this list in detail. Really notice what you like about your life. Linger over any items that draw you in. Savor them. If you find that doing this prompts you to call someone, send a note, go sit outside, take a moment in meditation or prayer, or do something so that these items appear more often in your future—great! As you begin to enumerate and appreciate what you *Have & Want,* you may notice that additional things you have and appreciate or enjoy come up. Feel free to include these on your list.

When you have completely reviewed your *Have & Want* list, in your mind's eye look over the previous week or month and notice what you have done with this book and program to improve the quality of your life and yourself. Notice the activities you've completed, what you've learned, and what you've achieved. Consider what you could do for yourself right now to appreciate or celebrate the investment and progress you've made.

Week 2: Persuasive Communication

Day 8: Finding and Transmitting Your Mission

To communicate your life mission is to speak what's in your heart. Men and women who live out their life missions are naturally charismatic. They have a compelling clarity, persuasiveness, and commitment that stems from their vision. All communication techniques pale in the face of simple words said by someone who truly believes them.

Before doing today's exercise, it's helpful to have taken at least two of your priority goals completely through the Well-Formed Outcome model. You need to have made these goals into compelling futures by enriching them visually, auditorily, and kinesthetically. If you haven't done this yet, make that today's exercise.

Having done that, get each of these important goals in mind simultaneously and ask yourself the following questions.

- What do these goals have in common?
- What themes or elements appear in all or most of them?
- How do these goals express your life's passion?
- How do they express your deepest values and principles?

Write down, draw, or even act out your answers.

Remember, you're in search of your life mission. This is not something you decide; it is something that *emerges from within you*. Take time to explore what deeply motivates what is most important to you. This could easily take more than the time you've allotted to complete today's activity. Begin now and find out what "bubbles up" for you—today, as well as in the days and weeks to come. Visions emerge from dreams, daydreams, and spontaneous thoughts. Be curious about how you'll discover yours.

Once you have a sense of your mission, share it with someone. Expressing it will help refine your mission and serve as an invitation to others. Who might want to participate in your mission or at least cheer you on, if he or she only knew about it?

Day 9: Listening with Rapport

As you know, listening is key to creating rapport and to understanding. The kind of listening that notices how another sees, hears, feels, and thinks demonstrates intention and invites you into someone else's world.

When someone is *face-to-face* with you, there's an incredible amount of information being communicated: the words, gestures, emotions, and unconscious cues. Although in-person communication is more complete, in today's environment much of our communication is done by phone, email, or texting.

Today, practice your listening and rapport-building skills when you're on the phone. While listening to the other person talk, play with speaking at the same speed or tempo as *they* are. Experiment with using *their* intonation patterns. If their voice is flat, flatten *your* voice. If they are expressive, try speaking more expressively.

Here's something you can do to build rapport on the phone or by email. Keep the following list of "process" words handy and begin to "feed back" to your callers the same kind of words they use. For more details on communicating in someone's preferred representational channel, refer to Chapter 7.

Generic or Unspecified Words:
Know, Understand, Believe, Notice, Discover, Consider, Communicate

Visual:
See, Look, Watch, Peak, Imagine, Appear, Reveal, Perception

Auditory:
Hear, Listen, Tell, Ask, Sounds, In Tune, Tonality, Whisper

Kinesthetic:
Feel, Touch, Grasp, Catch On, Contact, Push, Reach, Impression

Words that *imply* . . .

Visualization:
Color, Sparkle, Contrast, Flash, Snapshot

Sound:
Dissonance, Crackle, Silence, Orchestrate, Noise

Feelings & Sensations:
Weigh In, Curious, Warm, Soft, Impact

Day 10: The Magic of Physical Alignment

As you know from Chapter 5, 93 percent of the emotional content
of face-to-face communication is nonverbal—so words are only 7
percent of a communication. With every person you meet face-to-
face, practice matching his or her body language and gestures. If they
move slowly and deliberately, do the same. If they move quickly or
gesture a lot, then move more at their rate and add some gestures that
are similar to theirs.

For a completely different experience, first *mismatch* the other person's nonverbal behavior (moving fast when they move slowly, gesturing a lot when they don't gesture at all) and then, after rapport has
begun to drop off, reestablish it again by matching their rhythms and
gestures.

Day 11: The Secret to Wonderful Feelings

Today, make it your secret mission to encourage whomever you meet to feel better. You might compliment them, simply smile, or gently (and appropriately) touch their arm or shoulder. Experiment with different approaches in different situations. Write down your results at the end of the day.

You can also encourage yourself. Here's how:

- What emotion, if you could experience it at least several times every day, would make your life smoother and more wonderful?

- What are three things you could do to encourage this emotion in yourself?

- How will you begin to integrate these three things so you can enjoy your chosen emotion more often?

Day 12: Understanding the Values of the Heart

As you know from Day 9's activity, listening is much more than the physical act of hearing. Today, focus your NLP listening skills on noticing, understanding, and exploring the heartfelt values of others.

In your interactions, listen for their goals and values. Repeat aloud what you hear about their goals and values to give them an opportunity to confirm or clarify your understanding. Ask them what's important about achieving their goals and values. When you elicit their meta-outcome(s), you're asking for their higher and deeper values, their heartfelt values. Really listen to what they tell you. As you do this, you'll notice there are many different heartfelt values, and all of them are uniquely important to the individuals who hold them.

Because deeply held values drive people's goals and choices, you may even want to start a file of heartfelt values for the folks you frequently interact with. As you increase your acuity of noticing and understanding values, you're likely to discover that these are important criteria that must be met before a person will completely commit themselves to something. One of the most empowering things you can do is assist the people around you in finding ways to express their heartfelt values. Where people express their hearts and passion, they also release their talents.

Day 13: Finding Motivation and Giving Direction

An effective parent, teacher, manager, or other person in authority gives those he or she is responsible for clear and positive goals with measurable evidence of achievement. This way everyone in a partnership, team, or family not only knows what the goals are, they also know how to recognize when these have been achieved.

Successful leaders *also* communicate how the goals and values of the enterprise are in alignment with the goals and heartfelt values of all the individuals who are involved.

Review the previous day's list of goals, values, and heartfelt values. Pick one or two of the individuals from whom you've gathered information about their heartfelt goals and values.

Ask them what the fulfillment of their goals and heartfelt values will do for them—then listen for the motivation direction that's expressed in their answers. What do you notice? Do they want to attain or achieve something—moving ever closer *toward* it—or do they want relief and release in getting *away from* it? Notice whether they are more interested in solving problems (*away-from* motivation) or pursuing goals (*toward* motivation).

Build on this awareness whenever you're giving instructions or offering guidance; this will allow you to communicate with them in ways they will much more readily understand and appreciate. For more details, review Chapter 7.

Day 14: Appreciating the Love in the World for You

On this day of rest, take a few moments to reflect on the people in your life who love and care for you. You've obviously touched their lives in some way.

In your mind's eye, visit each one and imagine what it would be like to *be* this person and then notice what he or she appreciates about *you* most.

Most likely, you'll notice things you've done together and ways you've been "there" for this loved one, so far. You might have in mind some important situations or events you shared.

Also take time to notice the ways your presence—in silence, in jest, in seriousness, and in just being—have also touched this person. When you have given yourself an opportunity to appreciate this first loved one's perspective, do this again with another key person in your life. If time permits, do this appreciation process with *several* loved ones.

When you have done this imagining with at least two loved ones, notice any patterns of appreciation. Are they different from what you expected before this activity? Take a few additional moments and let yourself absorb as much as you can of the acceptance, acknowledgment, appreciation, and affection you've just discovered. If this prompts you to call someone, send a note, take a moment in meditation or prayer, or do something so this experience appears more often in your future—great! Take the actions you're inspired to take and see what happens.

Week 3: The Peak Performance Program

Day 15: Stepping out of Limitations and into Resources

When many people think of achieving peak performance, they often turn their attention to the obstacles they think are blocking their way. Henry Ford once said, "If you think you can or you think you can't, you're right." It's true, right? Achieving peak performance has much more to do with how we *think* about our experience than with our actual experience.

To demonstrate this for yourself, begin by noticing how you mentally "code" the positive and negative memories in your life. Are you associated (into the memories as if they are happening to you now) or are you disassociated (watching yourself on a TV or a movie screen) in your memories? Take enough time to sample *several* memories. You may even want to list them.

Very often, people find they have inadvertently coded many of their negative memories in the associated form and therefore reexperience them, and the negative feelings, strongly at inappropriate times. For example, they may vividly relive a social embarrassment as they are about to speak to a group, or they remember earlier rejections as they are about to explore a new relationship.

Now let's look at the other side. Check to discover if you are associated into your positive and resourceful memories. Too often, people have accidentally coded these in the disassociated form and thereby made their own resources inaccessible to themselves. Both of these memory codes can be changed for the better.

Begin by thinking of a single negative memory that is specific and associated. As you begin to reexperience it, vividly imagine yourself stepping out of it. Now see that memory at some distance away from you, with a big black frame around it and thick glass separating what is in the heavy picture frame from what is outside it. Examine the heavily framed picture to confirm that a younger you from that time is truly in that image and that you are outside it. Notice how different the feelings are now?

Take your time and repeat this process with another associated negative memory that you wish to change. If there are quite a few, make a plan to change several of them each day until you've shifted them all.

Day 16: Amplifying What Is Excellent

One way to achieve excellence is to remove the roadblocks and difficulties on the way to your goals. Another is to amplify the excellence so much that the roadblocks just become little bumps in the road.

Pick an area of your life where you're already excelling. Find a real and specific event, a memory of personal excellence you're pleased to remember—and relive it. As you begin to reexperience it, also begin to *amplify* it. Make it bigger and brighter and more colorful and compelling.

As you enjoy this excellence thoroughly, where would you like to experience it in your near future? Vividly imagine that happening now.

And where would you like to experience this resource in your longer-term future? Take this resource to that future time and notice how real that excellent future moment feels now.

Continue to place this amplified excellence in your future moments wherever you want or need them.

When you have "spread it around" to your satisfaction, let it go and recall another memory of personal excellence and repeat the process. By amplifying more and more moments of personal excellence and placing them in your future, you will raise the overall quality of your life—as well as the level of your performance—and you're making them a much more likely occurrence. For more details on using submodalities and anchoring, refer to Chapter 2.

Day 17: Accelerating Your Learning

In every endeavor, there are usually new skills to learn. How easily, efficiently, and effectively you learn them can make a tremendous difference, right? Two crucial aspects of learning are how to acquire good "form" *from the beginning* and how to successfully *reprogram* poor form created by habitual errors.

In Chapter 3, we talked about the study in which college students were asked to shoot basketball free-throws after mental rehearsal or actual practice. As you may recall, those that didn't practice at all showed no improvement, while the students who *mentally* rehearsed scored within a point of the students who actually got to *physically* practice. This study provided some of the first hard evidence about the power of visualization. Today athletes in every field—and professionals in other disciplines—practice some kind of visualization to perfect their performance.

NLP also recognizes how mental rehearsal stimulates and reinforces the same neural pathways and micromuscle movements as the *actual* activity. The mind and body are learning, remembering, and developing habits from both kinds of rehearsal. Whether your activity is rock climbing, a job interview, or a presentation to a client, you can use this for yourself.

And whenever your performance is extraordinary, you can increase the likelihood of a *repeat* performance by taking a moment to mentally rehearse your excellence. Since you just performed it, the patterns are fresh in your mind and body. Mental rehearsal will reaccess these pathways again each time you relive the experience—that day, the next day, and in the weeks to come. Replaying your excellence makes it more and more *your* consistent performance pattern.

On the other side, if you've developed a habit that no longer serves you, whether it's an athletic misalignment like a slice, or a useless behavior pattern like performance anxiety, you can eliminate it by "writing over it"!

You can do this by first reviewing your undesirable experience from a disassociated position. In your mental movie, see yourself with your undesired habit. Keeping the beginning of the movie the same, consider how would you like it to turn out differently. Watch the movie again starting from the beginning, only this time, watch yourself with a more useful response. Try several alternatives and pick one you like best. Now step into this new *revised* movie as a real and associated experience. Start at its beginning and vividly experience this new movie as if it's happening to *you* right now all the way through to its new ending.

When you have completed this, you have set yourself on a new track with a new natural response. To strengthen this new pattern, play the updated movie whenever you want.

Day 18: Making the Peak a Regular Part of Your Life

In NLP, we have a saying, "You don't have to be bad to get better." Improvement is always possible. So another way to encourage peak performance is to let your brain know you *want* to go there. Here's how you can use the Swish Pattern to take yourself to ever-higher levels of performance.

To start, recall a specific moment when your performance faltered or you felt yourself on a familiar plateau.

Bring this particular example vividly to your mind's eye, and in the center of it, see a dot. In the dot, there's an image of you having already exceeded your current level of success. You don't know how you did it. You just know you did. When the image moves closer, perhaps you'll see your satisfied smile and a gleam in your eyes that will let you know you accomplished this in alignment with your values and well-being.

Now watch as the performance-plateau experience rushes away from you, getting smaller and darker and farther away—until it loses all significance. At the same time, notice how the dot blossoms toward you, getting bigger and brighter and more real, until you are face-to-face with your exceptional self.

Clear your internal screen and repeat this process from the beginning at least half a dozen times. Notice if the performance-plateau image naturally fades away and/or the "exceptional self-image" automatically comes in.

This is just one example of a Swish Pattern. With a little bit of practice, this will become an automatic mental habit. If you'd like to learn more about this pattern, visit www.nlpco.com.

Day 19: Creating a Breakthrough Mind

When the British runner Roger Bannister broke the four-minute mile and the Russian weight lifters broke five hundred pounds, none of them knew they had done it! In both cases, their coaches had conspired to keep them from knowing they were even attempting to break the current record. In interviews after the record-breaking events, these different coaches were quite clear about their reasons for not telling their athletes. And even though these interviews were given *decades* apart, their explanations were quite similar.

These coaches believed their talented athletes could do what had never been done before. They noted that the numerical difference between four minutes and less than four minutes was a hundredth of a second, and the difference between five hundred pounds and more than five hundred pounds was less than an ounce. They were convinced that the limitations were not in their athletes, but in the *meaning* their athletes had attached to these numbers. This proved true for the runner *and* the weight lifters, for within months of each athlete's breakthrough, several others repeated the achievement—which had previously been thought impossible!

To create any kind of personal performance breakthrough, you need to change your own mental limitations. You may have had a personal experience that led you to conclude that something was not possible—or you may have come to believe it's not possible because others told you so. You may have thought this for so long that you only vaguely remember how and when this came to be true for you.

Begin by thinking of something that you decided years ago wasn't possible for you—it might be getting your dream job, becoming physically fit, finding your soul mate, or quickly and effortlessly mastering something complex—whatever it is to you.

With this limitation in mind, what experience—if you had had it *before* you acquired this belief or made this decision—would have transformed it from impossible to highly probable? Take a moment to create this enabling experience in your mind. It may be similar to something that happened later in your life, or it might be something that never happened to you but you could imagine it—or perhaps it happened to someone else.

Vividly create this enabling experience using the sub-modalities of a previous peak performance, a time when you really excelled, even if this example is from a completely different context. (You can also build on the sub-modalities you discovered in Day 16.)

Once you have created a rich and powerful reference experience, take that back in time with you and imagine it happened *just before* the situation that created your limiting memory. From this point, move ahead from that time—travel ahead with this new enabling memory and as you pass through the limiting memory, notice how having the enabling memory transforms the negative effects of the original limiting memory (and any other ones) into positive ones—all the way through your past into your present!

Now check to sense if that old limitation is completely gone. If you want to, repeat this last step to *strengthen* your new enabling memory. This new memory will not *guarantee* success, but it does guarantee that the limitations will be in the world, not in your mind.

Day 20: The Practice of Loving What You Do

Even as you transform your negatives, increase your positives, orient yourself to your *best* self, and raise expectations, there's still the need to practice. In *Outliers,* author Malcolm Gladwell's research revealed that people who really excelled—like the Beatles and Bill Gates— invested more than ten thousand hours in mastering their craft! He also pointed out that practice was not just something they *did* to accomplish a particular goal, but was something they were *drawn* to. For them, practicing is part of who they *are.*

Those who excel in any endeavor actually love to practice. Basketball great Magic Johnson has his own full-size basketball court. In addition to having his own court, Larry Bird would *find* a court wherever he went, spending hours a day there, all through the off-season. Rock- and-roll greats Eric Clapton and Bruce Springsteen play their guitars as much when they're off the road as when they are on. Chess masters the world over study and replay famous games. The great American architect Frank Lloyd Wright used to rebuild his own studio almost annually just to try out new ideas. These greats, and others like them, are attracted to practice. They want to find out what they have missed. They want to find out what they might do this time that they have never done before.

You can increase the attractiveness of practice in the important areas of your life with a simple NLP technique. Once you have decided to do something worthwhile, you might as well enjoy doing it, right? Most people do things for the results, yet everyone has a few things they do simply because they enjoy doing them. Find an example of a time when you wanted the results but getting them was not a lot of fun. Many people feel this way about doing their taxes. Identify something that you dislike doing. Then step into a *specific* experience of doing that to discover the sub-modalities associated with it.

Now think of an activity that you do simply because you enjoy it and the end result doesn't really matter. For many people, computer games, sports, or even puzzles have this quality. Step into the activity that you enjoy and discover the visual, auditory, and kinesthetic sub-modality distinctions of that experience.

Compare the two memories until you have found the sub-modality distinctions that make the difference between the two experiences. Use the worksheet on the next page to capture these differences. Be sure to identify a number of differences.

Next, associate into the *wanting results* experience—holding the content of its images constant—and transform its sub-modalities into the ones you found in the experience of *enjoying the doing*. Notice the effect this has on your experience. Better, right?

Now associate into the practice of a skill you would very much like to improve and transform its sub-modalities into the ones associated with *enjoying the doing*. The next time you practice that skill, notice how much more compelling and enjoyable it is to do so.

Worksheet to Increase Enjoyment
of Practicing & Doing Tasks or
Skills You Want to Improve

Sub-Modalities of Want the Results	Sub-Modalities of Enjoy the Doing

Day 21: It's a Wonderful Life—If You Notice

On this day of rest, it's time to appreciate you. You might begin by acknowledging that you've completed all the activities in this guide so far. And we invite you to "zoom out" and notice how others appreciate you.

Each of us has made a difference, in fact, many differences, in the lives of others. Frank Capra's classic movie *It's a Wonderful Life* reminds us all that our lives are deeply interconnected. Even though this movie is shown dozens of times a year, few of us take the time to notice the rich weave of connections that form the tapestry of our lives.

So take a few moments now, in your mind's eye, to go into your past and find small, as well as significant, ways you have affected the world around you in positive ways. Perhaps you helped your siblings with their homework, supported a friend at a crucial juncture, volunteered at a local shelter, or provided information that helped reveal unintended consequences to someone's important project. Identify the times you have touched others' lives with your words or your actions.

Use the worksheet on the next page to make a list of your positive words and/or actions (column 1) and their effects (column 2), even if these effects weren't obvious until years later. Because what we value isn't always what *other* people value, expand your yardstick to include how important you have been to others (as well as what's important to you).

With these experiences as proof of the importance of even your everyday actions, take a few moments to write down specific actions you would like to take in the *future,* actions that will add to the lives of others and the world. As you capture these in column 3, rehearse where you will take these actions and enjoy your participation in the world.

It's a Wonderful Life Worksheet

1 **Words Said or Actions Taken**	2 **Positive Effects on Others' Lives**	3 **Actions I'll Take in the Future**

What you do makes a difference—in your world *and* in the lives of others. Consider what you've learned from this book, and how you will be even more conscious of and active in making good things happen in the weeks, months, and years to come. Keep wishing, wanting, and dreaming. You can begin a new cycle tomorrow.

Today, do something *for yourself* that really delights you. Watch the sunset, smell the flowers, dance to the music, and touch another heart. Keep learning and growing to create the person you want to be and the rewarding relationships you want.

 Now that you've completed the 21-Day Guide, you may be ready for more information on NLP. If so, follow this link to a list of my favorite books and courses, http://eg.nlpco.com/21-4, or use the QR code with your phone.

Congratulations on making this commitment
to yourself and your well-being.

The work you do to improve yourself also affects your entire world,
and for that, you have our sincere thanks.

Best wishes for good fortune as you continue your journey.

—Tom, Tom, and Susan

A Lasting Legacy

Vikki Hoobyar

My darling husband, Tom Hoobyar, was an interpersonal genius. My first interaction with Tom was in an elevator that went from the garage to the entrance of a very popular bookstore in Menlo Park, California. A teenager was standing next to him, so I smiled my "I know what it's like to have teenagers" smile. When the door of the elevator opened, the kid skateboarded away and I was dismayed to discover that I had smiled at a man who was alone. Because I don't usually do that, I put my head down and marched into the store, not daring to look back.

A moment later, Tom offered to help me find a book after the salesperson "with too few brains and too many piercings" (as Tom described it) had blown me off. This was a *reader's* bookstore. He seemed so nice and knowledgeable about the bookstore that I took him up on his offer to help me.

We talked about what I was searching for. The book wasn't there, but it no longer mattered because we had begun an interesting conversation about NLP. There in the bookshop, Tom treated me to my first taste of NLP by having me visualize my favorite food and then my least favorite food. I was fascinated by this brief experience and what my brain was doing, so we went next door to grab coffee and continue the conversation. It was delightful.

At that point in my life, I was willing to be "friends" with men, but I was not willing to date a man until I really got to know him. Tom kept finding reasons to get together with me to continue our discussion about NLP. I knew he liked me a lot, but I really just wanted to be friends. He picked me up at work and took me to lovely restaurants. Afterward, I would always shake his hand.

On one particular day, although we had only planned an outing to an art fair for a couple of hours, we ended up spending the entire day together. That afternoon I said, "Aren't we spending too much time together on our first date?" What Tom heard was that I had called it a "date" and I had said it was the *first* one. About three months after meeting him, I fell completely, unreservedly in love with him. We married fourteen months later. Years later, I told him that had I been looking for a man to date; he would have been disqualified immediately as "too old, too tall, and too bald."

Tom had a lot of impact on others—people in business, NLP clients, and my family. When I met him, I was entering my first year of graduate school to get a master's degree in marriage and family counseling. As we got to know one another, he discussed NLP training with me and I was more than happy to learn the skill set. So while I attended college, I also attended several NLP trainings. When it came time to actually start counseling clients, I had a lot more confidence than my classmates because my NLP training had taught me that there was no objection a client could bring up that I couldn't handle. (How's *that* for "wow"?)

During our courtship, my youngest son quickly came to Tom's attention. He was fifteen, a high school dropout who was drinking a lot and taking drugs. His father had died when my son was eight years old, and he had had a very negative experience with his first stepfather. Tom started taking him out for dinner once a month. He told him that they were going to be in each other's lives whether they liked it or not. He explained to him that he was going to be the older guy in my son's life; that in fact, the day was coming when he would be calling Tom to bail him out of jail. (And that actually happened.)

Tom viewed my son as a very large fish he had to pull in with a very weak fishing line. So he would pull him closer and then let him retreat a little. One night when the three of us were watching TV, Tom turned to my son (who had no piercings in his face, his hair cut conservatively, and a baseball cap on his head, facing forward) and said, "Who are you and what have you done with our son?" We had a good laugh! No doubt about it, Tom saved the life of my younger son. He is now a very successful salesperson and an exceptional parent to his six-year-old son.

When Tom and I first married, my oldest son was in Ranger training with the U.S. Army. He called one night and said he was having some problems with impatient feelings toward his wife. Over the telephone, Tom had him notice the control panel that was in his mind. Tom helped him imagine installing a lever to control how many rpm's his mind was going. This way he could lower the rpm's when with his wife and increase the rpm's when doing Army tasks.

A couple of weeks later, my son called Tom and said, "I hope you don't mind, but I made some changes to the control panel." (Cute, huh?) Tom asked, "What did you do?" He explained that he had added a computer screen with handles to his control panel. On the screen, he put a picture of his physical training instructor. And when he held the handles, all of his instructor's power ran into his body. He taught the process to his fellow soldiers and they beat the Army Ranger physical training records.

Tom and I decided together that we would be really "present" for others. That meant that we made it a priority to really connect with people and to talk with people who were in crisis, no matter what we were doing at the time they called. (On more than one occasion, I sat in a Starbucks, in Boston, in New York, and in Philadelphia, while Tom coached a troubled friend over the phone.) We also attended every wedding and funeral we knew about. Over the thirteen years we were married, we had six more adorable grandchildren added to our large family. We made monthly trips to Reno, Nevada, to visit Tom's daughter, Tracy, and her family. We were present with each other—and with others.

Tom and I were blissfully happy together. Because we were always talking and he kept coming up with these "gems," I learned to carry a notebook so I could write down and refer to my favorites. One was "Behavior is high quality information." It wasn't a new concept, but the way it was worded really resonated with me. There were hundreds of these gems collected over the years. I would say, "Did you just hear what you said?" Describing things in an engaging way was so natural for him that he was unaware of how special this was. I told him he should write a book sharing those gems. Although he liked the idea, he was at that time extremely busy running his manufacturing company, coaching people, and running an alumni study group called the NLP Café. So any plans for a book went on the back burner.

We also hoped to someday in the not-too-distant future develop and offer a vacation-type retreat center in a rural setting. With his expertise and my training and experience in marriage counseling, we believed we could really help couples. We had a great relationship and even though we encountered challenges in our time together, there was no issue we couldn't resolve.

Tom frequently quoted John Lennon's line, "Life is what happens while you're busy making other plans." Perhaps that quote turned out to be a self-fulfilling prophecy. Sadly, Tom was diagnosed with stage IV pancreatic cancer in August 2009. He passed away one month later. He had the contract for this book under his belt and he had begun working on it. Thanks to Susan Sanders and Tom Dotz, Tom Hoobyar's dream of leaving a legacy has become a reality. All in all, Tom coached hundreds of people. He didn't just do NLP; he *lived* it. I hope to live up to Tom's glowing example of being a truly giving person.

Common NLP Terms

Accessing Cues: Behaviors that are correlated with the use of a particular representational system; e.g., eye movements, voice tones, postures, breathing, etc. (See Representational Systems.)

Anchor: A cue or trigger that elicits a response, similar to the stimulus response of classical conditioning. Anchors, mental sticky notes, can be auditory, visual, kinesthetic, or even spatial (mental sticky notes).

"As If" Frame: To pretend that something is possible or completed and begin thinking with that in mind.

Associated: Being in an experience or memory as fully and completely as possible (with all the senses); looking out from one's own eyes, hearing from one's own ears, feeling one's own feelings.

Auditory: The sense of hearing. (See "Representational Systems.")

Backtrack: A spoken or written review or summary of information, usually to build/maintain rapport and to invite revision or correction.

Beliefs: Generalizations about yourself, other people, and/or the world.

Behavioral Flexibility: The ability to vary one's behavior in order to elicit a desired response from another person (in contrast to repeating a behavior that hasn't worked).

Break State: To change a person's state dramatically. Usually used to pull someone out of an unpleasant state.

Channel: One of the five senses—sight, sound, feeling, taste, and smell. (Also see "Representational Systems.")

Chunk Size: The size of the object, situation, or experience being considered. This can be altered by chunking up to a more general category, chunking down to a more specific category, or chunking sideways or laterally to others of the same type. For example, beginning with "car," you could chunk down to a Ford or to a carburetor, chunk up to a "means of transportation," and chunk sideways to a plane or train.

Congruent: When all of a person's internal strategies, behaviors, and parts are in agreement and working together coherently.

Content: An aspect of meta-programs that addresses the five domains—people, place, information, activities, and things.

Context: The environment within which a communication or response occurs. The context is one of the cues that elicit specific responses.

Context Reframing: Placing a "problem" response or behavior in a different context that gives it a new and different—usually more positive—meaning.

Counter-Example: An exception to a proposed general rule, a specific instance of the falsity of a universally quantified statement, e.g., any hardworking teenager is a counter-example to the statement "All teenagers are lazy."

Criteria: Standards for evaluation; qualities that can be applied to a wide range of specific behaviors or events. Examples: fun, exciting, inexpensive, interesting, high-quality, bold, practical, new, etc.

Deletion: The process of excluding portions of experience of the world from one's internal representations, and one's speech.

Disassociated: Being outside of an experience—looking at or trying on things from an "Observer" or third position.

Distortion: Inaccurate reproduction of events in someone's internal experience. Distortion in language refers to demonstrably inaccurate comments on any subject.

Domain: The five elements of meta-program "Content"—people, place, information, activities, and things.

Ecology: Considering the effects of a change on the larger system instead of on just one isolated behavior, part, or person, e.g., considering how a specific outcome will support your beliefs, values, and important relationships.

Eye Accessing Cues: Unconscious movements of a person's eyes that indicate the representational system being accessed. (See "Accessing Cues.")

Feedback: The visual, auditory, kinesthetic information that comes back to you as a response to your behavior.

First Position ("Self"): Experiencing the world from your own perspective; being associated into yourself and your body.

Flexibility: Having more than one behavioral choice in a situation. (See "Behavioral Flexibility.")

Future Pace: Rehearsing in all systems so that a specific behavior or set of behaviors becomes linked and sequenced in response to the appropriate cues, so that it will occur naturally and automatically in future situations.

Generalization: Taking a specific situation or behavior and generalizing the content across contexts, as if it were a proven conclusion or fact, e.g., "That's just the way human beings are."

Generative or Evolutionary Intervention: An intervention that solves the presenting problem and also generates other changes that make the person's life better in many other ways.

Gustatory: Referring to the sense of taste. (See "Representational Systems.")

Hallucination: An internal representation of or about the world that has no basis in present sensory experience.

Incongruent: When two or more of a person's representations, parts, or programs are in conflict. Being "of two minds" or "torn between two possibilities," etc.

Installation: Teaching or acquiring a new strategy or behavior, generally by rehearsal or future pacing.

Intention: The underlying desire or goal of a behavior, assumed to be positive.

Kinesthetic: The sense of feeling. May be subdivided into tactile feelings (Kt: skin sensing, physically feeling the outside world), proprioceptive feelings (Kp: movement, internal body sensations such as muscle tension or relaxation), and meta feelings (Km: "emotional" responses about some object, situation, or experience). (See "Representational Systems.")

Lead System (also known as Preferred Representational Channel): The representational system initially used to access stored information, e.g., making a visual image of a friend in order to get the feeling of liking him/her.

Lost Performative (Lost Performer): A linguistic pattern in which the person performing the action or judgment is missing from the sentence, e.g., "It's important to know this."

Map of Reality: A person's perception of events. (See "Representational Systems.")

Matching: Mirroring an aspect of one's behavior (posture, tone of voice, breathing, etc.) to that of another person, usually to establish rapport.

Meta Model: A set of language patterns that focuses attention on how people delete, distort, generalize, limit, or specify their realities. It provides a series of outcome specification questions useful for making communication more specific, recovering lost or unspecified information, and for loosening rigid patterns of thinking.

Meta-Outcome: The outcome of the outcome: one that is at a higher level and an outcome of greater importance than the stated one, e.g., "having financial security or freedom and independence" might be the meta-outcome of "finding a better job."

Metaphor: A story, parable, or analogy that relates one situation, experience, or phenomenon to another.

Meta-Program: A thought pattern based on generalization that the brain uses for efficiency. These patterns act as automatic filters that help us make decisions; they tell us what's okay for someone and what's not. Examples include options/procedures, toward/away-from, proactive/reaction, general/specific, and internal/external.

Mind Reading: Imagining what someone else is thinking or feeling by asking yourself, "What must be going on inside that person for that to be true?" and going into second position with them to try on things from their point of view.

Mirroring: Matching an aspect of one's behavior (posture, tone of voice, breathing, etc.) to that of another person, usually to establish rapport.

Modal Operators: Literally "Mode of Operating." A linguistic term for one or more of four broad categories of acting: desire, possibility, necessity, choice.

Modality: One of the five senses—sight, sound, feeling, taste, and smell. (See "Representational Systems.")

Modeling: Observing and specifying how something happens, or how someone thinks or behaves, and then describing in detail or demonstrating the process for others so that they (or you) can learn to do it.

Motivation Direction (Meta-Program): A mental program that determines whether a person moves *toward* or *away-from* experiences.

Neuro-Linguistic Programming (NLP): The process of creating models of human excellence in which the usefulness, not the truthfulness, is the most important criterion for success. The study of subjective experience.

Nominalization: A linguistic term for the words that result from the process of taking actions (verbs) and converting them into things (nouns) that actually have no existence as things; in other words, you can't put them in a wheelbarrow. Examples of nominalizations are *love, freedom, happiness, respect, frustration,* etc.

Observer Position: A disassociated meta-position from which you can observe or review events, seeing yourself and others interact.

Olfactory: The sense of smell. (See "Representational Systems.")

"Other" Position or Second Position: To step into someone else's experience fully.

Outcome: Desired goal or result. (Also see "Well-Formed Outcome" and "Meta-Outcome.")

Pacing: Matching or mirroring another person's nonverbal and/or verbal behavior. Useful for gaining rapport. (See "Mirroring" and "Matching.")

Paralanguage: *How* something is said—or, more accurate, how it is *perceived* to have been said. Separate from the words themselves, paralanguage (such as volume, inflection, speed, intensity, tone, rhythm, pitch) provides audible cues that may telegraph information about someone's inner state and feelings. For example, tone of voice can indicate sarcasm, which the listener may find funny or hurtful.

Parts: A metaphoric term for different aspects of a person's experience. Parts are distinct from the specific behaviors adopted by the "parts" in order to get their positive outcomes.

Perceptual Filter: An attitude, bias, point of view, perspective, or set of assumptions or presuppositions about the object, person, or situation. This attitude "colors" all perceptions of the object, etc.

Perceptual Positions: The perceptual positions most commonly referred to: First Position (also called "self"), when someone is in their own body experiencing things from their own senses and point of view; Second Position (also called "Other"), when someone is imagining what it's like from *another* person's viewpoint and trying to "stand in their shoes"; and Third Position (also called "Observer"), when someone is observing something from outside the self and/or situation in a neutral or objective way.

Predicates: Words that express action or relationship with respect to a subject (verbs, adverbs, and adjectives). The words may reflect the representational system being used or they may be nonspecific, e.g., "That looks good," "Sounds right to me," "That feels fine."

Preferred Representational System or "Channel": The representational system or mode that a person habitually uses to process information or experiences; usually the one in which the person can make the most detailed distinctions.

Presuppositions (in NLP): Unifying beliefs of key individuals (Perls, Satir, Erickson, and Feldenkrais) who were studied to form the operating principles of NLP.

Rapport: A condition in which responsiveness has been established; often described as feeling safe or trusting, or willing.

Reframing: A process by which a person's perception of a specific event or behavior is altered, resulting in a different response. Usually subdivided into Context Reframing, Meaning Reframing, and Six-Step Reframing.

Representational Systems: The internal representations of experience in the five senses: seeing (visual), hearing (auditory), feeling (kinesthetic), tasting (gustatory), and smelling (olfactory).

Resources: A piece of knowledge, an understanding about the world, a belief, a behavior, a skill, a person, or an object, that contributes to the achievement of an outcome. When creating a Well-Formed Outcome, resources could also include time, money, support, etc.

Resource State: The experience of a useful response: an ability, attitude, behavior, characteristic, perspective, or quality that is useful in some context.

Second Position ("Other"): To "become" someone else fully by taking the perspective and the criteria, history, etc., of someone else—trying things on from their point of view, walking in their moccasins.

Self-Position: Experiencing the world from your own perspective; being associated into yourself and your body.

Sensory Acuity: The ability to make sensory discriminations to identify distinctions between different states or events.

Sensory based: Information that is correlated with what has been perceived by the five senses. (Contrast with "Hallucinations.")

Sensory Modalities: The five senses—sight, sound, feeling, taste, and smell.

Separator State or Break State: Eliciting a neutral state between two other states to prevent them from combining or connecting with each other.

Six-Step Reframing: A process in which the "part" (or parts) responsible for an undesirable behavior is contacted directly, the positive intention driving the behavior is uncovered, and new choices to satisfy that intention are created, resulting in an integration of conflicting parts. Also used to resolve interpersonal conflicts, especially on work teams.

State: A state of being, or a condition of body/mind response or experience at a particular moment.

Stimulus-Response: The repeated association between an experience and a particular response (Pavlovian conditioning) such that the stimulus becomes a trigger or cue for the response, e.g., accidental and intentional anchoring.

Strategy: A sequence of mental and behavioral representations that leads to a specific outcome, e.g., decision, learning, motivation, specific skills.

Sub-Modalities: The smaller elements within a representational system; for example, a visual image can be bright, dim, clear, fuzzy, moving, still, large, small, etc.

Swish: A generative sub-modality pattern used to change habits and responses.

Third Position ("Observer"): A disassociated position from which one can more objectively or neutrally observe or review events, seeing oneself and others interact.

Universal Quantifier: A linguistic term for words that are applied to all cases and all situations without exception, e.g., *all, every, always,* and negations such as *never, none,* etc.

Visual: The sense of seeing. (See "Representational Systems.")

Well-Formed Outcome: A goal that is stated in positive terms, obtainable, chunked down appropriately, within the individual's control and contextualized, and helps satisfy your or someone else's outcome.

References

Chapter 2

Cornell College of Hospitality research source: a paper by Michael Lynn, Ph.D., http://www.hotelschool.cornell.edu/research/chr/pubs/reports/abstract–13602.html.

Leslie Cameron, "Outcome Frame," *NLP Home Study Guide,* published by NLP Comprehensive, ©1984–2007.

Chapter 3

Research on visualization and shooting free-throws. L. V. Clark, "Effect of mental practice on the development of a certain motor skill," *Research Quarterly* 31, no. 4 (December 1960): 560–69; Tony Morris, Michael Spittle, and Anthony P. Watt, *Imagery in Sport* (Champaign, IL: Human Kinetics, 2005), also mentioned at http://www.vanderbilt.edu/ans/psychology/health_psychology/mentalimagery.html.

Francesco Cirillo, *The Pomodoro Technique,* 2009. This work is licensed under the Creative Commons Attribution-Noncommercial, No derivative Works 3.0 License—http://www.pomodorotechnique.com.

"Eye Movement Integration" process originally created by Steve and Connirae Andreas, http://www.nlpco.com/library/therapy/eye -movement-integration-therapy.

Navy SEALs training tips, http://www.menshealth.com/best-life/ mission-save-you/page/5.

Chapter 4
Herbert Benson, *The Relaxation Response* (New York: William Morrow, 1975).

Excerpt about meta-programs from Joseph O'Connor and John Seymour, *Introducing NLP* (London: Thorson's, 1990).

Chapter 5
GGNEE model created by Rick Middleton, founder of Executive Expression in Los Angeles; mentioned in Mark Goulston's *Just Listen* (New York: American Management Association, 2010).

Chapter 6
Emotional content in communication based on research by Albert Mehrabian, *Silent Messages*, 1st ed. (Belmont, CA: Wadsworth, 1971).

Research on sports teams and touching, Benedict Carey, "Evidence That Little Touches Do Mean So Much," *New York Times*, February 22, 2010, http://www.nytimes.com/2010/02/23/health/23mind .html. "To see whether a rich vocabulary of supportive touch is in fact related to performance, scientists at Berkeley recently analyzed interactions in one of the most physically expressive arenas on earth:

professional basketball. Michael W. Kraus led a research team that coded every bump, hug, and high five in a single game played by each team in the National Basketball Association early last season. In a paper due out this year in the journal *Emotion,* Mr. Kraus and his co-authors, Cassy Huang and Dr. Keltner, report that with a few exceptions, good teams tended to be touchier than bad ones."

Allen Bluedorn, *The Human Organization of Time* (Stanford, CA: Stanford University Press, 2002).

Phil Zimbardo, *The Time Paradox: The New Psychology of Time That Will Change Your Life* (New York: Simon & Schuster, 2008). Animated presentation at http://www.youtube.com/watch?v=A3oIiH7BLmg.

Chapter 7
Mark Goulston, *Just Listen* (New York: American Management Association, 2010).

Touch Research Institute, University of Miami School of Medicine. "Research by Tiffany Field of the Touch Research Institute in Miami has found that a massage from a loved one can not only ease pain but also soothe depression and strengthen a relationship." Best source: http://books.google.com/books/about/Touch.html?id= 1fBdoaBC9-YC.

Cincinnati Children's Hospital: "Research has demonstrated that patients who receive healing touch experience *accelerated* wound healing, relaxation, pain relief, and general comfort."

Robert Cialdini, *Influence: The Psychology of Persuasion* (New York: HarperBusiness, 2006).

Chapter 8

Robert Dilts, *Strategies of Genius* (Capitola, CA: Meta, 1995).

Keith V. Trickey, "The Walt Disney Creative Strategy," http://www
.wiredportfolio.com/blog/wp-content/uploads/2008/10/DisneyPaper
.pdf.

21-Day Guide

Stephen R. Covey, *The 7 Habits of Highly Effective People* (New
York: Fireside, 1989).

Malcolm Gladwell, *Outliers* (New York: Little, Brown, 2008).

Acknowledgments

We gratefully acknowledge Dr. Robert Dee McDonald, NLP innovator, author, and trainer for creating:

- and testing this version of the "Auditory Swish" in eighteen countries.

- his extended version of the NLP Presuppositions.

- the taxi-driver metaphor, which is the foundation of his Destination Method, a Transpersonal Coaching Strategy.

- the Mission Detection Process, which informed sections of this book.

Robert McDonald is coauthor of two NLP books titled, *Tools of the Spirit* and *NLP: The New Technology of Achievement.* His website is TelosCenter.com.

Index

Note: Italic page numbers refer to illustrations.

About the Authors

 Tom Dotz is a real entrepreneur. That means he's experienced business and life from every side. He's ridden the rocketing financial start-up bubble, and had it explode along with the rest of his life. He knows a brilliant business plan with the best financing can evaporate through no fault of your own. He knows you need resilience. When Tom took his first NLP training, he was so impressed that he founded the NLP Institute of California. Using NLP to market NLP, he created a powerhouse community and grew it to the largest organization of its kind in the U.S. in just four years. Now the owner of NLP Comprehensive, he leads the design of programs and products for real-life problems and opportunities.

 Tom Hoobyar, NLP Master Practitioner, engineer, and high tech CEO, used his NLP skills and life experience to help individuals and businesses grow. He held thirty-seven patents in the biotech industry, including the original Radial-Diaphragm valve, as founding CEO and marketing strategist for ASEPCO, Inc. He took even more delight in his accomplishments as a happily married family man with three adult kids and seven

grandchildren. He founded the NLP Café, and the international NLP Alumni study group. Through the NLP Café he conducted advanced programs in NLP for fifteen years, and served on the board of NLP Comprehensive, a world-leader in NLP training.

 Susan Sanders helps organizations make learning and working easier, fun, and more meaningful. Her understanding of how people "work," love of words, attention to beliefs and metaphor, and unique ability to organize ideas distinguish her approach and ability to create lasting change. A decade-long study of NLP enables Susan to integrate NLP concepts and strategies into writing and editing, instructional design, and training delivery.